Frigates, Sloops and Brigs

D1354936

PEN & SWORD MILITARY CLASSICS

We hope you enjoy your Pen and Sword Military Classic. The series is designed to give readers quality military history at affordable prices. Pen and Sword Classics are available from all good bookshops. If you would like to keep in touch with further developments in the series, telephone: 01226 734555, email: enquiries@pen-and-sword.co.uk, or visit our website at www.pen-and-sword.co.uk.

Published Classics Titles

The
Frigates

An account of the lesser warships of
the wars from 1793 to 1815

by James Henderson CBE

Drawings by
Ernest E Relf

PEN & SWORD MILITARY CLASSICS

The Frigates was first published in Great Britain in 1970,
Sloops and Brigs was first published in Great Britain in 1972,
both by Adlard Coles Ltd.

Reprinted in this format in 2005 by
Pen & Sword Military Classic
An imprint of
Pen & Sword Books Ltd
47 Church Street
Barnsley
South Yorkshire
S70 2AS

Copyright © Estate of James Henderson CBE, 1970, 1972, 2005

ISBN 1 84415 301 0

The right of James Henderson CBE to be identified as Author of
this work has been asserted by him in accordance with the Copyright,
Designs and Patents Act 1988.

A CIP catalogue record for this book is
available from the British Library

All rights reserved. No part of this book may be reproduced or transmitted
in any form or by any means, electronic or mechanical including photocopying,
recording or by any information storage and retrieval system, without
permission from the Publisher in writing.

Printed and bound in England
By CPI UK

Pen & Sword Books Ltd incorporates the Imprints of Pen & Sword Aviation,
Pen & Sword Maritime, Pen & Sword Military, Wharncliffe Local history,
Pen & Sword Select, Pen & Sword Military Classics and Leo Cooper.

For a complete list of Pen & Sword titles please contact
PEN & SWORD BOOKS LIMITED
47 Church Street, Barnsley, South Yorkshire, S70 2AS, England
E-mail: enquiries@pen-and-sword.co.uk
Website: www.pen-and-sword.co.uk

To Captain James Rowland, DSO and bar,
RN (retd) whose feats of warfare in command
of HMS *Wolverine* and her consorts in the
North Atlantic showed that the lights kindled
by the frigate captains still burn undiminished

The Frigates
Contents

Plates

Notes on the plates, are on pages 179 to 181

The author is indebted to the Trustees of the National Maritime Museum, Greenwich for their kind permission to publish the plates reproduced in this book

Author's notes

A good deal of confusion often arises in reading early accounts of this period, due to the fact that so many ships were captured from the enemy and put into service under the same name. Thus at Trafalgar there were both an English and a French 'Swift-sure', an English and a French 'Neptune', with a Spanish 'Neptuno' to make it more difficult. To avoid all difficulty, the name of any ship under British command is printed in SMALL CAPITALS, while the ships of all other nations are printed in *italics*. At the moment a ship changes hands it changes typography. Thus there is no difficulty in knowing immediately under which command the BONNE-CITOYENNE was in May 1798.

An awkwardness often arises from the fact that many of the best early histories are compiled directly from the log of the ship engaged, an excellent method up to a point. The log noted the change of the year on 1st January, and the month on its first day but no other day; this was reasonable in a log which was intended to be read through, when submitted to Admiralty; but it can be intensely annoying when one reads, 'On the 21st., at 6 a.m., sighted a large sail, ENE about 8 leagues', and then has to turn back page after page to find out what month it was, and as many more to find out what year. I have therefore been particular in writing the full date unless obviously redundant.

The term 'starboard' has always been used for that side of the ship which is on your right as you face forward; at the time about which I write, and earlier, the other side was called 'larboard'. During most of the nineteenth century this was the name, but owing to the verbal difficulty of distinguishing larboard from starboard, it became customary to call larboard 'port'; this was easier, since not only was the port light red, but after dinner one passed the port to the left. However, I have retained 'larboard', because in print there is no confusion, and it corresponds with the contemporary accounts.

In helm orders one has to recall that all ships were steered by a tiller; in small ships this might appear on deck, and the sweep of deck-space required for the tiller was quite a serious tactical consideration. In larger ships the tiller was well below decks, perhaps twelve or fifteen feet long, operated by rope and tackle from the wheel on the quarter-deck, but still a tiller. Hence if one put the tiller over to starboard, the rudder and consequently the ship's head went round to larboard; therefore the helm order 'starboard' meant that the ship was to go to larboard. Much later, after steam and steam steering became almost universal, helm orders were changed by international agreement; the order 'port' meant 'turn to port' and the order 'starboard' meant 'turn to starboard'. I have retained the helm orders of the period, but have done what I can to avoid confusion.

The most important moment in an officer's career was his promotion to post captain; from this point on his seniority was assured. No other post captain could get ahead of him, however strong his 'interest'. At the same time, a lieutenant commanding a small ship, or promoted 'Commander' into a ship of less than post rank (twenty guns) was called 'Captain' so long as he was in command. To avoid confusion between an actual post captain, on the ladder which must inevitably lead him to flag rank if he survived long enough, and a junior officer in temporary command; I have used the substantive ranks of commander and lieutenant to indicate non-post captains, and 'Mr' to denote a warrant officer in temporary command. This is only of interest as regards ancillary ships, as a frigate could only be commanded by a post captain except in case of incapacity (wounds or death) in which case the lieutenants assumed command according to seniority. It was usual that after a meritorious action the first lieutenant of the British ship should be promoted commander, and given some ship of less than post force to show what he could do in actual command; thus gradually, as the war went on, was built the best cadre of naval officers that the world has ever seen.

It is a difficult point to determine how far a writer should interrupt himself to explain terms that are probably familiar to most of his readers. This I have dealt with by a fairly copious first chapter giving a sufficiently detailed general description of the frigates; an indexed sail plan (see endpapers) and a glossary. Thus the reader new to the period can inform himself as fully as he wishes, while those who know it well are not irritated by incessant explanations in the text.

Foreword

by Admiral of the Fleet
Sir Algernon Willis G.C.B., K.B.E., D.S.O., D.L.

This book by Mr James Henderson is particularly commended to those interested in the sea and in national defence.

In the 22 years of the Revolutionary and Napoleonic Wars (1793 to 1815) this country was engaged almost continuously in hostilities with France and, at times, with Spain, the Netherlands, and America as well. Our survival depended on supremacy at sea and this island produced a magnificent body of fighting seamen, who raised the efficiency of the British Navy to a state which has seldom been equalled. While the great victories over the enemy's battle fleets, such as St Vincent, the Nile and Trafalgar, gave us command of the sea, it was the smaller ships, notably the frigates, which exercised the control of sea communications enabling our trade to flow freely while cutting off most of that of the enemy.

These efforts led to countless frigate actions which our sailors fought with success, often against odds.

The graphic accounts of these actions and of other activities of the frigates related by Mr Henderson in this book make stirring reading, and take one back to the great days when, in the words of the younger Pitt: 'England saved herself by her exertions and Europe by her example.' Pitt, of course, intended to include the Scots, the Welsh and the Irish in this eulogy!

I wish this book the success it certainly deserves.

Petersfield
Hampshire

A. U. WILLIS
Admiral of the Fleet
August 1970

1

The Frigates

'Frigates!' cried Nelson, 'Were I to die this moment, *want of frigates* would be found engraved on my heart!' He was chasing round the Mediterranean in search of the French expedition to Egypt, the biggest overseas invasion ever mounted, with 75 warships, 400 transports, 10,000 sailors and 36,000 troops, horse, foot and artillery. Had Nelson had the four frigates which were originally detailed to join his squadron, he would inevitably have caught the expedition on the high seas and the whole of history would have been different; General Buonaparte would have ended his career, in all probability, in 1798 as a prisoner of war in England, or Naples if he were unlucky.

The term frigate appears to have originated in the Mediterranean, French *frégate*, Italian *fregatta*, and to have been at first applied to the galleass type of warship, about 250 tons, fitted with oars as well as sails. The first English ship to be called a frigate was the CONSTANT-WARWICK, about 380 tons, launched in 1646. According to Samuel Pepys, who was in a position to know, she was built on the lines of a captured Dunkirk privateer. The word came to be used rather loosely for any swift ship of some force, until the eighteenth century when the frigates came into the strict rating system of the Royal Navy. They were almost all fifth-raters, except for the small 28-gun class which were sixth-rate, which rate included anything down to a 20-gun post-ship, the smallest that could be commanded by a post captain. Smaller vessels were not rated, although well defined.

Because 'fifth-rate' sounds a long way down the list, many

have thought that a frigate was a small ship of little force; but this was very far from the truth. Table I on page 185 gives a view of the rating system in 1794, when the 'ready' ships had been commissioned, and in 1814, before the run-down commenced. In this table, 'relegated' means out of commission and relegated to harbour or other duties; still useful, but not sea-going. Even VICTORY was relegated after the battle of Cape St Vincent, and served as a prison ship before being again commissioned as Nelson's flagship in the Mediterranean fleet.

The table shows at a glance that both at the beginning of the wars, and more especially at the end, by far the most numerous rates were the third rate, mostly 74-gun line-of-battle ships, and the fifth-rate frigates. The first and second rates, all three-deckers, were few in number, all fitted as flag-ships. In the third rate, the 64-gun ships were phased out as the war went on, and by 1814 there was only one in commission, the line being almost all 74s. The fourth-rate two-decker was a very small class, not fit to lie in the line of battle, unable to fight a ship of the line but too slow to get away. The fifth-rate 44-gun two-deckers were obsolete, having been built in 1744 to a design which even then was already obsolete. They were cranky, slow and unhandy, used mostly for convoy duties, and gradually relegated or broken up. The 28-gun sixth-rate frigates were gradually phased out during the period, so that at the height of the conflict the main strength of the Royal Navy was in the third-rate 74s and the fifth-rate frigates.

At a distance, hull down below the horizon, it was impossible to distinguish a frigate from a ship of the line; the difference in length was negligible, the sail plan was identical, and it was only when she came hull up that the higher sides and double row of ports showed the 74. Nevertheless, their roles were quite different. The 74 was built to carry as many and as heavy guns as possible, and to fight anything that floated. She was much higher, broader and deeper than the frigate, and consequently slower and less manoeuvrable. Battleships almost always operated in squadrons (less than ten ships) or fleets (more than ten); if a single one was detached, it was almost always because there was no frigate available.

The frigate, on the other hand, was not called upon to take

on *anything*, only ships of her own class. From the battleship she was to stand away, and this she could do 'with ease and honour both', keeping well out of fighting range but having the enemy under constant observation, while she could fight any ship she could not avoid. Attached to a fleet, the frigates were the eyes and ears, ranging in line abreast over an immense expanse of sea while the battleships kept steadily on in line ahead, repeating signals and carrying despatches. In a fleet action, they assisted disabled ships and took possession of captured enemies. At that period, it was against the etiquette of war for a battleship to fire on a frigate during a fleet action, unless the frigate asked for it by firing first. Thus the frigate EURYALUS, Captain Blackwood, remained in the thick of the battle of Trafalgar, repeating signals first for Nelson and later for Collingwood, but sustained no damage or casualties, and was able to tow off the dismasted ROYAL SOVEREIGN. Detached either singly or in small squadrons, the frigates might be sent anywhere in the world to attack enemy commerce and protect their own, to hunt down privateers or pirates, or to take part in the conquest of yet another colony. The best voyage of all was to sail 'under Admiralty letter', that is, not under any senior officer but with direct instructions from Admiralty — usually sealed, to be opened at a stated latitude and longitude, so that no hint of destination might leak out before departure.

Quite surprisingly for a leading maritime nation, Britain produced no outstanding naval architect during the eighteenth century, and most of the frigates were built on the lines of captured French vessels, which were always superior in size and speed to their British counterparts. The *Danaé*, 941 tons, was captured in 1759 and from her were built the 36-gun 12-pounders of the beginning of our period. In 1782 the RAINBOW captured the *Hebé*, 1063 tons, 40 guns, and from her were built the earlier 36- and 38-gun frigates, 18-pounders. In April 1794 a frigate squadron under Sir John Borlase Warren captured the *Pomone*, 44 guns, 1239 tons, and she became the prototype of all the later heavy frigates.

In more than twenty years of warfare there were naturally changes in the ships engaged; a glance at Table II, page 186, will show the change from a majority of small and light frigates in 1794 to almost all large and powerful ships in 1814. Of frigates with a main battery of 12-pounder guns there were only 12 left in commission out of 68, while the 18-pounder classes had gone up from 20 to 113. The 40-gun 24-pounder class was taken from the lines of the *Pomone*, but the 44s had a different origin. When the *Pomone* was examined, it was realised that she had only been taken by the excellent handling of the British squadron, and that there was no frigate in the Royal Navy that could match her single-handed: how many more did the French have? Admiralty was beginning to have doubts about the 64-gun two-deckers, which were not really a match for the French 74s; three 64s were therefore cut down by having the whole of the upper deck removed, and the forecastle and quarter-deck rebuilt on the main deck: retaining their powerful batteries of 24-pounders and the masts and rigging of 64s, they were real frigates for speed and handiness but were more than a match for any French frigate then afloat. They did notable service for many years, but were gradually phased out as they aged, and it was found that the new 38s and 36s could meet any French frigate afloat.

As these last two classes came to dominate the rating of frigate, I shall describe them in particular; the others differ merely in size and armament. A frigate was a long and fairly low ship, carrying its main battery of 18-pounders on a single deck, 14 or 13 ports each side according to whether she was a 38- or 36-gun frigate. Above this main deck the quarter-deck extended from the mainmast right to the stern, and the forecastle from the foremast to the bow. In both types the quarter-deck carried eight 9-pounder and the forecastle two 12-pounder long guns, plus four carronades on the quarter-deck and two on the forecastle, usually 24-pounders. The carronade was a very fair attempt to produce a short light gun which could nevertheless throw a heavy shot at comparatively short range, and many of the smaller ships of the Royal Navy were armed entirely with carronades; on the larger ships, however, frigates and 74s, the few carronades were generally reserved, loaded with two shot and a keg of musket-balls, to discourage any prospective boarding party on the opposing deck. Between the quarter-deck and the forecastle the bulwarks were carried well up, and deck-beams were laid over from side to side, just as if there were to be a complete second deck. On those beams, on each side of the ship, a gangway about six feet wide connected the two raised decks, and the larger boats and the spare spars were laid on the beams between the gangways.

Although there were a few experiments with other timbers when the ship-building programme was at its height, almost all the frigates were built entirely of oak, the main beams being at least a foot square in cross-section, and the planking four to five inches thick. This was proof against the musket-ball of the period, but cannon shot smashed through the planking and even the timbers, scattering deadly splinters all around, which caused far more casualties than shot. This was one of the reasons why officers opposed the use of teak, long after the Bombay-built ships had shown the superiority of teak for all maritime purposes: a splinter-wound from teak almost always goes septic, while an oak wound usually stays clean. The masts and spars were of pine, usually from the Baltic, and other timbers were used for particular purposes. All the frigates were extremely well built, fit to go to sea and stay at sea in any weather whatever. During the whole twenty-two years of war, only three frigates foundered at sea, and these were all very old ships, not really sea-worthy by frigate standards, and in each case it is clear that they met the centre of a tropical hurricane.

The frigates could carry six months' provisions, which meant that they could sail anywhere in the world without having to touch at any port. Full use was made of this mobility. In all the wide oceans of the world there was nowhere that the frigates were not sent, and nowhere that they did not find work to do. Well might Napoleon say bitterly, 'Wherever you find a fathom of water, there you will find the British.'

It has often been supposed that the frigates were very cramped for accommodation, as compared with the line-of-battle ships, but a simple comparison of known figures will show that it was quite the reverse. Take the favourite 38-gun 18-pounder which has been described: with a main deck about 150 feet long and 40 feet wide, and measuring at 1,060 tons, the whole complement was 277, officers, men and boys; very nearly four tons per man. No other class of warship had so much man-room. The 74 was usually about 1,700 tons, with a complement of

594 —less than three tons per man. The big 112-gun first-rater, of 2,350 tons and a complement of 841, had just over 2¾ tons per man; and in addition had to provide the very considerable space required for an Admiral and his staff, who were not included in the ship's company. In the smaller ships, the 20-gun post-ship had about 3 tons per man, while the smallest were really packed. Of the brig SPEEDY, fourteen 4-pounders, 158 tons, Lord Cochrane, her commander, wrote, 'She was crowded, rather than manned, with a crew of eighty-four men and six officers, myself included.' This is 1¾ tons per man. It is therefore clear that the frigates had more tonnage per man than any other class, rated or not. The nearest modern comparison I can make is the now obsolete 'Admiralty V' class of destroyer, which served well in both great wars: 1,090 tons, complement 134. When one allows 425 tons for engines and boilers and 350 tons for fuel oil, it is clear that the balance of 'liveability' is all with the sailing frigate.

There was, of course, no pretence at equality in allocating this ample living space. Inequality was emphasised. The captain was not first, he was on a different plane altogether. Almost always a post captain of more than three years seniority, he wore a pair of epaulettes, which were worn only by the Marine officers in the rest of the complement. His accommodation was quite different from that of anybody else; under the quarter-deck, right aft, he had a dining-room, another day cabin, and two night cabins, even on the smallest 28-gun frigates. He had his own cook, steward, clerk and coxswain, who served nobody else. At the entrance to his quarters a Marine sentry was stationed night and day. When he appeared on the quarter-deck, the whole of the windward half was instantly cleared for his solitary promenade. Nobody dared to address him without permission. He might, once or even twice a week, invite his first lieutenant and one or two other officers to dine with him, and might include an occasional midshipman who had been recommended to him by some person of influence; but these were very formal occasions. Discipline had to be maintained, and maintained all the way; nobody thought very highly of a captain who was in the least familiar with his officers.

The only other commissioned officers on the ship were the lieutenants, usually four, and the two Marine officers. These were the commissioned officers of wardroom rank, to whom were added the sailing master, the surgeon, the purser, and the chaplain, if any; these were the warrant officers of wardroom rank, and could walk the quarter-deck, but their sleeping quarters were below, the surgeon and the chaplain near the cockpit, which was their action station, and the purser next his stores. The sailing master had a cabin below, but at sea he was hutched under the quarter-deck near the captain's quarters. The commissioned officers were housed in a row of cabins each not much more than a cube of six feet, all opening off the wardroom and fitted in, as best might, between the guns. All partitions were light and movable, for when the ship cleared for action the cabins and all their furnishings were thrown down into the hold. The wardroom officers had usually a common mess, to which everybody contributed equally, although there was nothing to stop anybody from opting out, either to live economically on the ship's rations or to indulge in private luxuries.

A deck below, the gunner presided in the gun-room over the senior warrant officers — boatswain and carpenter — and petty officers such as sailmaker, cook and armourer, master's mates and surgeon's mates, and also the very youngest boys in the ship, the 'captain's servants', young gentlemen not yet rated as midshipmen, although they could walk the quarter-deck, which the gun-room warrant officers could not. The midshipmen berthed in and around the cockpit, which became the surgery in action. Between the officers aft and the ratings forward were berthed all the lesser petty officers and also the Marines, about thirty of them, with a sergeant and three corporals. This was a precaution against nocturnal mutiny; the Marines were reckoned to be reliable under all circumstances.

Forward of the mainmast lived the ratings, a very mixed lot: professional warship sailors, very few, less than a sixth of the whole; fishermen and merchant sailors who had been conscripted by the press-gang — few ever volunteered; landsmen who had volunteered for the 'bounty', or to avoid gaol or debtor's prison, or to escape from difficult social circumstances. It was the business of the boatswain and his mates, under the first lieutenant, to make this mixed bag into a taut, close-knit ship's company, and usually they were successful.

Living was hard before the mast, but the hardships are often exaggerated by comparison with modern shore living; by comparison with shore living, for the same class of people at that time, it was still hard but far from intolerable. Below decks the atmosphere was close and stuffy; but men whose blood is thoroughly oxygenated by a vigorous life in the open air invariably prefer a comfortable fug when they turn in. Hammock allowance was 14 inches per man, but of course as half were on watch this meant in effect 28 inches per man, 4 feet 8 inches per pair, a shade better than a double bed; and a clean hammock was infinitely superior to some straw on a damp floor. In a well-run ship great pains were taken to keep the ship and the men clean; vermin-borne diseases such as typhus which decimated armies on shore were very rare in the ships of the Royal Navy. Food was coarse and monotonous, but few had ever had much better, and at least they were sure where the next meal was going to come from. Drink was only too plentiful. The allowance of beer was a gallon a day, and of rum half a pint; but this rum was almost pure alcohol, and when cut down, as it was, with two pints of water it was still equivalent to very nearly two bottles of rum at the strength at which it is retailed today. Anybody today who drank eight pints of beer and the best part of two bottles of spirits every day would be put down as an alcoholic, yet this was the daily ration for every man in the Navy. It was eagerly expected. The severest punishment less than flogging was to cut a man's rum ration off for a week; the withdrawal symptoms must have been very unpleasant, but no doubt a popular type would get 'sippers' from his mess-mates. To be drunk was a serious naval crime, but many men must have been at least tipsy every afternoon. Far more men lost their lives through drink than by enemy action, and lunacy was all too common, mostly from frequent head injuries caused by running against overhead beams while drunk. Admiral Lord Keith considered that almost every crime, and the majority of casualties, were caused by excessive rum; yet he dared not suggest to cut the ration. Did not Solomon advise, 'Let him drink, and forget his poverty, and remember his misery no more.'

To understand the importance of sea-borne cannon, it is necessary to compare with land guns. At that time, the standard field-piece was a 6-pounder, and owing to difficulties of transport they were few; even at Waterloo Wellington could deploy only 156 guns of assorted nationalities. The twenty-eight 18-pounders of the 38-gun frigate would on land form the siege train for the assault of some major fortress, hauled up by hundreds of animals at a few miles a day; but the frigate, under favourable conditions, could carry her formidable battery two hundred miles in the twenty-four hours. The 18-pounder was nine feet long, weighed two tons, and required ten men to handle it. On firing, the force of the recoil sent it running inboard on its carriage to the full length of the breeching-tackle which secured it to the ship's side; it was then sponged out with a swab, the powder in its cloth cartridge rammed down with a wad on top, then the shot and another wad; the cloth of the cartridge was pierced and a little fine priming-powder poured into the touch-hole. The gun-crew then ran the gun out by heaving on the breeching-tackle, after which the gun-captain adjusted his aim. The modern guns were fired by flint-lock and lanyard, but slow-match was always kept ready in case of emergency. The management of the gun was heavy work, especially in rough weather. Under good conditions with a well-trained crew, a shot every two minutes was a very good rate of fire.

While during the twenty-two years of the wars Britain was at some time or other in conflict with every maritime Power except Portugal, it was, of course, the French who were the most frequent antagonists, and the most carefully studied by British officers. For equivalent gun-power, the French frigates were larger, better designed, and more numerously manned (up to a hundred more) than their British counterparts. In tactics, the desire on either side was to get athwart the enemy's stern, where the whole broadside could rake the whole length of the ship with only two or four guns able to reply; but usually it came to a mutual cannonade at about fifty yards range. The British fired low, on the downward roll of the ship; the French fired high at the rigging, on the upward roll. The British idea was to kill the crew and dismount the guns; the French wished to disable the sailing power of their enemy, hoping to be able to take a favourable position for cannonade, musketry or boarding with their superior numbers. The British tactics were much more

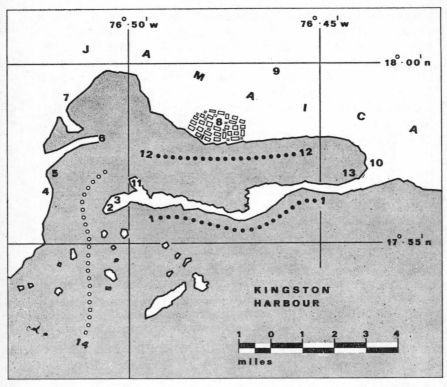

1 The Palisades. 2 Fort Charles. 3 Port Royal, Headquarters, C-in-C, West Indies Station. 4 Apostles Battery. 5 Port Henderson. 6 Fort Augusta. 7 Passage Fort. 8 Town of Kingston. 9 Military Camp. 10 Fort Nugent. 11 Gallows Point. 12 Kingston Harbour. 13 Harbour Head. 14 Passage into the Harbour through the reefs.

effective; in almost every action the French casualties were much heavier than the British, and the French usually lost. During the period 1793 to 1815, the British lost 17 frigates to the French, of which 9 were recaptured; whereas in the same period the French lost 229 frigates to the British. Very few were sunk; it is very difficult to sink a wooden ship by above-water bombardment: the accepted form was that when a ship had sustained such damage and losses that she could not continue the action with any hope of success, she should haul down her flag and surrender.

Engaging in war has always an element of risk, so has going

to sea, and in those days especially so had going to a tropical climate. Those not closely acquainted with the period may be surprised that of these three hazards climate was the chief, sea-going next, and combat almost negligible. Taking the whole of the wars, more than half the deaths were by disease, chiefly tropical. Scurvy was still a danger, though not so fearful as in 1740, when Anson lost by scurvy two-thirds of the complement of his squadron between Britain and Juan Fernandez. For the rest, about forty per cent of all deaths were from the hazards of the sea — shipwreck, fire, explosion, falling from rigging, and personal accidents, mostly when drunk. In the whole Royal Navy during the whole period, less than ten per cent of the deaths were in action; and in frigates, which were not required to take part in the great fleet encounters, deaths in action cannot have been more than five per cent of the total death-roll. In a frigate duel, on the British side ten killed and twenty wounded was a pretty heavy casualty list.

The mosquito was far deadlier than the French cannon. Most histories ignore or play down the incidence of disease, and play up the great battles; but it is all the same to a widow's husband whether he meets a cannon-ball in an action or dies in a stinking hospital in the Caribbean; and the latter was at least ten times more likely. During only two years of operations in the West Indies, the army lost by 'Yellow Jack' twenty times as many British soldiers as were killed at Waterloo. The British seamen were not supplied with statistics, but they were perfectly well aware of how many of their shipmates they had seen more or less buried at the Palisades* compared with the number they had seen killed in action. Given good officers, they looked forward eagerly to battle, not only with the natural zest of warriors, but with the hope of gain; prize money might very well set up a man for life in his sphere of society. Under any good captain they engaged with every confidence: under a great captain — and at least fifty of the frigate captains were born leaders of men — they went into action in the highest spirits, each man sure of his comrades, each determined to do his duty and absolutely confident of victory.

* The Palisades was a beach at Jamaica, where the dead from the hospitals were buried in very shallow graves in the sand. The land crabs completed the disposal. This Aceldana is now the airport.

2

Success Story

When the French National Convention declared war on Britain on 1st February 1793, it took some time to get the great battle fleets to sea. Of the ships already in full commission, squadrons had to be sent to distant stations to carry the news and to assemble the merchants into convoys, protect their own and harass the enemy. The British stores had been so well assembled by the Comptroller of the Navy, Sir Charles Middleton, volunteers came in so readily and the press-gang was so busy, that by July the number of line-of-battle ships in full commission had been increased from 26 to 54, and the Royal Navy could put out powerful fleets into the Mediterranean and the Channel, as well as meeting its distant commitments in India and the West Atlantic. Almost immediately on the declaration of war, however, there sailed from the ports on both sides of the Channel swarms of small vessels, both of the regular navies and of privateers, all anxious to snap up some richly-laden merchantman of the other side who had not yet heard of the war.

A privateer was a ship owned and fitted out by private persons, who received 'letters of marque' from a sovereign power; these entitled them to carry on war at their own risk and expense, and for their private profit, and at the same time ensured that if captured, the crews were to be treated as prisoners of war. It was in effect licensed piracy, and in fact many known pirates, especially in the West Indies, applied for and received letters of marque, thus legalising their trade so long as they confined it to the ships of the enemy. Many British privateers were fitted out, but as the war continued and the grip of the British blockade tightened and the French overseas colonies were captured, British privateering practically disappeared, simply because it was no longer profitable. French merchantmen were so scarce, so well armed and so well escorted, that the distant profit just wasn't worth the certain expense and probable risk. The French privateers, on the other hand, were a thorn in the side of the British marine during the whole of the wars. Built for the purpose, well armed, and manned by the bold and experienced mariners of Brittany, they could run from any ship of war and over-awe almost any merchantman except the heavily-armed ships of the Honourable East India Company. Immediately on the outbreak, the small warships of both Navies, brigs, sloops, and a few frigates, were sent into the Channel and its approaches, to look for enemy ships and of course snap up what prizes they could.

In May 1793 the frigates VENUS and NYMPHE left Falmouth on a cruise in the Western Approaches, and finding little of interest, they separated to cover a wider field. Early in the morning of the 27th May the VENUS, about 300 miles west of Cape Finisterre, came across the *Semillante*, a frigate of about twenty-five per cent more force; a sharp action ensued, of which the *Semillante* had much the worse; but just as the VENUS was closing in for the kill there hove in sight the *Semillante's* consort, the *Cléopâtre*, a fresh and powerful frigate, and the VENUS could only run as well as her damaged rigging would permit. The *Cléopâtre* chased her for two days, until she was rejoined by the NYMPHE, when the *Cléopâtre* in turn made off. Both the French ships went into Cherbourg, then quite a small port, while the British pair made Falmouth.

The NYMPHE was a frigate of the 36-gun class, 938 tons, mounting twenty-six long 12-pounders on the main gun-deck, with two long 6-pounders and eight carronades, 24-pounders, on the quarter-deck and forecastle, and with a total complement of 240 officers and men. She was commanded by Captain Edward Pellew, a Cornishman who had already been favourably noticed for seamanship, knowledge of the dangerous French coast, and capacity for training a crew. The VENUS being under repair, Pellew left Falmouth on the 17th of June, 1793, to cruise in the

Channel, with some hope that the *Cléopâtre* might be doing the same, she being, as far as was known, the only French ship of force north of Brest; the *Semillante* was safe enough for a few months.

Once, in the Roman Senate, a Commander-in-Chief was chosen on the grounds that in addition to all his military virtues 'He is favoured by Fortune'. Thus it was with Pellew: he was always lucky. Early the very next morning, about twenty miles south of Start Point, a large sail was observed to the south-east, and this was none other than the *Cléopâtre*. She was of almost exactly the same force as the NYMPHE, but with eighty more men in her crew. At first she bore away, and both ships continued under full sail in a fair breeze on that fine June morning. The NYMPHE was overtaking, and when Captain Mullon of the *Cléopâtre* recognised her, he shortened sail and cleared for action until the NYMPHE came up with her about six o'clock. A curious ceremony now took place, reminiscent of an earlier generation; of course the war was yet young, and very few in either ship had ever been in action. As the ships closed, the captains hailed each other and saluted by taking off their hats; the crew of the NYMPHE shouted 'Long live King George' and gave three cheers, led by the captain waving his hat from the quarter-deck. Captain Mullon waved a cap of liberty to his men, who shouted 'Vive la République', and nailed the cap to the mast-head. Then, as the guns came to bear, Captain Pellew put on his hat and the NYMPHE's broadside thundered out. The *Cléopâtre* answered immediately, and at little more than a ship's length apart a furious cannonade carried on for three-quarters of an hour, the raw crews serving their guns like veterans, the captains gravely walking the quarter-decks amid the storm of shot. Suddenly, at the same time, both the mizzen-mast and the steering wheel of the *Cléopâtre* were shot away, and, out of control, she swung around head-on to the NYMPHE, her jib-boom passing between the fore and main masts of her opponent. She kept on swinging, until the jib-boom was pressed so hard against the mainmast of the NYMPHE that it looked as if it would carry away the damaged mast; but the jib-boom broke. The two ships remained hooked together by the rigging, and Captain Pellew, thinking that the enemy intended to board him with their superior numbers, ordered his own boarders up to repel them. However, the *Cléopâtre* was in no condition for boarding, all her commissioned officers having been killed or wounded, and seeing some sign of confusion, Captain Pellew instantly gave the order to board. His men leapt over the bulwarks on to the forecastle of the *Cléopâtre*, and through the gun-ports on to her main deck. With a fierce rush along the deck and the gangways they reached the quarter-deck, and in less than ten minutes hauled down her colours.

On the quarter-deck they found the heroic Captain Mullon mortally wounded, his left hip and part of his back having been carried away by a round-shot. Resolute in his duty to the last, he remembered that he had in his pocket a list of private coast-signals, and as he lay in his death-throes he pulled a paper from his pocket, bit it to pieces and was trying to swallow it when he died. In fact the paper he destroyed was his Captain's commission, and the signals fell into British hands; but no mistake could dim his heroic devotion to duty.

In so close and fierce an action, it was to be expected that casualties would be heavy. The NYMPHE had 23 killed, including 5 warrant officers, and 27 wounded, including 2 lieutenants and 2 midshipmen. The *Cléopâtre* had 63 killed and wounded, including her captain killed and all 3 lieutenants wounded. Both ships were extensively damaged, but repairable, and both arrived at Portsmouth on the 21st.

As has been said, Pellew was always lucky. This was the very first naval battle of the war which was fought out to a finish between ships of equal force manned with equal courage and resolution, and the result was a decisive British victory, with the captured vessel brought into a British port. King George III came down in person to Portsmouth and knighted Captain Pellew, the first hero-knighthood of the wars. His brother, Commander Israel Pellew, had been with him as a volunteer, having no ship at the time, and the King of his own authority made him a post captain. First-Lieutenant Amherst Morris was promoted Commander by Admiralty, which also bought in the prize, changing the name to OISEAU as there was already a CLEOPATRA in the Royal Navy. A tidy bit of prize-money nicely rounded off the honours.

Captain Israel Pellew was perhaps unlucky in that he spent the whole of his naval career under the shadow—the beneficent shadow—of his elder brother. He had a satisfactory career, ending up a knight and an admiral, but he was always being compared with his big brother. Israel commanded the CONQUEROR at Trafalgar, and early in the battle took possession of the French flag-ship, the *Bucentaure*. He sent his Captain of Marines on board to arrange the formalities of the surrender of the Commander-in-Chief, Vice-Admiral Villeneuve, who asked to what ship he had surrendered. 'The CONQUEROR, Captain Pellew.' 'Ah, I am happier to know that I have to give my sword to so distinguished an officer as Captain Sir Edward Pellew.' Perhaps Israel was a better name for a patriarch than for a captain; perhaps he was just not so lucky. His first frigate command, the AMPHION, was lying in harbour at Plymouth on 22nd September 1796 when she took fire and blew up, killing most of the crew and their visitors from shore.

Sir Edward Pellew was now given the 38-gun frigate ARETHUSA, while the NYMPHE, after repairs, was commanded by Captain George Murray. In the spring of 1794 they formed part of a squadron of five frigates cruising off the Breton coast, under the command of Commodore Sir John Borlase Warren in the FLORA, the others being the MELAMPUS, Captain Thomas Wells, and CONCORDE, Captain Sir John Richard Strachan. On the 23rd of April, before dawn, they descried a strange squadron, which turned out to be the French frigates *Engageante*, *Resolue* and *Pomone*, with the corvette *Babet*, standing in line ahead in that order. The *Babet* was out of her class, having only twenty 8-pounders and two brass 6s. The FLORA overtook the *Babet* at 6.30 a.m., and firing into her, passed ahead and engaged the *Pomone*, a very different proposition, being the most powerful frigate in the world at that time. The ARETHUSA, next ahead, now engaged the *Babet*, which surrendered at 8.30 a.m., after a most courageous resistance to very superior force. By this time the FLORA had had such a hammering from the *Pomone* that she had to drop astern, and now stopped to take possession of the *Babet* while the ARETHUSA and CONCORDE pushed on to overtake the *Pomone*, which had also been much damaged by the fire of the FLORA. Under the cannonade of the two British frigates, both her main and mizzen masts crashed down, and the shattered spars took fire; thus crippled, she hauled down her colours at 9.30 a.m., and was taken over by the ARETHUSA.

The Commodore now signalled the CONCORDE and MELAMPUS to chase the remaining two frigates, the NYMPHE being too far in the rear to have much hope of catching up. The CONCORDE, being the better sailer, intended to engage the *Engageante* in passing, hoping to do her enough damage to slow her down until the MELAMPUS could come up. However, the *Resolue* came to the aid of her consort, and together they did so much damage to the CONCORDE's rigging that she was glad to hang back and refit. The *Resolue* now stood ahead, and Sir Richard Strachan decided to make sure of the *Engageante* and let the other go. The battle lasted until 1.45 p.m., when the French frigate, having been so knocked about that she could neither fight nor flee, at last surrendered.

The British squadron was so superior in force that the result was to be expected: the great interest was the capture of the *Pomone*. Admiralty was surprised at her size and force; it had not been thought in the least likely that the Revolutionary Government could so quickly produce an entirely new and superior class of warship, and steps had to be taken to cope, as already described (p. 18). The *Pomone* was taken into the Royal Navy, and later became for a time the flagship of Sir John Borlase Warren; the *Engageante* was too much battered to go to sea, and became a hospital ship; the *Babet* was added to the Royal Navy as a sloop, but was lost in 1801 with all hands, in a West Indian hurricane.

Sir John's squadron continued to make things difficult off all the coast of Brittany, especially in the vicinity of Brest, where a formidable French fleet was gathering. On the 23rd August 1794 they attacked a French frigate and two corvettes, and drove them on to the rock-bound shore. The squadron was becoming the theme of the ballad-mongers —

> '*If they run, why we'll follow, and run them ashore,*
> *And if they won't fight us, what can we do more?*'

The ARETHUSA had a good name for balladry, lucky again:

> '*Come all ye jolly sailors bold,*
> *Whose hearts are cast in honour's mould,*

While English glory I unfold,
Huzza for the ARETHUSA!'

On the 21st October 1794 Sir Edward Pellew in the ARETHUSA found himself in command of a small squadron: ARTOIS, Captain Edmund Nagle, DIAMOND, Sir William Sidney Smith, and GALATEA, Captain Richard Goodwin Keats. It is striking how many of the frigate captains of those early days became famous admirals before the wars ended; of course at that time ships were scarce, and Admiralty could give each one a picked captain and a picked crew too. On this day they sighted a big French frigate and gave chase; the ARTOIS sailed so much better than the others that she was alone when she overhauled the *Revolutionnaire*. Action lasted less than three-quarters of an hour, when the French crew refused to fight any more and forced the captain to surrender after a loss of eight killed and four wounded, as against three killed and five wounded in the ARTOIS. While the French ship was definitely more powerful than the British, she was on her first cruise. Being little damaged, she was a valuable addition to the Royal Navy, and Captain Nagle was knighted.*

What with captures and what with building, more ships were becoming available, and for the 1796 campaign there were two powerful frigate squadrons to cruise the waters around Brest, one under Sir John Borlase Warren in the POMONE, and the other under Sir Edward Pellew in the INDEFATIGABLE, one of the new 44-gun frigates made by taking a deck out of a 64-gun ship of the line. In his squadron was the recently captured REVOLUTIONNAIRE, Captain Francis Cole. The squadron sighted a French frigate, and Pellew ordered Cole to get between her and the land, being a few miles off Ushant. This Captain Cole was able to do, but the night falling misty, he lost sight of her until after 9 p.m., when he made all sail and chased at great speed, coming up with her about midnight. Captain Cole hailed the French frigate, inviting her to surrender without fighting, in view of the powerful squadron coming up; this the French captain refused, but after a couple of broadsides the crew called out that they had surrendered. The ship was the *Unité*, Captain

---

* The ARTOIS, Captain Sir Edmund Nagle, wrecked on the French coast, 31st July 1797.

Durand-Linois, of considerably less force than the REVOLUTION-NAIRE, and having had nine killed and eleven wounded, while the British had no casualties at all. The fact that both the *Revolutionnaire* and the *Unité* were surrendered by their crews against the wishes of their officers shows that the French Navy had not yet recovered from the anarchy of the Revolution. The surrender did not affect the career of Captain Linois, as we find him later as a Rear-Admiral commanding a squadron in the Indian Ocean. In this case, as well as having a mutinous crew, he was handicapped by the presence on board of the wife of the Governor of Rochefort with a large family and domestic staff; Captain Pellew stopped a neutral merchant ship and put the family and retainers on board to continue their journey.

On the 20th of the same month, when the squadron was returning to Plymouth, a strange sail was sighted and the recognition signal was not replied; Pellew went in chase along with the AMAZON and CONCORDE. The chase went on for fifteen hours at high speed, 168 miles being run at an average of 11 knots; the INDEFATIGABLE was well ahead of her consorts, and brought the enemy to action about midnight. The fight continued under full sail for two hours, during which time the French ship lost her mizzen-mast and main top-mast, and the INDEFATIGABLE lost her gaff and her mizzen top-mast. The action was broken off while both made what repairs they could to their rigging, when the AMAZON and CONCORDE came up, and after they had taken up good positions the French ship surrendered. She was the *Virginie*, Captain Bergeret, who was highly praised by Sir Edward in his official despatch, having had fifteen killed and twenty-seven wounded, and four feet of water in the hold, before he surrendered to an overwhelming force. The INDEFATIGABLE had no casualties whatever. The *Virginie* was a very fine new frigate of over 1,000 tons, and after repair was a most acceptable addition to the Royal Navy.

Aggression was the keynote of the policy of the French Directorate; *l'attaque, l'attaque, et toujours l'attaque.* Indeed, this policy had won them astounding victories over all Europe, and had battered most of western Europe into either submission or alliance. Of the maritime nations, Holland declared war on Britain in May, Spain in October of 1795. The combined fleets far out-numbered the British, who also could not abandon their far-spread responsibilities. The Directorate planned an attack on British soil; in the summer of 1796 General Hoche had a conference at Basle in Switzerland with Arthur O'Connor and Lord Edward Fitzgerald, the Irish patriots or traitors, depending on the angle of view, when a plan for a major invasion of Ireland was roughed out, and Wolfe Tone came to France to assist in the preparations and action. The French had contemplated landing 25,000 troops; the Irishmen thought 15,000 was enough (neither of the delegates had ever seen an army assembled) and were able to assure the French (who had no experience of negotiating with Irishmen) that immediately a French army landed it would be joined by a quarter of a million armed patriots. Their own imagination fired, the Directorate thought up a two-fold plan: the French Navy, having landed the Army in Ireland, was forthwith to proceed to India and conquer the British empire there; however, sanity broke through, and it was decided that the conquest of Ireland would be enough for one campaign. The plan was well worked out; the disembarkation was to be in Bantry Bay, and three different landing places were selected, according to the wind which might be blowing at the time; if none was feasible, then the troops were to debark at the mouth of the Shannon; should the fleet scatter during the approach, the ships were to rendezvous off Mizzen Head and remain thereabouts for five days to gather again. The only things left out of the calculations were the Royal Navy and the weather; as things turned out, the Channel Fleet was absent, and the job had to be done by Admirals December and January, plus a few frigates.

By November, General Hoche and Vice-Admiral Morard-de-Galles had everything in readiness at Brest, awaiting only two reinforcing squadrons; one, under Rear-Admiral Richery, did not arrive until 11th December, and the Toulon squadron under Rear-Admiral Villeneuve (he who lost at Trafalgar nine years later) did not seem to be coming at all. It was decided to set out, and on the 15th December the great fleet moved out of harbour and anchored in Camaret Bay; there were 17 line-of-battle ships, 13 frigates, 6 corvettes, 7 transports and a partially disarmed frigate serving as a powder transport. In addition to the large crews, the fleet had on board an army of probably 18,000 men, horse, foot and artillery, with vast quantities of stores; thus encumbered, they were to face the Royal Navy and the Atlantic in mid-winter.

The main Channel Fleet, under Lord Bridport, had gone into Portsmouth for the winter, agreeable to Admiralty instructions, leaving off Brest a strong squadron of line-of-battle ships under Vice-Admiral Colpoys, cruising about forty miles offshore, with an inshore squadron under Captain Sir Edward Pellew in the INDEFATIGABLE, having under his command the REVOLUTION-NAIRE, Captain Francis Cole, the AMAZON, Captain Robert Reynolds, the PHOEBE, Captain Robert Barlow, and a small armed lugger the DUKE OF YORK, Mr Sparrow. Immediately on observing the decisive movement of the French fleet, Sir Edward despatched the PHOEBE to inform Colpoys and, probably having doubts as to the promptitude of that very senior officer, at the same time sent the AMAZON to Portsmouth.

The French fleet had intended to sail out by the passage d'Iroise, the direct route from the port, but seeing the frigates so bold about the entrance, the Vice-Admiral concluded that they must be strongly supported, and he would run the risk of his ships being destroyed in detail as they came forth; so, the wind being fair from the east, he decided to take the southward passage through the dangerous Raz de Sein. Darkness falling and the wind rising gusty, he changed his mind and made for the passage d'Iroise, followed by those of the fleet who could divine his intentions. As a guide, he stationed a corvette at a suitable spot, with directions to fire guns, rockets and blue-lights to keep the fleet on the right track. Pellew thought he would like to join in the fun, so he took the INDEFATIGABLE right in among the French fleet, where he too fired guns, rockets and blue-lights, greatly to his own pleasure and the confusion of the French, so much so that the 74-gun *Seduisant* went ashore on the Grand Stevenet rock near the entrance of the Raz; here she too, as signals of distress, began to fire guns, rockets and blue-lights, to add to the general mayhem. During the night she became a total loss, with more than half her complement of 1,300 men.

Having satisfied himself that the whole fleet had put to sea, and, in the prevailing easterly wind, could not get back into harbour, Pellew sent the REVOLUTIONNAIRE with this information to Vice-Admiral Colpoys, and his little lugger to Falmouth with the same news. Later in the same day, having completed his job of watching the enemy and reporting their movements, he decided that he would not do much good hanging about there and went off to Falmouth himself, arriving on the 20th December and reporting to Admiralty by the semaphore telegraph.

Meanwhile the French fleet had got fairly to sea, but in three separate detachments, out of sight of each other and, fortunately for them, out of sight of Colpoys' fleet of thirteen ships of the line; and also out of sight of their leaders, who had, for reasons doubtless clear to themselves, embarked together in the fast frigate *Fraternité*. Colpoys was somewhat at a loss, but on the 20th sighted a squadron of French line-of-battle ships and gave chase; this, however, was the tardy reinforcement from Toulon, which in the dirty weather got clean away and went into L'Orient. In the chase and the weather the British fleet was damaged and scattered, and Vice-Admiral Colpoys turned up at Spithead on the 31st with only six ships left under his command.

Somehow the fragments of the French fleet met at the rendez-vous off Mizzen Head in a spell of fine weather on the 21st, lacking only the *Seduissant*, wrecked, and missing the *Nestor*, 74, the *Fraternité*, frigate, with the two commanders-in-chief, and two other frigates. Rear-Admiral Bouvet, an excellent sailor, took command of the ships, and General Grouchy (who did *not* distinguish himself at Waterloo eighteen years later) took over the Army; but try what they could, they could not get up Bantry Bay. Christmas Day, when Lord Bridport was trying to get the Channel Fleet out of Spithead, was the coldest in living memory; indeed, the coldest since 1708; moreover, a bitter east wind drove a thin snow along with it. Now the French could appreciate the sailing directions given to the Great Armada two centuries before: 'Take great heed lest you fall on the island of Ireland, for fear of the harm that may befall you on that coast, where the ocean sea raiseth such a billow as can hardly be endured by the greatest ships.' Some went ashore, some collided with each other; all the survivors were blown out of the Bay, and eventually, despairing of success and short of provisions, they made the best of their separate ways back to France, harried by six frigates out of Cork.

One of the last to leave the coast was the *Droits de l'Homme*, 74, Commodore la Crosse, a very good officer, having also on board the famous General Humbert. Pursuant to orders, the Commodore went to the second rendezvous, the mouth of the Shannon, where he captured a small British privateer and took her crew and passengers on board as prisoners. On the 7th January, as nobody else appeared, he left the station and made for France, intending to make a landfall on Belle Isle and then go into one of the harbours in that vicinity. On the 13th January he thought himself in the correct latitude and about seventy or eighty miles west of his objective, the weather coming up foul from the westward. He sighted through the mist and rain two large ships to windward, turned away, and was glad to lose sight of them: actually they were French. Two hours later, with the storm rising and the sea very rough, the *Droits de l'Homme* descried two more ships to leeward, between her and the land, wherever that might be; and what ships were these but the INDEFATIGABLE and the AMAZON, back on station!

Commodore la Crosse was a brave and experienced seaman, and knew very well what an immense superiority a ship of the line had over two frigates, even if one was larger than usual; but he also had on board a valuable battalion of soldiers, many of whom must inevitably be killed in a gunnery battle, and also an important General. The wind was rising, and backing to south-west, a bad sign; and just after he sighted the British frigates a sudden squall carried away both his main and fore top-masts, cumbering his decks with wreckage and reducing his power of manoeuvring. This made up his mind, and after clearing the fallen spars he set off before the wind to the eastward, under mainsails only.

Sir Edward Pellew was no swashbuckler, to rush into battle regardless of any consideration; he knew the rule that frigates did not engage line-of-battle ships, and also that if he did engage and lost his ship he would be in serious trouble for hazarding her against odds which all experience showed to be impossible, the *Droits de l'Homme* having almost three times his fire-power and at least five times his man-power. But he had that quality of all the great captains, a cool head amid tumult, which could assess the enemy's situation as accurately as his own. He had seen the topmasts fall, and knew how that would handicap the handling of the Frenchman; he knew she was overcrowded and overloaded, and he saw the rising tempest as an ally; in such a sea the lower ports of the 74 would have to be kept shut, only opened briefly when the guns were ready to fire; a serious drawback for that formidable battery of 32-pounders. Above all, he knew his men and they knew him; there was complete mutual confidence; the battle was only to be won by discipline and seamanship, and his men knew well that there was no more consummate seaman afloat than Sir Edward Pellew.

The INDEFATIGABLE came up with the *Droits de l'Homme* about 5.30 p.m., as darkness was falling; shortened sail to close-reefed topsails only, drew across the enemy's stern and opened with a raking broadside, to which there could be no immediate reply; the battleship, however, was able to draw alongside, and pour in her powerful broadside, as well as a very heavy fire of musketry from the soldiers on board. Pellew now drew ahead, intending to cross the bows of his opponent and rake her again; this attempt was foiled, and the *Droits de l'Homme* tried to run him down and board with her six hundred soldiers; but the INDEFATIGABLE evaded and continued the cannonade.

The AMAZON had been about eight miles astern when Sir Edward commenced the action, but made for the gun-flashes under all the sail she could carry; she came up at about 6.45 p.m., fired a broadside at close range into the quarter of the *Droits de l'Homme*, and tried to pass under her stern to rake her with the other broadside, but with great skill Commodore la Crosse so manœuvred as to bring both his antagonists together on his weather side, where the heeling of his ship enabled him to open his lower-deck ports. Such a broadside was more than frigates could stand, and at 7.30 p.m. both British ships went on ahead; the AMAZON because she had too much sail on, which she could not shorten during the engagement, and the INDEFATIGABLE to repair her rigging and sway up more shot from her hold. The *Droits de l'Homme* was very glad of the respite, for one of her 24-pounders on her upper deck had just burst, no doubt due to a breaking wave having stopped the muzzle with water just as the gun was fired. A gun-burst is as bad an accident as can happen; apart from the actual casualties caused by a 2½-ton gun flying into fragments, every other gunner thinks his gun may be next.

At 8.30 p.m. the British ships re-engaged, and the desperate action continued for almost the whole of the winter's night. No bald description can give the slightest idea of the scene; the howling of the gale, the tossing of the ships, the thunder and flame of the guns, the crashing of the shot and the incessant musketry. The frigates stationed themselves as well as they could, one on each bow of the battleship, where their broadside could rake her with best effect and she could not bring her great batteries to bear. By yawing first on one side and then on the other she was able to fire at least her forward guns into the frigates, and was always intent on the least chance to run in and board, which must have been decisive; but the seamanship of both the frigate captains frustrated every attempt.

The wind veered to the westward again, still rising. So high ran the sea, that in the INDEFATIGABLE the gun-crews on the main deck were waist-deep in water; and in the *Droits de l'Homme*, every time they opened the lower ports to fire the 32-pounders, the water poured down on to the prisoners in the cable tier. So violent was the tossing that several of the main deck guns of the INDEFATIGABLE broke the ropes of their breeching-tackle, and others drew the ring-bolts out of the ship's side; the force of the recoil added to the tossing of the ship being more than any sane shipwright could be expected to think about. A gun breaking loose in a tempest was the ultimate disaster; Sir Edward, who thought of everything, had thought of this too, and had ordered such a quantity of spare rope to be rove that every accident was dealt with immediately it occurred.

The fire of the frigates was deadly among the French gun-crews; but as fast as they fell others took their place, whether sailors or soldiers; no Frenchman hung back. At 10.30 p.m. the mizzen-mast of the *Droits de l'Homme* was observed to be tottering, and shortly after Commodore la Crosse ordered it to be cut away, so as to fall clear of the deck. The driver, the main fore-and-aft sail of the ship, was rigged on the mizzen, and this loss made the ship very difficult to manage. The British frigates now took station on the quarters of the battleship, where their fire had even greater effect, as it was on the quarter-deck that most of the officers had their station. Several of them were wounded; on the other side, Lieutenant Bendall Littlehales, first of the AMAZON, was promenading the quarter-deck with his captain when he was knocked unconscious by the wind of a 32-pound shot from the lower-deck battery of the *Droits de l'Homme*. Captain Reynolds had him carried below; as soon as he came round he insisted on returning to his post; but it was months before the bruising disappeared: one of the earliest examples of super-sonic shock.

Shortly after midnight the *Droits de l'Homme* had fired off all her round-shot and started firing shell, which, according to her log, made the British stand off a little further. She must have fired at least 4,000 rounds to have exhausted her shot, all 24 or 32 pounds. By four o'clock in the morning of the 14th January, exhaustion was beginning to show, after eleven hours of furious combat under the worst possible conditions. The AMAZON had three feet of water in her hold, only the stump of her mizzen-mast standing, all her other masts and yards seriously damaged, and she had repaired her rigging so often that she had not a yard of spare cordage left. Her casualties, however, were only three killed and fifteen wounded. The INDEFATIGABLE had four feet of water in her hold, and all her masts damaged, although, by the diligence of her crew, still standing; she had no killed and nineteen wounded. It was far different on the *Droits de l'Homme*, where there were 103 killed and 150 wounded.

Still the exhausted crews stood to their guns, and still the fury of the cannonade thundered out over the fury of the tempest; until at half-past four a break in the flying clouds allowed the moon to enlighten the scene, and Lieutenant George Bell, fourth of the INDEFATIGABLE, whose action station was on the forecastle, saw land dead ahead to the north-east, less than two miles away and with breakers in front of it. By the time he could get to the quarter-deck with this news the breakers were clearly seen from there. Pellew's appreciation of the situation was instantaneous; thinking of everything, he ordered the signal for imminent danger to be made to the AMAZON; ordered his lieutenants to cease fire, and his sailing-master to put the ship about across the wind. One can imagine the thoughts of the exhausted crew as the successive orders came through: 'Cease fire! Hands to the braces! Stand by to go about!' Everybody knew what was involved.* In such weather. the amount of sail carried must be exactly right; if too much, the ship would be dismasted and drive ashore; if too little, as she turned into the wind she would lose steerage-way and broach-to in the trough of the waves. Very well: but what of her shot-through masts, her cut rigging, her torn sails? Would she stand? Orders were given and carried out as steadily as if at sail drill in Spithead; round she swung into the wind, hung in stays for a sickening moment, and then with a thunderous clapping the close-reefed top-sails filled on the other tack, and she sped away from the breakers like a frightened gull. Not so her consort; not so her enemy. Lacking her mizzen-mast and driver, the AMAZON could not bear up into the wind; she tried to wear round with it, but had not sea-room enough, and before five o'clock ran ashore. The *Droits de l'Homme* tried to bear up into the wind, but instantly her fore-mast and bowsprit carried away, leaving only the torn mainsail standing; she tried to anchor, but the anchor would not hold, and shortly she struck heavily on a sandbank; struck again, carrying away her mainmast with the shock; swung broadside on to the sandbank, struck again, turned on her side and remained fast, with the great seas breaking right over her.

The INDEFATIGABLE was far from safe. This glimpse of land had looked like the island of Ushant, and there was plenty of sea-room on her new course, if that were the case. But at first light breakers were seen ahead again, and there was nothing for it but to go about again. Dawn came about half-past six, and again breakers were seen ahead, and again she had to go about. As the light improved, the AMAZON was seen ashore, and, two miles south, the *Droits de l'Homme* on her side, with a great surf beating right over her. No attempt at rescue could be contemplated, for now they could make out where they were:

* There is always a certain amount of tension at such times. The author had twice occasion to put his little 60-tonner about in heavy weather, in a gale, force 8, in the Irish Sea, and in a hurricane, force 12, in the Firth of Forth. The difference in pitch between the howl of the gale and the shriek of the hurricane is quite remarkable.

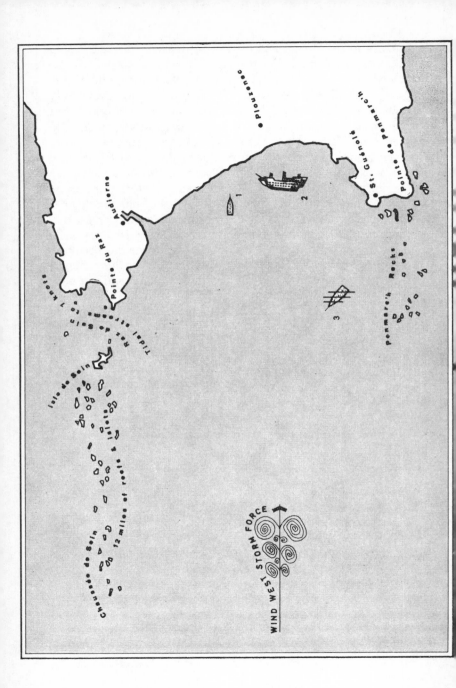

right in the dangerous Bay of Audierne, and ahead of them Penmarck Point, with the dreaded Penmarck Rocks around it, the breakers leaping to top-mast height. But the situation, though desperate, could at least be seen; no more knocking about in the darkness from one hazard to another. For four, mortal hours the worn-out sailors toiled at the ropes, beating up against the relentless storm, desperately clawing off the spouting reefs; until at eleven o'clock the INDEFATIGABLE cleared the last of the rocks and stood out to the open sea.

Shortly after the AMAZON struck, six of her crew stole a small boat and tried to go off on their own; but she soon swamped and all six were drowned. Captain Reynolds set his men to constructing rafts, and when there was flotation for everybody the whole ship's company including the wounded were enrafted and drifted to shore, where they all arrived safely by nine o'clock that morning, having struck about five. Of course they became prisoners of war.

Things were quite different on board the *Droits de l'Homme*. One of the English prisoners taken off the Shannon, Lieutenant Pipon, wrote a long account of the wreck. As soon as she struck the prisoners were brought up from the cable tier to the deck. They could see the AMAZON on shore, about two miles away, and to seaward the INDEFATIGABLE, beating off the Penmarcks under close-reefed topsails in a tremendous sea; from the *Droits de l'Homme*, she appeared to be doomed. On board the French ship all was chaos, men rushing about screaming and shouting without any apparent purpose; the same men who had served their guns so steadily during the most bloody battle seemed now

Position in Audierne Bay, 8 a.m., 14th January 1797

1 AMAZON ashore; crew prepared to enraft
2 *Droits de l'Homme* on her side, dismasted; panic on board
3 INDEFATIGABLE beating to windward under double-reefed topsails only

If more detail is required, the appropriate Admiralty Chart is No. 2351. There is a detailed description of the Bay in the Channel Pilot, Part II.

to be quite unnerved. The officers had given up all command and responsibility, and the men's only thought was *sauve qui peut*. As a consequence, although the wreck was scarcely two hundred yards from the shore, where hundreds of people had assembled from the adjacent town of Plouzenec, it was five days until the rescue was completed, and two-thirds of the survivors of the battle perished of starvation and exposure.

This was the last frigate action fought by Sir Edward Pellew. When next we hear of him, he was in command of a squadron of line-of-battle ships. About the time of Trafalgar he was for some years Rear-Admiral, Commander-in-Chief, East Indies. After the death of Lord Collingwood, Vice-Admiral Sir Edward Pellew, Bart., became Commander-in-Chief, Mediterranean, flying his flag in the new CALEDONIA of 120 guns, having with him on board—surprise!—Rear-Admiral Israel Pellew as Captain of the Fleet. He finished the wars as Admiral Viscount Exmouth, Knight Grand Cross of the Order of the Bath, and reputed to have amassed £300,000 in prize-money. His descendants bear his title to this day. But amongst all his well-won honours and rewards, the story men always told of him was how the INDEFATIGABLE fought a French 74 in a tempest the whole of a winter's night, ran her on shore, and then weathered the Penmarcks. It was a feat of arms and seamanship such as had never been done before, and never was done again.

3

Mutiny and Retribution

A verity that enthusiasts forget is that things keep on happening, even after the most resounding victory or the most disastrous defeat, and very seldom do they happen as expected. When the British were rejoicing over Wolfe's conquest of Canada, it did not occur to anybody that it made inevitable the secession of the American Colonies; and when Louis XVI triumphantly signed the treaty which finally established the United States, he did not know that he was signing his own death-warrant for nine years later. Such an explosion as the French Revolution had a world-wide fall-out, and while Britain was at war with the Republic, nevertheless the ideas of the revolution spread and took root. British sailors would fight and run ashore the *Droits de l'Homme*; but they might reflect that they too were men and possibly they too had rights. Then the numbers in the Navy had been expanded from 20,000 to 120,000, so that five out of six were recent recruits or conscripts, and among them, we may be sure, were many on whom the ideas of the revolutionaries had made a deep impression. There was always a sufficient cadre of com-missioned officers to command any probable number of ships; but even this had its dangers, for many of the senior officers were too old, too set in their ways, to realise that fresh winds were blowing. The mutiny at Spithead was really more of a strike; the sailors had legitimate grievances, and they refused to go to sea until these were redressed. They had the full sympathy of all the younger officers such as Nelson who, however, detested the mutineers at the Nore, where politics played a part. Even after those Fleet mutinies were appeased and suppressed there were sporadic outbursts of unrest in the ships throughout the world.

It was easy enough, given Treasury approval, to meet most of the grievances: the sailors had not had a rise in pay since the rates were laid down by Samuel Pepys; the method of paying was quite archaic, so that the sailors had often to sell their warrants at a huge loss for ready money or else wait interminably for their pay in cash. The food was often much worse than necessary, and the pursers cheated the men all too often. Oddly, the most difficult problem was the demand for fresh vegetables when in port; Pepys' regulations made no mention of such a thing, and gentlemen on a well-varied diet could see no reason to introduce any such novelty. But the real root of discontent was the discovery the men had made from their prisoners — there was no flogging in the Republican Navy. The Nelson generation of officers knew that they could only lead their men, but there were still too many who thought that they could drive them; they would flog their crews into what they thought was discipline but was only subjection. At Spithead, the most objectionable officers were put ashore and declined to reassume command; Admiralty was unable to find other ships for them, and they went on half-pay for the rest of their lives. Henceforth every captain knew that his log would be carefully examined when he submitted it to Admiralty at the end of his voyage, and if a lot of floggings were recorded he would require good justification, or strong influence, if he were to get another ship. But the weeding-out took a long time; too many weak men thirsted to display their authority, and too often unbridled sadism was the compensation for the complete absence of anything like a normal sex life.

The family of Pigot was most distinguished in naval records, and for generations had given to the Navy officers noted for their bravery and efficiency; unfortunately, several of them were also noted for their severity in enforcing discipline, which in one case went far beyond the limits of standing orders, or even of sanity. The disciplinary difficulties must be recognised. A captain could not impose the death penalty, and even if he could he would only be reducing a not too numerous complement;

imprisonment would scarcely be considered as a punishment, but rather as a blessed cessation from toil, even if in fetters. Extra duty might hazard the ship, since every man was already working up to the fatigue limit. Cutting off grog might be effective with really unpopular men, but in general it was evaded by the culprit's messmates making up his allowance amongst them. At the same time the highest standards of discipline had to be maintained amongst a rough illiterate body of men, of whom a high proportion were society's drop-outs. Even in 1944, it is generally believed that Major-General Wingate employed corporal punishment in his memorable 'Chindit' jungle campaign. It is quite a large problem, not to be readily solved by 'gentlemen in England now abed' whose most difficult disciplinary problem has been an encounter with an inebriated Cypriot waiter.

A flogging was a serious matter which had to be entered in the ship's log; all hands were called 'to witness punishment' and the stated offence and the sentence were read out before execution, but on a long cruise it would be years before the captain had to send in his log to Admiralty, and meantime he was in a position of absolute authority seldom granted except to sovereigns. This authority was taken for granted and seldom used by the great captains such as Nelson, Pellew, Hoste and Maxwell; they punished with the greatest reluctance, and felt that there must be some inadequacy on their part if it became necessary. Most of the modern captains followed their example, but there were a number of captains whose severity was known and dreaded throughout the fleet; consequently, they had great difficulty getting a crew together, and when they did, it was usually the sweepings from the receiving ships, whose stupidity and disaffection gave great grounds for severity at the very beginning of a commission. These severe captains fell into two categories: the hard-bitten old salts of previous wars, who felt that an occasional flogging kept the whole crew on their toes; and young captains who had come to Captain's rank far too quickly, by family influence, and whose arrogance and perversities had full .play in such a position of limited but absolute command.

Of the latter type was Captain Hugh Pigot, of the 32-gun

12-pounder HERMIONE, on the West Indies station in 1797 under Sir Hyde Parker, Commander-in-Chief. Captain Pigot was a brave and efficient officer, but of a most unfortunate disposition, combining discourtesy to his officers with savage brutality to his crew. On the 22nd of March 1797 the HERMIONE carried out a neat boat-action; the ship's boats, commanded by the first and second lieutenants, Samuel Reid and Archibald Douglas, went into an anchorage of Puerto Rico, spiked and dismounted the guns of a battery guarding the anchorage, and took out thirteen prizes, including three armed privateers and a richly laden brig. In April of 1797 Captain Pigot was acting Commodore of a small squadron consisting of his own and two similar frigates, a brig and a cutter, detached to act against some privateers and their prizes which had taken refuge in Port Jean-Rabel, in San Domingo, under the protection of two batteries. On the very dark night of the 20th–21st April all the boats of the squadron, after a long row, boarded the vessels and by 4 a.m. brought them all out on the land breeze, despite the fire of the batteries, with no loss whatever, the prizes being a full-rigged ship, three brigs, three schooners and two sloops. This was a useful and meritorious service, but in his official letter Captain Pigot did not give any name of the many lieutenants and junior officers engaged, thus, of course, depriving them of a good mark towards ultimate promotion. He himself was not personally engaged in either of these services, except in getting the lion's share of the prize-money; this was in fact according to the general rule that the captain should stay with his ship and send his lieutenants in the boats, but it was also the general rule that in such cases the captain should take all the trouble necessary to see that they got full credit.

On the 22nd September 1797 Captain Pigot was cruising in the HERMIONE off the west end of Puerto Rico; deciding to shorten sail, he ordered the topsails to be reefed. When the top-men were on the mizzen-topsail yard, directly over the quarter-deck, he shouted at them that he would flog the last man off the yard. It is difficult to believe that his mind was not quite unbalanced when he made this threat, for not only are the top-men the best sailors in the ship, but the best of them take the outside ends of the yards, at the clew-earrings, so that inevitably it must be the best men who are last off the yard. One thing they could be sure of, and that was that the captain would carry out his threat. As they were all rushing down the rigging, the two yard-men, finding their way blocked, made a leap through the air, hoping to catch hold of some part of the rigging lower down. Both missed, and both crashed at the same time on to the quarter-deck. The boatswain and the sailing-master examined them and reported to the captain that they were both dead. 'Throw the lubbers overboard,' was all the captain said, and it was done.

Nobody knows what was thought on board the HERMIONE that evening. The captain, alone in his cabin must have reflected, if he were not in fact insane, that he had two lives to account for and a very poor account to give. The first lieutenant and the sailing-master must have been wondering what the captain was going to write in the log, and whether they dared to share his guilt by signing it (as was their duty), or whether they dared to defy him by refusing to sign it (as was their duty also). There cannot have been much gay talk and happy laughter in either ward-room or gun-room; forward, there were 'low whispers and black frowns'. Apart from the psychotic sadism of the captain, which had already driven them as far as men could be driven, the whole crew felt the insult of their murdered comrades being hove overboard to the sharks. They expected their dead to be treated with proper ceremony; sewn up in canvas by the sail-maker's mates, with a couple of round-shot at the feet; laid out on the gratings on the gangways, and the burial service read over them; the gratings tilted till the bodies slid overside, to the wail of the pipes. To throw them overboard like galley-slops was the ultimate insult, after the ultimate injury of a causeless death. They would take no more.

As the night came on, dark and moonless, the watch on deck began rolling round-shot about the deck. This was very often the precursor of mutiny; even a 12-pound shot would 'take the feet' from anybody walking on the deck who met it, while the barefooted sailors could make their way anywhere without touching the deck. The trundling of the shot caused the first lieutenant to come out to see what was amiss; he was wounded in the arm with a hatchet, and then hacked down, his throat cut, and his body thrown overboard. On hearing the tumult, the captain ran out, but was driven back into his cabin (the Marine sentry taking no action) where he was stabbed by his own coxswain, and after several cutlass-wounds was pushed out of the cabin window, still alive. No officer attempted to interfere, but the mutineers now entered the ward-room and killed all the ward-room officers most bloodily with axes and cutlasses: not a shot was fired. Those murdered in the ward-room were the other two lieutenants, the lieutenant of Marines, the purser and the surgeon. The mutineers then went down to the gun-room, where they murdered in the same way the boatswain, a midshipman, and the captain's clerk. All the bodies were immediately thrown overboard, whether quite dead or not.

The only warrant officers allowed to survive were the sailing-master, the gunner, the cook, the carpenter, and one little midshipman. It was clear that they could not navigate the ship without the sailing-master, nor fight an action without the gunner; do repairs without the carpenter, nor subsist without the cook; but why the midshipman was spared is a mystery. Perhaps even in that night of fear and horror some gleam of pity fell on the poor boy.

It might possibly have been the original intention of at least some of the mutineers merely to detain the captain in his cabin and then desire the first lieutenant to take the ship to the Admiral at Jamaica. The possibility might then exist that they might have been forgiven, especially if the captain was held to be insane; but once the first lieutenant was wounded every man on board was under sentence of death, or what was worse, flogging round the fleet. The systematic murder of the officers does not seem the outcome of panic or blind rage, since they carefully preserved those who were indispensable to them. They killed everybody they could do without, and whose testimony might later help to convict them.

Perhaps they had some idea of making off to the great South Seas, like the BOUNTY's men, but they must soon have been convinced that they were not victualled nor equipped for either the voyage round the Horn against the weather, or for 15,000 miles on the route round the Cape of Good Hope. They may have thought of turning pirates, but in the West Indies every man's hand would have been against them; all the warships and privateers of both sides. Eventually they decided to surrender the ship to the Spaniards, now at war with Britain, and they obliged the sailing-master to take her into La Guayra, on the north coast of South America.

Here they handed the ship over to the Spanish Governor, stating that they had turned their officers loose in a boat; but the surviving warrant officers would have none of this, dissociated themselves from the crew, and insisted on being made prisoners of war. They made the truth clear to the Governor, and as news leaked out the nearest British Admiral made a formal demand for the ship and the mutineers to be handed over to him. However, the Governor fitted out the *Hermione* as a Spanish frigate with a Spanish crew, and let the mutineers go free, although it does not appear that he did anything to help them. They led an Ishmaelite kind of existence, harried wherever the power of Admiralty could extend, especially after 1808 when the Spaniards changed side again. Those who could, took service with the navy of the United States; but sooner or later, over the next twenty years, most of them were hunted down and hanged. There could be no mercy shown for such a crime, yet some pity might be felt for the perpetrators. They were the scum and scrapings of the sea-service, yet if they had fallen into the hands of Sir Sydney Smith or Lord Cochrane something might have been made of them; but such commanders could pick and choose from hundreds of volunteers. It was inevitable that the worse crews should fall to the worse commanders, and that a really bad commander should drive his crew into despair and desperation.

The Spaniards gave the *Hermione* a thorough refit and put more guns into her, making the total 44. There were comparatively few ships-of-war in the Caribbean, for its extent (twenty degrees of latitude and thirty of longitude), and a powerful frigate like this was a constant menace not only to British merchant vessels but also to the numerous small ships-of-war which were always in employment, on convoy duty and putting down privateers and pirates. It was not for two years that definite and useful information about the *Hermione* reached Sir Hyde Parker, then Commander-in-Chief at Jamaica; she had sailed from Les Cayes in San Domingo, and was now lying in Puerto Cabello, in Venezuela, about seventy miles west of Caracas. It was believed that from that port she was next to sail to Havana.

Captain Edward Hamilton was on the Jamaica station, in command of the 28-gun frigate SURPRISE. This had been a French 24-gun corvette, but on capture had been armed almost entirely with carronades, mostly 32-pounders, which made her a formidable ship at close quarters, but a sitting duck for any long-gun frigate which could keep out of range of her carronades. To help her speed, Captain Hamilton (who seems to have been on good terms with the Dockyard) had her fitted with the mainmast and yards appropriate to a 36-gun frigate. When the news about the *Hermione* was known, Captain Hamilton proposed to the C-in-C that he should be given an extra twenty men and another boat, and he would try to cut out the *Hermione* by boarding from boats; but Sir Hyde Parker, always more noted for caution than for dash, turned it down. However, when Captain Hamilton sailed next day on sealed orders, he found that they were to proceed to Cabo de la Vela, west of the Gulf of Venezuela, and about 200 miles west of Puerto Cabello; he was to cruise off the Cape as long as his stores would allow, and in particular to look out for the *Hermione*, which would be bound to follow the channel between the Lesser Antilles and the mainland, if sailing for Havana. It was highly typical of British practice to send a 28-carronade ship to seek out and destroy a ship of 44 long guns; but no doubt if they *had* met on the high seas the SURPRISE would have done the job.

No *Hermione* turned up, however, although the SURPRISE cruised about for some weeks, until Captain Hamilton began to fear that she must have slipped past at night; to satisfy himself, he made the long beat to windward right up to Puerto Cabello. There, sure enough, was the *Hermione*, in an impregnable position, moored head and stern so that her broadside covered the entrance, which was further strengthened by formidable batteries on either bank; when later Captain Hamilton was able to make some contact with the land, he was informed that the shore batteries mounted no less than 200 guns between them. Clearly he would be unwise to engage a force eight times more powerful than his own, especially as the long guns of the defences would shatter the SURPRISE to matchwood before any of her carronades could range. Moreover, the crew of the *Hermione*, including soldiers, was little short of 400 men, while the whole complement of the SURPRISE was less than 200. As Captain Hamilton had sailed close in, the enemy was well aware of his presence, and there was little chance of surprise; anyhow, the entrance was patrolled by gun-boats by day and by night.

All this was rather discouraging, especially to an officer who knew that he had already somewhat exceeded his orders; but being a Scot, and a Hamilton at that, the captain was unwilling to put his tail down and go home. For three days he cruised around, speaking to nobody, but writing a good deal in his cabin. On the 24th October 1799 he invited all his wardroom officers to dine with him, and was as gay as befitted a captain; then, when the cloth was drawn and the stewards had left, he told them what he was going to do, and asked for their support, for some of them were not bound to the orders he proposed: they drank his health and success resoundingly. The whole ship's company was summoned aft, and the captain addressed them from the quarter-deck. He informed his men that it was impossible to wait there any longer; the supply position would compel him to leave the station, and that frigate must become the prize of some more fortunate ship. (Deep groans and murmurs.) There was only one alternative, and he intended to take it. 'I shall cut out that frigate this very night!' (Loud cheers.) 'I shall lead the boats myself!' (Louder cheers.) 'Will you follow me?' (Loud and prolonged cheers.) 'Then listen carefully, here are my orders; I want every man to know what he is to do, his station and his officer.' The challenge was to be 'Britannia'; the answer 'Ireland'. Everybody was to be dressed in blue or dark clothes, not a rag of white or light colour. The men specifically detailed for boarding were to take the first spell at the oars, so as to be rested before they went into action; but if necessary all were to board, leaving only the bowman in each boat, to hang on if he could. The six boats were arranged in two divisions, each three being roped in tow, one division to go round the *Hermione* and attack the starboard side, the other the near or larboard side. The pinnace, with the captain, the gunner

(Mr John Maxwell), a midshipman and sixteen men, was to board at the centre, on the gangway; the launch, with a lieutenant, a midshipman and twenty-four men, was to pass the pinnace and board at the starboard bow, cut the cable with axes provided, and set the fore-topsail; the little jolly-boat, with a midshipman, the carpenter, and eight men, was to board the quarter-deck, cut the stern cable, and set the mizzen-topsail. The gig, with the surgeon in command (Mr John M'Mullen) and sixteen men, was to board the larboard bow, one cutter with a lieutenant, a Marine officer, and sixteen men, was to board the larboard gangway, and the other cutter, with the boatswain and sixteen men, was to board the larboard quarter. The rendezvous was to be the quarter-deck.

These were excellent orders, the best that could be made for so desperate an enterprise. The only officer left on board was the sailing-master, being the only man who could take the ship out if the attempt was a failure, in which case few officers could be expected to rejoin. But in war there are no certainties, least of all in sea warfare; Nelson had his best captain go aground at Aboukir, and three ships at Copenhagen; not to be provided for in the most detailed orders. In this case the advancing boat-flotilla was discovered by two gun-boats, who opened fire, and some of the boats held back to engage the gun-boats. The pinnace, while rounding the *Hermione*'s bows, caught her rudder in a buoy-rope, and Captain Hamilton and his men had to scramble as best they could on to the forecastle. By this time the whole of the *Hermione*'s crew were fully alerted, mostly gathered on the main deck, whence they kept up a brisk fire of musketry on a dark mass consisting of their own gun-boats and some of the attacking boats, which they imagined to be two frigates bearing down to attack them. The captain and his party made a rush along the gangway, but on the quarter-deck some of them were borne back; the surgeon's party now advanced along the other gangway, catching the Spaniards in a cross-fire. For a time Captain Hamilton stood alone on the Spanish quarter-deck, where he was attacked by four men and knocked down by a musket-butt. At this moment the Marines boarded, and after a single volley rushed the main deck with the bayonet; all the boats, however delayed, boarded and carried out their tasks;

the cables were cut; the fore-topsail and the mizzen-topsail filled on the breeze off the land; the gunner and two others, all wounded, took the wheel; and the HERMIONE stood out of Puerto Cabello. The batteries opened fire and scored several hits; the Spanish prisoners were restive down below, and the Marines had to fire down the hatchways; but when this resistance was quelled, Captain Hamilton ordered no shot to be fired and no light to be shown, and under the random fire of 200 guns the HERMIONE stood out to sea, and joined the SURPRISE before 3 a.m.

A striking feature of this desperate adventure was the casualty list; on the British side, none killed and twelve wounded, including the captain and the gunner; on the Spanish side, 119 killed and 97 wounded. How was this possible? How was it that sixteen men could clear the forecastle, charge along a gangway and clear the quarter-deck, before their supporting forces arrived, and in the teeth of nearly four hundred alerted men? How could thirty Marines drive below two hundred Spaniards, at the point of the bayonet? Partly the answer lay in the detailed and public orders; every man knew what he was expected to do, and was determined to do it. Another answer was that known to all great captains: the overall numbers do not matter, what matters is the number, force and quality at the point of contact. The British, on the attack, had every man his task; they were encountering only the Spaniards who happened to be there at the time, and no doubt wished themselves elsewhere. In a quick fierce rush in a confined space, the leading rank was all-important; let the first line of defenders look but just one glance over their shoulders, all fell into confusion and the action was lost.

The SURPRISE and HERMIONE arrived at Port Royal, Jamaica, on the 1st November 1799, to be acclaimed as they deserved; especially the gallant surgeon, John M'Mullen, who had no possible business to be commanding a boat in a desperate boarding action, but who in fact saved the battle: his was the only boat which carried out orders precisely, and his timely arrival and determined advance decided the quarter-deck affray.

Sir Hyde Parker took the HERMIONE into the Royal Navy, but under the name of RETALIATION; which was afterwards altered by Admiralty to RETRIBUTION. Captain Hamilton was knighted by the King; the House of Assembly of Jamaica presented him with a sword of 300 guineas value; and the City of London made him a Freeman. In the action, however, he had suffered many and serious wounds, from which he never quite recovered. He was sent home to recuperate in the ordinary packet-ship, which was captured by a French privateer and he was sent as prisoner of war to Paris. The First Consul took particular notice of Sir Edward Hamilton, and in consideration of his wounds allowed him to be exchanged for six midshipmen, and he arrived safely home in the summer of 1800, honoured by both friend and foe.

4

Invasion

On the 17th of February 1797 there slipped out from Brest a
small squadron, under the command of Captain Jean-Baptiste
Montaignes Laroque: it consisted of two powerful frigates,
Résistance and *Vengeance*, both rated as 40 guns but mounting 48,
a 22-gun corvette *Constance*, and a lugger, *Vautour*. The lugger
was unarmed but was packed with men; they were embarked
on one of the most extraordinary expeditions ever sent out.

The French Directory, in spite of the failure at Bantry Bay,
still had designs of a landing in force in Ireland, and to further
this decided on a demonstration against England. Raking the
gaols, they picked out 1,200 men, mostly bandits and deserters,
put them into uniform, gave them muskets and bayonets, and
ammunition, not, however, to be distributed until after landing.
The command was given to an American mercenary named
Tate, who was given the rank of Colonel, and who seems to
have been admirably suited for such a command. His orders
were to land at Bristol, sack and burn the city, and then march
overland to Liverpool, sacking and burning *en route*. No arrangements were made for taking the party off. They had no cannon,
no camp equipment, no transport, and no supplies. The men
were promised a free pardon and all the loot they could lay
their hands on. Quite clearly, the Directory considered the party
expendable.

On the 20th of February the squadron anchored off Ilfracombe,
where some attempt at a landing was abandoned on news of
organised resistance. The commodore had probably got some

information about the tides and currents of the Bristol Channel, for he gave up that objective and sailed north, anchoring in Fishguard Bay towards dusk on 22nd February. The stop at Ilfracombe was of course imbecilic; nothing was accomplished, and on the other hand the alarm was given, and all round the coast the militia were assembling. During the night all the 1,200 men were landed, and having got rid of them, the squadron made off immediately.

During that night the local magnate, Lord Cawdor, assembled the local Yeomanry, Militia, and Volunteers, and by full day marched to meet the invaders. Seeing the ordered lines of resolute men, and especially, no doubt, the cavalry, of which he had none, 'Colonel' Tate at once put up the white flag and surrendered. Not a drop of blood was shed. It has been said that Tate was further influenced by mistaking some red-shawled women for soldiers, and a correspondent of the *Daily Telegraph* (19th February 1969) has said that this was in fact a ruse organised by Lord Cawdor, who issued the women with a yard and a half of military scarlet apiece and set them to march round and round a hillock, like a stage army.

This expedition, however ludicrous it seems at this distance, did in fact have one of the effects the Directory hoped for: it caused a run on the banks, which had already been under increasing pressure. This became so serious that on the 26th of February an Order in Council was issued, authorising the Bank of England to issue £1 and £2 notes as legal tender, and this Order was subsequently legalised by Act of Parliament. This important step, which would never have been taken under ordinary conditions, was of the greatest benefit to the war effort; paper money freely accepted freed the country's gold for the foreign subsidies without which the war must have collapsed.

The second effect was that the British public, seeing the miserable condition and behaviour of these 'troops', at once concluded that all French soldiers were miserable, cowardly, half-starved tramps, an illusion which was rudely dispelled by the splendid armies of Napoleon.

At dawn on the 9th of March 1797 two British frigates made a reconnaissance of Brest Roads. They were the SAN FIORENZO, 36 guns, 18-pounders, Captain Sir Harry Neale, and the

NYMPHE, 36 guns, 12-pounders, Captain John Cooke. Having ascertained that the French fleet, fourteen battleships and six frigates, was still in the port, they were returning to inform Lord Bridport, commanding the Channel Fleet off Ushant, when they sighted two sails to the westward, apparently making for Brest. The complication was that Brest was only ten miles away, and the wind was fair for leaving the port, so that anything to be done must be done quickly before overwhelming force could be brought out.

The two British frigates hauled close to the wind until they had the weather-gauge of the enemy, and then bore down on the leading ship, which was the *Résistance*, with the commodore of the Fishguard expedition; she did not resist long, however, but after an engagement of about ten minutes hauled down her colours and was taken into possession. The second ship now arrived, the corvette *Constance*, Captain Desauney, and was in a hopeless position, but made a spirited fight for ten minutes, until she lost her mainmast and surrendered. The frigate had nineteen casualties, the corvette fourteen; the British ships had no damage and no casualties.

The *Résistance* was one of the finest frigates afloat, nearly 1,200 tons, and was taken into the Royal Navy under the appropriate name of FISGARD; rated as a 38-gun frigate, she did excellent service for a long period. The *Constance* was also taken into service, under her own name, and was rated as a 22-gun post-ship. Thus the net result of the Fishguard expedition was to save the Bank of England, to present the Royal Navy with two fine ships, and to confer a nice bit of easy prize-money on two lucky ships' companies.

It is perhaps to be remarked that this was the very last time that an armed enemy force ever stood on the soil of the Island.

5

The East India Station: The Far East

Edward Cooke was fortunate in his education. As a very young lieutenant, he had spent quite a part of the ten years' peace between 1783 and 1793 in France, with the special intention of learning the language. (Nelson had intended to do the same, but was deterred by the senile entreaties of his father for his company.) By the time he was recommissioned in 1793, he was not only proficient but perfect in the language of the enemy. He quickly attracted the keen eye of Vice-Admiral Lord Hood, who had him as one of his lieutenants on his flag-ship, the VICTORY, when he sailed for Toulon in the middle of 1793, with another twenty ships of the line and a sufficiency of frigates and small craft. To be a lieutenant on a flag-ship, with its strict ceremonial and constant calls, was perhaps not much fun, but it was regarded as an almost certain promise of early promotion, so long as one did not attract the unfavourable attention of the Admiral.

The situation at Toulon was quite tricky: the citizens and the Councillors were almost all Monarchists, and so was the Rear-Admiral Trogoff, commanding the fleet in the harbour; but the sailors deposed him and elected Rear-Admiral Julien, a strong Revolutionary. Lord Hood was given to understand that the city authorities were willing to treat for the conditional surrender of the town and the fleet, and he sent his best French-speaking officer, Lieutenant Cooke, ashore to conduct these extremely delicate negotiations. It was quite remarkable that out of a fleet carrying six flag officers and about forty post captains, a lieutenant should be sent on such a mission, not as interpreter but as plenipotentiary. It was sufficiently hazardous, for the Revolutionary fleet lay in the way; Cooke had to make two calls, with a day between, and on each of the four passages he had his difficulties. For instance, on his second return a French frigate saw him (rowing himself) and lowered a boat to intercept him; and, when this failed, fired upon him several times with her whole broadside, as he scampered along the beach from rock to rock and up the steep way to the cover of some trees. He was probably the only man ever to have half a dozen broadsides of a frigate directed against his single person.

With such a background, it is not surprising that five years later Edward Cooke found himself not only a post captain, but in command of one of the finest frigates in the Navy, and on the East Indies station, where there was plenty of action and plenty of prizes. His ship was the SYBILLE, rated as 38 guns but actually mounting 46; she was French-built in Toulon, of what was then called Adriatic oak, now called Jugo-Slavian, still the finest oak in the world. Every captain thirsted to command a Toulon-built capture. SYBILLE had been captured in the Mediterranean by the ROMNEY, 50 guns, on 17th June 1794.

The main base of the East Indies was at Fort St George, Madras, where a powerful force was established, sufficient to send out several detachments at a time as requisite, but always keeping a strong reserve in case of some unexpected move by the enemy. The purpose was to protect the immense convoys of the Honourable East India Company's ships from China, Indonesia and India, and of course to do as much depredation as possible on French and Dutch warships and convoys. Ships were also stationed at Calcutta, to cover the Bay of Bengal, and at Bombay, to look after shipping in the Arabian sea, where Arab pirates were the chief danger. Britain's only ally in these waters was Portugal, which had a port at Goa, not much use when Bombay was so near, and at Macao, of the very greatest service, since the great China convoys assembled at Canton, a little way upriver. Portugal also had part of the island of Timor, but this was a little out of the trade routes.

The French had had land settlements at many places on the

coast of India, but these were all seized by the British shortly after news of the declaration of war was received; only Pondicherry, which was heavily fortified, made a respectable resistance. The main French naval base was at Port Louis, on the Île de France, now Mauritius, about a thousand miles SW by W from Madras. This was deemed impregnable, owing to the reefs which surrounded the island on all sides except off the heavily fortified entrance to Port Louis. Here a large naval force was stationed, mostly of powerful frigates, to protect French commerce, that of the Dutch, and of course to prey on the traffic of the Honourable East India Company. Holland had already lost to the British the Cape of Good Hope and Ceylon, and her bases were principally on Java, Batavia (now Djakarta) at the west end, and Gresik (now Sourabaya) at the east end; they had several line-of-battle ships, 64s, and a number of frigates, but showed little inclination to risk them outside Indonesian waters. Spain had an important naval base at Manila, but she was principally concerned with the Pacific, and any of her goods passing through the Indian Ocean were carried by the French Philippines Company.

The area of the East India command thus extended about six thousand by five thousand miles, including the most valuable trading countries in the world, and containing several enemy naval forces, some of them very active and aggressive: 'ample room, and verge enough' for the most ambitious officer.

Late in 1797 Cooke was sent to China, to convoy to Fort St George the fleet of the Honourable Company, then assembling at Canton. He was given also the small 32-gun 12-pounder frigate FOX, Captain Pulteney Malcolm, a man after his own heart, who also was a competent French linguist; and a pilot for the dangerous China seas, Mr Bernard, who spoke both French and Spanish; he shipped in the FOX, which, with her shallower draught, was intended to be the leading ship in tricky waters. They duly arrived at Macao at New Year, but found that the India fleet, although almost ready, did not intend to sail until March, as the monsoon period was upon them, when constant stormy weather was to be expected, varied with typhoons of the utmost violence. This did not daunt the frigate captains, who had never experienced a typhoon, and they determined to perform some service rather than lie idle at Macao, which they knew would be bad for the morale as well as the morals of their crews. They took on board a good supply of fresh beef and vegetables, and on the 5th of January sailed with the intention of reconnoitring Manila; they felt that their C-in-C would be pleased to have a reliable report, and the possibility exists that they may have been influenced by the alleged presence there of two ships of rich lading, bound for Panama.

They duly sighted the island of Luzon some distance north of their destination, and coasted southwards. They were flying French colours, and captured a small vessel which had just left Manila. The master of this ship informed his captors that in Manila there were four ships of the line and four frigates, but only one battleship and one frigate were fit for sea, the others being under repair during the monsoon season. In consideration of this information, Captain Cooke let the ship and lading go free, only robbing the till of about 4,000 Spanish dollars. The two captains now laid their plans for entering Manila Bay; they decided to be a detachment from Rear-Admiral Sercey's squadron, the SYBILLE to be the *Seine*, and the FOX the *Prudente*. On the 13th January 1798 they arrived at Manila Bay towards evening.

Manila has a large bay, about twenty miles each way, formed by the projecting peninsula of Bataan on the westward side. The city of Manila lies at the head of the bay, fairly open, although protected by a mole; but about ten miles to the south the curving peninsula of San Roque forms the magnificent harbour of Cavite, two miles deep, which was the naval base, dockyard and arsenal. Both the city and the dockyard were heavily fortified and quite recently strengthened, for in the war of 1762 the British had captured Manila by a surprise attack from India. The Manila galleon was the longed-for mark of every warship, privateer or pirate in those waters, but it was only taken once, by Commodore Anson in June 1743, who brought the CENTURION into Spithead with two millions sterling in gold and silver. It is not generally understood that fifty years before Drake entered the South Seas, the Spaniards were running a regular liner service across the Pacific: one ship a year in each direction. From Acapulco they ran along the 13° north

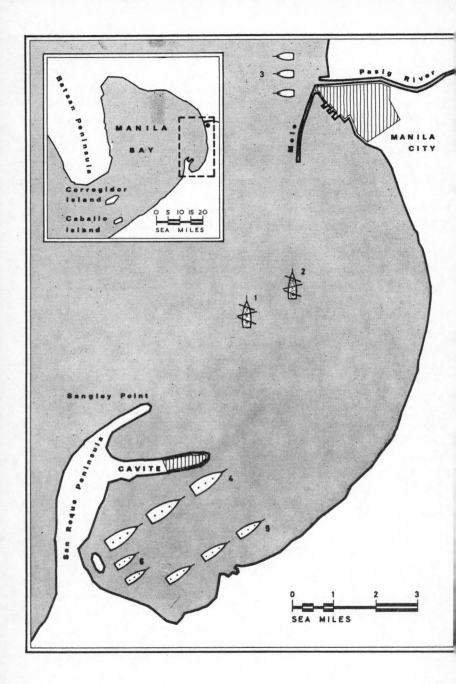

line of latitude (very convenient before longitude could be calculated) for 8,000 miles till they came to Guam, rising out of the great deeps (5,000 fathoms) to over 1,300 feet, a fine landfall; here they refreshed before sailing the remaining 1,500 miles to Manila, the whole voyage on the North Equatorial trade wind. Returning, they stood away north into at least 30° north, where they picked up the North Pacific trade wind which carried them securely to the coast of Mexico. Manila was the entrepôt where all the riches of the East were assembled to lade the galleon.

The entrance to the bay is about ten miles wide, and contains the fortified island of Corregidor and the smaller one of Caballo. The frigates passed through unchallenged in the darkness, and before midnight anchored in the bay. At first light on the 14th January they weighed anchor and started up the bay, on a very light wind. By 9 a.m. the FOX was sufficiently advanced to see into Cavite harbour, at a distance of three miles, and descry three sail of the line and three frigates; none of them, however, ready for sea, since two of them had all their topmasts struck and the other four had all their masts out. The wind now died away altogether, leaving the frigates becalmed about half-way between Manila and Cavite, and about five miles from the shore of the bay between those places.

At 11 a.m. a twelve-oar guard-boat was observed approaching; it came alongside, and a Spanish captain came on board to make the usual inquiries. Mr Bernard told him that he was on board the *Prudente*, and the larger consort was the *Seine*; they

The head of Manila Bay, 10 a.m., 14th January 1798

Reference:
  1 SYBILLE, hove-to
  2 FOX, hove-to
  3 Three Spanish gun-boats, manned, anchored off Pasig River
  4 Three Spanish line-of-battle ships, under repair
  5 Three Spanish frigates, under repair
  6 Two Spanish merchant ships, one unloading, one aground

Note: ships are *not* on the same scale as the map.

Inset: General view of Manila Bay, on smaller scale

had been detached from the squadron of Rear-Admiral Sercey to cruise on the China coast, and had come in for fresh provisions, and to find if any part of the Spanish squadron would like to join them. The Spanish captain told them that the Governor had already directed that all their requirements should be supplied, but he did not think any of the warships in the port would be able to go to sea for at least two months; which was very good hearing for the British officers.

Captain Cooke now came on board and was introduced as Commodore Latour, a well-known officer in Sercey's squadron; Latour had actually been dead for some time, but as the news had not yet reached Manila, everything went down very well. Captain Malcolm now invited the officers to have some wine in his cabin, and suggested that the boat's crew should come on board and have some refreshment forward. This was accepted, and while the officers had an instructive chat in the cabin, the men were shown down to the lower deck, where as they came off the ladder one at a time they were seized, disarmed and tucked away in the orlop. After about an hour, in which they pumped the Spaniard dry of all available information and replaced it with Madeira, the two British captains disclosed their identity, to the astonishment and horror of the Spanish captain. However, Captain Cooke assured him that he would not be taken away as a prisoner, and urged him to have another glass.

Meantime two large twenty-oar boats approached, bringing the Governor's nephew, and one of the aides of Admiral Alaba, commanding at Cavite, with all hospitable intentions. The officers were shown into the cabin and informed that they were temporary prisoners, while the crews were shown below and dealt with as before. But now a large party of British sailors required the Spaniards to exchange clothes with them; they then entered the three row-boats and made for three large gun-boats, which lay off the mouth of the river Pasig, which then bounded the city. Taken completely by surprise, the gun-boat crews surrendered without firing a shot, and were duly brought alongside the FOX. The gun-boats were in excellent condition, each with thirty oars and a heavy gun in the bows, one 32- and two 24-pounders, with four swivels apiece.

A fourth boat now came alongside, and the Captain of the Port came aboard, to inquire what was going on, and to demand the instant restoration of the gun-boats; otherwise the frigates would be treated as enemies. Talking volubly but not very understandably, Captain Malcolm escorted him to the cabin, while his crew were invited below. It was now 4 p.m., the dinner hour of the period, and Captain Malcolm regaled his captive officers with the best his stores could provide, and at the same time ordered a good meal and copious grog for his two hundred prisoners forward. Festivities over, all the prisoners were escorted to their boats, and allowed to go ashore without parole or conditions of any kind; but the British captains thought it a good idea to retain the gun-boats as a souvenir of their visit.

A good wind came up, and the two frigates left the bay, with the three gun-boats in tow, with prize crews. They were not unhappy; they had exposed the inherent weakness of Spanish rule in the Pacific, although it was to be exactly a hundred years until Commodore Dewey destroyed the Spanish fleet at Cavite and the U.S.A. annexed the Philippines. They had acquired a great deal of valuable information; they had not taken their merchantmen, which were well into the safety of Cavite, either aground or unladen, but they had three large copper-bottomed gunboats, three heavy brass guns, a dozen swivels, and an amplitude of small arms and ammunition; and not a drop of blood had been shed on either side. An interesting day; and all because both captains could speak French!

Note: The subsequent short career of Captain Cooke will be found in Chapter 6, 'Bay of Bengal'. Captain Pulteney Malcolm had a long and honourable career in the Royal Navy. In 1809 he commanded the DONEGAL, 74, under Admiral Gambier off the Basque Roads; and in 1829 Admiral Pulteney Malcolm was Commander-in-Chief, Mediterranean.

6

East Indies: Bay of Bengal

Really large frigates, mounting 24-pounder guns in the main battery, were very scarce in 1799. The first was the *Pomone*, captured in 1794 (page 30) which gave Admiralty quite a shock; they cut down three 64-gun ships by one deck, and laid down the ENDYMION on the same lines as the *Pomone*. The U.S.A. had three, which had been laid down as 74s, quite the largest; the French had the *Romaine*, launched at Cherbourg in 1795, on the lines of the *Pomone*, and the much larger *La Forte*, launched at Rochefort in the same year. This was the largest frigate in the world, which had been built as a frigate from the keelson up. All the British 44s were in the Channel fleet, but the *Forte* was sent to Mauritius (then Île de France) where she was for a time the flag-ship of Rear-Admiral Sercey. In 1799 her main armament was thirty 24-pounder long guns, fourteen long 8-pounders, and eight bronze 32-pounder carronades, a total of 52 guns, plus eight swivels mounted on her waist bulwarks. In addition, her sides above water were thickly lined with cork covered with stout netting, the idea being to reduce the effect of splinters. Her displacement of 1,400 tons enabled her to carry her armament and protection with ease.

This formidable vessel, under the command of Captain Beaulieu-de-Long, was sent from Île de France at the end of 1798 to cruise in the Bay of Bengal and make prize of as many of the Honourable Company's ships as she might come across; there was nothing to be feared from their resistance. There was no British frigate on the station which, in the French view, could fight the *Forte*; and she could walk away from any 74. The complaints of the Honourable Company became such that something had to be done about the *Forte*, and as the SYBILLE had completed her convoy duties and was in Madras, it was determined to send her forth to 'seek for, sink, burn or destroy' the French frigate.

SYBILLE was still commanded by Captain Edward Cooke, whom we have seen playing pranks at Manila; this, however, was a serious matter, with every prospect of a desperate and possibly losing battle, so that he had to take stock of his capacity. The SYBILLE was a Toulon-built capture, of 1,091 tons, rated as a 38-gun frigate, actually mounting twenty-eight 18-pounders as her main battery, with six long 9-pounders and fourteen 32-pounder carronades on her quarter-deck and fore-castle; she was thus much more lightly armed than the *Forte*, and so far as the main battery was concerned, which is what really matters, she had a broadside of 268 pounds against 360 pounds in the *Forte*. In man-power she was also woefully deficient; the *Forte* was reputed to carry at least 500 men, although it was understood that this number must have been depleted by the number of prize crews she had had to furnish, to take her prizes to the Île de France. The established complement of the SYBILLE was 297 men and boys, but this was now reduced to 221 officers and seamen, 10 boys, and 9 Marines, having no Marine officer. Her numbers were made up in various ways. Her previous consort, the FOX, was cruising, and had sent a prize into Madras with a prize crew under Lieutenant Tuckey, who were very gladly received into the SYBILLE. Captain Davies (of the Army), an aide-de-camp of the Governor-General, came as a volunteer; and the Governor-General drafted on board a detachment of the Army, from the Scots Brigade; a total of 131 supernumeraries altogether, making the total complement 371, or 74 above her establishment; a very different matter, however, from the same number of trained seamen.

The SYBILLE sailed from Madras, northward-bound, on 19th February 1799, and on the 23rd met a cartel* going to Madras with some British prisoners out of the *Forte's* prizes; Captain

* A cartel is a ship, usually a small prize, unarmed and flying a white flag, proceeding to an enemy port with prisoners for exchange.

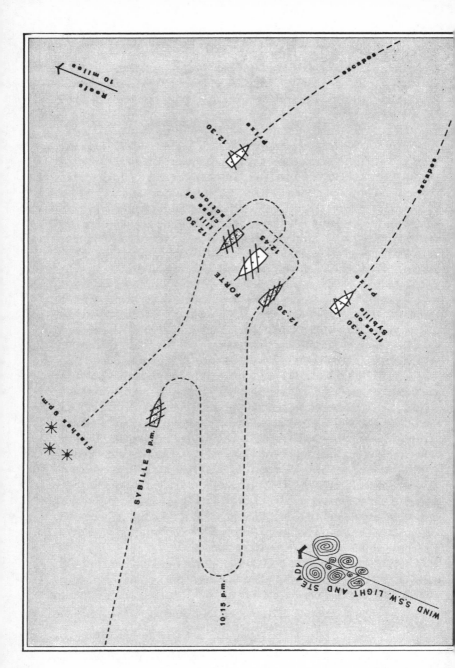

Cooke desired the cartel to accompany him into Balasore Roads, south of Calcutta, where they anchored on the 26th. He was unable, however, to get any positive information about the movements of the *Forte*; although he was sufficiently informed, both by the French crew of the cartel and some of the prisoners, that his ship was by no means a match for his wished-for opponent. Nothing daunted, Cooke let the cartel go on her way, while he sailed to cruise about the Sandheads off the mouth of the Hoogly river which leads up to Calcutta: this seemed a likely area in which to find a French commerce raider.

On the night of the 28th at about 8.30 p.m. the *Forte* fell in with two country ships, the ENDEAVOUR and the LORD MORNING-TON, bound from Canton for Calcutta with rich cargoes. After a desultory cannonade of about half an hour, the two surrendered and all three hove-to in the light breeze, while the *Forte* lowered boats to put prize crews on board the merchantmen and bring their officers on board the frigate. This business of 'taking possession' might require three hours or more, as the merchant-men's manifests and other documents had to be examined.

On this night, at 8.30 p.m., the SYBILLE was standing to the south-east, with a light breeze from the south-south-west, the night being very dark, when flashes were observed on the north-east horizon. This was taken to be low lightning, a common phenomenon in that area, but the steady repetition of the flashes until almost 9 p.m. aroused suspicion, and SYBILLE extinguished all lights and made sail to the westward. At 9.30 p.m. they descried three ships to the south-east, the central and largest of which they supposed to be the *Forte*; she made a most formidable appearance, her lights shining through every port; 170 feet long, she was longer than most British 74s, and with two ports in her gangways she looked exactly like a two-decker 74 which had perhaps two ports obscured. All three ships were

Narrative: 9 p.m., SYBILLE sights flashes, and goes to windward; 10.15 p.m., enough to windward, goes about; 12.15, *Forte* leaves her prizes and turns to engage SYBILLE, opening fire at 12.30, supported by one of the prizes. SYBILLE does not reply, but turns sharply under the stern of the *Forte*, firing a broadside into it at 12.45; continues to go about, and at 12.50 fires a broad-side into the starboard side of the *Forte*. The action continues in the same position until 2.30 a.m.

lying-to, about two miles to the windward of the darkened SYBILLE, which stood on steadily to the westward, in order to get the weather-gauge. At 10 p.m., having got sufficiently to windward, the SYBILLE went about, furled some of her sails, and made towards the *Forte* at only two knots, under spanker, topsails and one jib only, the wind still light and steady from the SSW.

In spite of the darkness, the SYBILLE's sails must have been clearly visible on board the *Forte*; but no movement was made. What was in the captain's mind will never be known, for he had not an hour to live: one theory is that he thought the advancing ship was an East Indiaman, and lay in wait for yet another easy prize; on the other hand, British prisoners on board said that the SYBILLE was clearly recognised, but was allowed to come on as close as possible lest she should make her escape. Whatever the reason, the *Forte* made no move until just after midnight, when she squared off to the wind and advanced to the lee of the SYBILLE, firing a ragged broadside at about three-quarters of a mile range, which cut down her jib but did no other damage. One of the prizes also fired, and the *Forte* gave another partial broadside; but the SYBILLE kept steadily on, completely darkened, completely silent. One may imagine the tension on board among the officers on the quarter-deck, the sailors at the braces, the soldiers crouched behind the bulwarks, the gun-crews beside their guns: all tense, all waiting the word of command. It is at such a moment that a commander experiences the reward of all the weary months of training in which he forged the tremendous weapon to his hand.

When the stern of the *Forte* was on a line with the mainmast of the SYBILLE, Captain Cooke gave the order; the helm was put hard over, so that she passed close under the stern of her enemy, within twenty-five yards; and the whole of her larboard broadside crashed into that stern, raking the *Forte* right to the bows; still keeping the helm hard over, the SYBILLE ranged close along the lee side of the *Forte*, and crashed in a second broadside. At the same time the men of the Scots Brigade sprang to their feet, and fired across the decks of the *Forte* such a volley of musketry as she could never have expected from a British frigate.

These two broadsides from twenty-four heavy guns, plus the

simultaneous volley from more than a hundred muskets, practically decided the engagement. Captain Beaulieu-de-Long and his first lieutenant were both killed, several guns dismounted, and many of the crew killed and wounded; nevertheless the *Forte* kept up a furious and long-continued cannonade. As usual, the French fired high, perhaps higher than usually, certainly much too high, as most of their shot took effect only on the upper rigging of the SYBILLE, whose every shot crashed into the hull of the *Forte*. Nevertheless the French stuck bravely to their guns, while the flame of the cannonade illuminated the scene beneath the canopy of smoke.

At 1.30 a.m. on the 1st of March — Woe worth the day! — Captain Cooke fell, mortally wounded by a grape-shot, and the command devolved on Lieutenant Lucius Hardyman. At 1.45 a.m. Captain (Army) Davies, who had volunteered, met a 24-pound ball which nearly cut him in halves. The cannonade continued unabated for another half an hour, when the fire of the *Forte* began to slacken and ceased altogether about 2.30 a.m. The SYBILLE now stopped firing, and hailed to ask if the *Forte* had surrendered. No reply was received; SYBILLE fired another broadside, and hailed again. Again no reply was received, but now men were seen in the *Forte's* rigging, as if setting sail with a view to escape. SYBILLE now fired continuous broadsides, and in a few minutes the mizzen-mast of the *Forte* came down, followed shortly by her foremast, mainmast and bowsprit,so that she lay a dismasted hulk. At 3 a.m. all firing ceased, and the cheers of the SYBILLE's crew were the signal for the British prisoners in the *Forte* to come on deck. Lieutenant Manger, third of the SYBILLE, was sent over by boat to take possession.

It was only after going on board that the British sailors became aware how terribly destructive had been their fire. The whole of the engaged side, above the water-line, was practically stove in; all of the bulwarks on that side had disappeared; the boats and spare spars were shot to pieces; and of all the furnishings of the deck, such as capstan, wheel and binnacle, no trace was left. Later, it was found that more than 300 shot had pierced the hull. The deck was strewn with dead and dying, a frightful spectacle; her casualties were 145 killed and wounded, including almost all the officers on board. By contrast, the SYBILLE came off lightly; she had lost most of her cordage and sails, and there were bad scars on her masts and yards, all of which were still standing; she had only six shot in her hull, and her casualties amounted to twenty-two killed and wounded.

After unsuccessfully pursuing the prizes, which made off when the outcome of the battle was plain, the SYBILLE anchored in seventeen fathoms and spent two days making such emergency repairs as enabled the two ships to make their way up the treacherous Hoogly River to Calcutta. The FORTE took a lot of repairing, but she was taken into the Royal Navy and rated as a 44-gun frigate, the largest class. Lieutenant Hardyman was given command, and this appointment was ratified by Admiralty, and Captain Hardyman made post captain. The unfortunate Captain Cooke lingered for almost three months, and died on 25th May, being of course buried with all possible military honours.

This encounter had several unique features. There was nothing unusual in the French ship having a considerable advantage in tonnage and gun-power; what is surprising is the little use she made of that superiority. Usually the French ships had much larger crews than the British, and made more use of musketry; but in this case the French had depleted the crew seriously, from 513 to 370, by the numbers she had to detach to man her prizes, which of course meant officers too; so that she had actually a man less than the British ship, and made very little use of small arms. The presence of a comparatively large body of good troops on the British ship was probably the reason, as their volley fire made the French keep their heads down. Captain Cooke was a very good officer, who had not only the confidence but the affection of officers and crew alike; moreover he had exercised his men at the guns far more than was customary at that period. The engagement is a striking illustration of the old adage, that the best defence is a rapid and accurate fire on the enemy.

7

Inglorious Defeat

The difficulties of manning the Royal Navy have already been described: by 1795 the barrel had been scraped clean of real seamen, and the Quota Acts of that year prescribed that the Justices of the Peace of each region must produce a quota of men — any kind of men — amounting to about one half per cent of the population each year. Naturally, the quota men were mostly society's discards, although there were many tempted by the handsome bounties offered to volunteers — but many of these volunteers were from debtor's prisons. By 1798, a freshly commissioned ship could be sure that most of the crew supplied from the receiving ships would be landmen of poor quality, and knocking them into the shape of seamen a difficult task for the first lieutenant and the bosun.

Such was the manning of the frigate AMBUSCADE when Captain Henry Jenkins assumed command; but she was even worse than usual, having far too large a proportion of boys. To enable the ship to be worked at all, Captain Jenkins was allowed to take a party of about thirty experienced seamen from the CARNATIC, 74, in which he had been first lieutenant; as these were volunteers, he must have been quite a popular officer, perhaps easy-going, perhaps even lax. He was certainly totally unfitted to weld a raw crew into an efficient fighting force; instead of encouraging the inexperienced to profit by the experienced, while maintaining a steady impartial discipline, he made no secret of his contempt for the original crews, whom he called 'blackguard Ambuscades', and of his partiality for the men he had brought aboard, whom he denominated 'gentlemen Carnatics'. Thus he added jealousy and distrust to the other shortcomings of his raw hands.

The AMBUSCADE was a smallish frigate of about 700 tons, 32 guns, 12-pounders, and 8 carronades, 24-pounders. She left Portsmouth on the 5th of December, 1798, to cruise on the west coast of France. She made some prizes, which had to be supplied with prize-crews, which took off her second lieutenant and twenty good sailors, leaving her with no more than 190 men and boys. On the 14th December she was lying-to off Bordeaux, waiting to be joined by the frigate STAG, 32 guns, Captain Yorke. At 7 a.m., a sail was sighted to seaward, bearing directly for them; it was taken for granted that this was the STAG, and at eight, officers and men went for breakfast, leaving only the usual watch on deck. Before 9 a.m., the approaching ship was within half a mile, when suddenly she put about and made off to sea, hauled as close to the wind as possible. This was reported to Captain Jenkins, who ordered a chase under all sail.

The ship they were chasing was the *Baionnaise*, commander Lieutenant Richer; the French called her a large corvette, the British a 28-gun frigate; she mounted twenty-four 8-pounders, six 6-pounders, and two 36-pounder carronades, plus eight swivels mounted on her bulwarks: she had thus little more than half the weight of broadside of the AMBUSCADE. She was, however, much better manned, her establishment being 280 men and boys, not all of which may have been present, as she had been to the West Indies; she had also on board a platoon of the famous regiment of Alsace, thirty men and an officer, whom she was bringing back from a tour of duty in Cayenne.

The AMBUSCADE sailed somewhat better than the *Baionnaise*, and about noon came within gunshot of her, whereupon she shortened sail and the cannonade commenced, the AMBUSCADE making full use of her heavier and longer-ranging main battery. After about an hour it appeared that the *Baionnaise* must surrender in a few minutes; she was very much knocked about in her hull, masts and rigging, and had sustained heavy casualties including both her captain and first lieutenant wounded, so that there was only one commissioned officer left to command her.

The AMBUSCADE, on the other hand, had little damage and very light casualties, all her officers being still on the quarter-deck. At this moment AMBUSCADE suffered a catastrophe: one of her main deck guns burst, shattering the adjacent hull and badly wounding eleven men; such an accident is disturbing for even the best-disciplined crew, and the ill-trained men of the AMBUSCADE went into temporary panic. Taking advantage of the lull in the firing, the *Baionnaise* made sail, in the hope of escape.

The officers of the AMBUSCADE were able to quell the panic, and sail was made in pursuit; but having hoisted far more sail than was necessary to overtake a crippled opponent, she shot past and had to be brought around again to renew the engagement. During this pause the commander of the troops on board the *Baionnaise* approached the only sea officer left on the quarter-deck, with a suggestion: they had no chance in a gun duel, and could not escape by sailing; why not try boarding, and see what the regiment of Alsace was made of? 'Short time there was, ye well may guess, for musing or debate.' The suggestion was instantly adopted, and the *Baionnaise* laid on a collision course with the advancing AMBUSCADE, while the platoon fell in on the forecastle.

The attempt to board was a common manœuvre by the French, whose ships were generally much more numerously manned than the British; but it was seldom successful, as all British officers knew how to take avoiding action. Nothing would have been easier in this case than for the British, with rigging intact, to avoid the attempt and resume the cannonade; but no order was given. The captain did nothing, and nobody else dared to give an order. With a rending crash the *Baionnaise* ran into the starboard quarter of the AMBUSCADE, carrying away with her bowsprit the mizzen-mast with its rigging, the wheel, and, worst of all, the starboard bulwark of the quarter-deck, leaving it perfectly open to the fire of thirty veteran musketeers at a range of a few yards.

The British Marines on the quarter-deck stood firm, and returned the fire; with some effect, for the officer commanding the troops, who had advised the action, fell dead; but the fire of his men swept the quarter-deck. The first lieutenant, Dawson

Main, received a mortal wound in the groin. Next, Captain Jenkins had part of his hip and thigh shot away, and was carried below. Lieutenant Sinclair, commanding the Marines, was wounded in thigh and shoulder. Mr Brown, the sailing-master, was shot dead through the head. In default of the second lieutenant (away with prizes), the command now devolved on the third, Joseph Briggs, who was very ill below; but he struggled up to the quarter-deck, only to be shot in his turn. Now Mr William Murray, the purser, was left in command, and of course fighting was not part of his duties; but he did his best.

At this moment a loud explosion was heard below, and an alarm of fire was raised. The gunner had ordered a gun to be shifted, in order to fire through a cabin window at the bow of the *Baionnaise*. The cartridges had been carelessly laid in such a position that the flash from the touch-hole, or perhaps an end of slow-match, ignited them, and thirty or forty pounds of gunpowder went up in a flash, blowing out part of the stern and severely burning every one of the gun's crew. Such accidents, of course, do not happen in well-run ships. This completed the panic of the crew; they bolted below, in spite of every effort of Mr Murray to rally them, and hid themselves in the bowels of the ship. The French soldiers now came over the bowsprit to the quarter-deck; the crew swarmed after them, and in a few minutes had complete possession of the AMBUSCADE.

The casualties in the AMBUSCADE were ten killed and thirty-six wounded, mostly by the two accidents related, and the fight on the quarter-deck. The *Baionnaise* had thirty killed and thirty seriously wounded plus probably as many slightly wounded, showing the effect of the fire of the AMBUSCADE, and the almost certain victory had the normal precautions to avoid being boarded been taken; four more broadsides would probably have brought the French flag down, especially since both her senior officers were below, wounded.

There was great rejoicing when the *Baionnaise* brought her prize into Rochefort, and the news was immediately spread over Europe, that a French corvette had taken a British frigate. Lieutenant Richer was given a double promotion to 'Captaine de vaisseau', which he probably merited, although he was below, wounded, when the fateful decision was taken, and took no part in the action which followed. It was, however, the greatest triumph the French Navy was to have during the twenty-two years of warfare.

The ship's company of the AMBUSCADE, now *Embuscade*, were soon exchanged, and in August of the same year a court martial sat three days at Portsmouth on the loss of the ship. Eventually the whole company was acquitted, in somewhat restrained terms. Clearly there had been rank cowardice among some of the crew, but it was very difficult to sort out the punishable from the pardonable. There had been a woeful lack of discipline and seamanship, and had Captain Jenkins been unwounded he would probably have been cashiered; but he was a poor wreck, crippled for life, who could obviously never again serve afloat. Then there was the fact that every officer of the ship had been killed or badly wounded at his post; the ship had been overwhelmed, not surrendered; she never struck her flag.

There was, of course, a sequel. On 28th May 1803 the *Embuscade* was on the last few days of a passage from the West Indies to Rochefort, just entering the Bay of Biscay. The positions of the British blockading fleets were known, and also the usual whereabouts of the patrolling frigates, so that *Embuscade* had little to fear, although she had a much depleted crew and some guns dismounted. But she was never a lucky ship. She now met with the VICTORY, 100 guns, Captain Sutton, on her way to the Mediterranean to become Nelson's flag-ship. *Embuscade* tried her heels, but VICTORY was the fastest three-decker of her day, in spite of her age (sixty-three years); to fight was out of the question, for one broadside from the VICTORY would have reduced the *Embuscade* to firewood. (The first broadside the VICTORY fired at Trafalgar, on the *Bucentaure*, 80 guns, flag-ship of Vice-Admiral Villeneuve, caused four hundred casualties, dismounted twenty guns, and left the ship practically defenceless.) There was nothing for it but to surrender, without a shot fired, and a prize crew took her to Portsmouth, where the AMBUSCADE was re-entered in the list of the Royal Navy.

On the 27th November of the same year the *Baionnaise* was cruising off the north-west coast of Spain when she was sighted and chased by the 64-gun ship of the line ARDENT; here again the French ship could neither fight nor flee; but as she was not far from the coast, she was run ashore near Cape Finisterre and burnt by her crew. Thus sadly ended the sad story.

8

Successful Defeat

In February 1805 the frigate CLEOPATRA, 32 guns, 12-pounders, Captain Sir Robert Laurie, Bart., was homeward bound from the West Indies. By this time the 32-gun frigates were considered obsolete, and the very last of them was on the stocks, to complete the last order; henceforward there were to be no frigates which did not mount a main battery of 18-pounders at least. To compensate for her now insufficient fire-power, her four quarter-deck 6-pounders had been removed and replaced with ten 24-pounder carronades, bringing her broadside up from 174 pounds to 282; always supposing, of course, that she could get within carronade range. She sailed very well, however, and with her excellent captain and efficient crew could expect to overhaul most enemy ships; she was a little short-handed, having only 200 men and boys instead of her establishment of 214, and she had several of her men down sick with the usual diseases inevitable at that time during a West Indies cruise.

On the 16th of February she was about 250 miles south-west of Bermuda, on the edge of the Sargasso weed, and still in the justly feared Bermuda triangle, the angles of which rest on Bermuda, Florida and Puerto Rico; an area in which more ships have been lost without trace than any other in the world. Not only in the eighteenth century: it has been stated that in the middle of the twentieth century nearly a thousand lives have been lost in this triangle, all without trace. Various theories have been propounded, from frightful monsters emerging from under the Sargasso weed (where, incidentally, all the eels of the Atlantic world go to breed) to the sounder one that, in that sector of a revolving storm in which the hurricane winds were opposed to the current of the Gulf Stream, such a sea would be raised as would overwhelm almost any small ship. Quite probable; but it does not explain the loss, in 1945, of five U.S. Navy torpedo bombers, and of the air-sea rescue ship which went out to look for them; all fitted with radio, all lost without word or trace.

On the 28th January 1805 the French 40-gun 18-pounder frigate *Ville-de-Milan*, Captain Jean-Marie Renaud, sailed from Martinique for France with important despatches, and with strict orders to speak no vessel by the way. To emphasise this stand-offish attitude, her four 36-pounder carronades were removed, and replaced by eight 8-pounder long guns, giving her four long 8s on her forecastle and sixteen on her quarter-deck; to compensate for the extra weight aft, her two aftermost 18-pounders were removed, leaving her with a main battery of twenty-six 18-pounders, and twenty 8-pounders, sixteen of which could be traversed to act as stern-chasers; an admirable arrangement for enabling her to carry out her present orders. She was a large frigate of nearly 1,100 tons, with a crew of 350 and a broadside of 340 pounds, all long guns.

It was at dawn on the 16th February that the CLEOPATRA sighted the *Ville-de-Milan* in the south-east, the wind being north-west, and bore up to speak her. By noon it could be descried that she was a large frigate with fifteen broadside ports to her main deck, indicating the 40-gun rate, so that the CLEOPATRA was chasing a ship which must have at least half as much force again as she had. Many a captain in such circumstances would remember a pressing engagement elsewhere, especially if he had reason to believe that the opponent was speedier. A prudent captain would shadow the bigger ship right across the Atlantic, if necessary, in the hope that some other British ship might come in sight to swing the balance of strength the other way; a possibility which would increase the nearer they came to the blockaded shores of France. Sir Robert Laurie, however, was more noted for courage than caution, and his order was to make more sail in pursuit. To the surprise and elation of his officers and crew, who did not know the French captain's orders, the *Ville-de-Milan* also made more sail and positively ran away. More and more sail was spread in both ships, studding-sails were boomed out, and they both tore along under every rag they could carry. Before dark it appeared that the CLEOPATRA was gaining. On both ships studding-sails were carried all night, somewhat hazardously in that area, where sudden squalls such as might dismast an over-pressed ship were quite frequent.

Daylight on the 17th February showed the two ships within four miles of each other, the CLEOPATRA still gaining. By 10.30 a.m. it was clear to Captain Renaud that in spite of his serious attempt to carry out his orders, his audacious opponent was going to bring him to action, so he took in his studding-sails to wait for her. When within gun-shot the CLEOPATRA also took in her studding-sails, and both ships hauled up their main-courses in preparation for action. At noon, observation on board the CLEOPATRA showed that they had chased 180 miles since sighting. At this time, being about half a mile behind, the CLEOPATRA fired her bow-chasers, two long 6-pounders; but the heavy fire returned from the powerful stern-battery of the *Ville-de-Milan* quickly caused her to steer clear, trying to approach the quarter rather than continue a direct stern-chase.

The CLEOPATRA was within a hundred yards at 2.30 p.m., when the *Ville-de-Milan* luffed up close to the wind and gave her opponent two broadsides. The CLEOPATRA closed to within fifty yards before replying, when a furious cannonade commenced and was kept up without intermission all afternoon, while the wind grew stronger and a heavy sea arose. By 5 p.m. both ships had suffered severely, but the rigging of the CLEOPATRA was so much shot about that her sails could scarcely be managed. She now tried to cross her opponent's bow, in the hope of raking her, but while doing so a shot struck her wheel and completely jammed the rudder. The *Ville-de-Milan* was to windward and squaring her sails, she ran right down on the CLEOPATRA, with such force that her bow actually mounted the quarter-deck just aft of the main mast, and she lay with her head and bowsprit right athwart her opponent; from which favourable position she poured in a heavy fire of musketry from her forecastle and fighting tops, to cover an attempt at boarding. This was gallantly repulsed, and the crew of the CLEOPATRA tried to set some sail on her, in the hope of disengaging somehow from the big ship which was pressing her into the sea; but the continuous musketry at so short a range was too much for them. At 5.15 p.m. the *Ville-de-Milan* boarded again, and all resistance ceased.

The fury of the cannonade, and the resolution with which it was continued on both sides, is demonstrated by the damage and casualties. Almost immediately after she was boarded for the second time, the CLEOPATRA lost her foremast, mainmast and bowsprit; and during the night the mainmast and mizzen-mast of the *Ville-de-Milan* went overside. Out of a complement of rather less than 200, the CLEOPATRA had fifty-eight killed and wounded, including all her commissioned officers except the captain, her sailing-master and her boatswain. The loss of the *Ville-de-Milan*, out of a crew of 350, has not been definitely ascertained, but was probably about thirty killed and wounded, including, however, her Captain Renaud killed, nearly at the close of the engagement, and her second captain, Capitaine de frégate Pierre Guillet, wounded.

Captain Guillet managed to get the two ships detached, and they lay alongside each other for three days, while a prize crew of fifty officers and men was put on board the *Cleopatra*, a number of the prisoners transferred to the *Ville-de-Milan*, damage was patched, jury-masts rigged and rigging repaired. All this was not helped by the dirty, squally, weather, but by the 21st February the two ships were able to get under way, however slowly.

The 50-gun two-decker LEANDER had had a somewhat chequered career since the Battle of the Nile; under command of Captain John Talbot she was making her way towards the North America station. On the 23rd February, at noon, in a clear spell between squalls, she espied a sail in the distance, to the south, and made sail in chase, losing sight very shortly but continuing on the same course. At 2.30 p.m. the weather cleared, and the chase was made out to be a frigate, jury-rigged; and shortly a much larger ship was seen ahead of her, also under jury masts. They closed, apparently for mutual support, and hoisted French colours. These were, of course, the *Ville-de-Milan* and the *Cleopatra*, neither in any state for another battle.

At 4 p.m. the LEANDER came up within gun-shot, when the two frigates separated, the *Cleopatra* running before the wind (she was in no condition to do anything else) and the *Ville-de-Milan* hauling up to take the wind on her quarter, which was about the nearest to the wind she could manage. The LEANDER followed the *Cleopatra*, overtook her in half an hour, and gave her one shot from her 32-pound lower battery; whereupon she hauled down her French colours and lay-to.

Those of the British prisoners who had been left on board now came on deck to take over the ship again, and hailed Captain Talbot to inform him what was happening; he ordered them to follow him as best they could, and immediately went off in pursuit of the *Ville-de-Milan*. The presence of a sufficient British crew was a very fortunate circumstance, as otherwise two hours would have been lost in putting a prize crew on board. As it was, by 5.30 p.m. the LEANDER was alongside the *Ville-de-Milan*, which surrendered without a shot being fired. After providing prize crews and arranging for the security of the prisoners, the LEANDER conducted her prizes into Halifax, where they were thoroughly repaired. The larger was taken into the Royal Navy as the 38-gun frigate MILAN, and the command was, very properly, given to Sir Robert Laurie.

Had the *Ville-de-Milan* met the LEANDER without first fighting the CLEOPATRA, two courses were open to her: no doubt, in accordance with her orders, she would have sailed away, as she was very well able to do, being much faster than the clumsy old two-decker; but had her captain so wished, she might have fought with about equal chances, being somewhat larger in tonnage, more numerously manned, and only slightly lighter in weight of metal, while being much more nimble in manœuvre. However, the hammering she had taken from the CLEOPATRA precluded all thought either of flight or of resistance, and her captain was absolutely correct in surrendering immediately. Sir Robert Laurie, therefore, while he had incurred heavy casualties and temporarily lost his ship, had nevertheless inflicted such damage to his opponent that she was bound to fall a prey to almost any well-found frigate which might encounter her, and this was accomplished only by the bold chase and intrepid encounter with a ship so much superior in every category. This was the sort of engagement Nelson had in mind, when with six ships he went in search of a fleet reported from seventeen to twenty. He assured Earl St Vincent that none of his ships would surrender, 'And before we are destroyed, I have little doubt but they will have their wings so completely clipped, that they may be easily overtaken.' Laurie never had the opportunity to command great fleets like Nelson, but he had the same ideas.

Prospective Admirals, however, will note that the 'successful defeat' went out with the wooden walls. The very last instance of a weak fleet successfully attacking a stronger was the Battle of Lissa in 1866; but there the weak Austrian fleet was commanded by Tegetthof, one of the finest naval officers ever, while the strong Italian fleet was under an officer whose conduct can only with charity be called irresolute. Ever since then, any naval encounter which was pushed home resulted in the destruction of the weaker with negligible damage to the stronger: there is no place in modern warfare for facile optimism.

9

The Young Star-captains

'Where the fleet of stars is anchored, and the young star-captains glow.'

Samuel Pepys laid down excellent rules for promotion in the Royal Navy: an aspirant to a lieutenant's commission had to have had at least six years at sea, been a midshipman or master's mate, and must be examined by a Board of three post captains; once commissioned, his further promotion to commander and captain depended on the view taken by his seniors; once he was captain, nobody could possibly be promoted over his head; only seniority mattered. No doubt if Pepys had exercised his authority for a century or so, things would have been better, but the rules became sadly bent during the eighteenth century. Some sort of influence, or interest as it was then called, was necessary even to get a captain to take a boy on board his ship at all, and from then on influence counted far more than ability. It was especially necessary to get the young man made post captain as early as possible, so that he might attain flag rank before he was *too* senile, and for this end influential persons got the rules broken with complete impunity. Especially was this the case on distant stations, where the Admiral C-in-C could appoint post captains at his discretion, subject always to confirmation by the Board of Admiralty. Thus Admiral Rodney made his son a post captain at sixteen, and Admiral Parker made *his* at seventeen, and both appointments were confirmed by the Board; but neither of them attained any subsequent distinction of his own.

Had Sir John Suckling not been Comptroller of the Navy, it is very unlikely that his nephew Horatio Nelson would have become post captain at twenty, and consequently rear-admiral at thirty-eight, qualified by seniority to command fleets. Of course, the whole system of eighteenth-century patronage was modified by the fact that people of great influence preferred to use it on behalf of youngsters who were likely to do them credit. Moreover, although a captain must inevitably advance by years alone in rank, this did not mean that he *must* have a command. Even when the Navy was at its most numerous in ships, not much more than a third of the captains commanded one; the rest were ashore on half pay. Thus at the beginning of 1811 the active list included 181 flag officers and 753 post captains, but there were only 264 post ships in commission, from 120 guns to 20 guns. And although the Board could be very obliging in allowing an early *rank* to the favoured of 'interest', *command* was a different thing, decided much more by the professional officers of the Board than the political. Where the choice was between two officers of more or less equal suitability, influence might swing the scale; but it would never get an incompetent officer appointed to an important command.

Thomas Byam Martin had dedicated himself to the Navy since early boyhood; not surprisingly, for his father, Sir Henry Martin, was Commissioner for Portsmouth in 1780, and Comptroller of the Navy in 1790. When he first went to sea, at the age of thirteen, it was in the PEGASUS, Captain Prince William Henry, afterwards King William IV. There was no difficulty about his examination and commission as lieutenant, which he received when he was seventeen; and when the great wars began in 1793, he served in the great fleet at Toulon, under the eye of Vice-Admiral Lord Hood.

The Republic of Genoa was of importance in this part of the Mediterranean, occupying 150 miles of strategic coastline, difficult of access from the rest of Italy. Theoretically it was neutral, but there was evidence that its many harbours were in fact being used as bases by French warships. On 5th October 1793 the BEDFORD, 74, Captain Mann, with the CAPTAIN, Captain Reeve, went into the harbour of Genoa itself, and took out the French 36-gun frigate *Modeste*, after a token resistance.

On rejoining the fleet off Toulon, Admiral Hood took the frigate into the Royal Navy under its existing name, and made Byam Martin post captain in command of her; he was now twenty years of age.

On the 8th of June 1796 two British frigates were on patrol about fifty miles west of the Scilly Islands. They were the 32-gun 18-pounder UNICORN, and the 36-gun 12-pounder SANTA MARGARITA, Captains Thomas Williams and Thomas Byam Martin respectively. At dawn they saw three strange warships to the south, only three miles away, and made after them. They turned out to be two frigates and a ship-corvette, keeping close together for mutual support. Shortly after noon the frigates hoisted French colours and opened fire with their stern-chasers, doing some damage to the rigging of the pursuers. At 4 p.m. the smaller frigate bore away from the heavy fire of the UNICORN, and cut across the bows of the SANTA MARGARITA, intending to rake her with a broadside; but Captain Byam Martin very neatly evaded this by running alongside his opponent and engaging her in a fierce cannonade broadside to broadside. Twenty minutes of this was enough, and the French captain hauled down his colours, having had 32 killed and 19 badly wounded, against the British loss of 2 killed and 3 wounded. Captain Byam Martin was very pleased to find that his prize was the *Tamise*, formerly the British THAMES, which had been captured in October 1793, after a desperate action with the *Uranie*, of almost twice her force; they fought each other to a standstill, the *Uranie* made off, but three more French frigates came up and took the crippled THAMES.

Meanwhile the UNICORN was in pursuit of the larger opponent, which turned out to be the *Tribune*, a large 36-gun frigate actually mounting 44 guns. After a running fight of ten hours, and a total chase of more than 200 miles, Captain Williams got to close quarters, dismasted his opponent and forced her surrender. She was rather larger than the UNICORN, but the extraordinary thing about this engagement is that while she had thirty-seven men killed and fifteen wounded including her captain, the UNICORN had not a single casualty.

On returning to port, both the first lieutenants of the two frigates were promoted commander, and Captain Williams, the senior captain, was knighted. At twenty-three, Byam Martin could afford to wait.

The TRIBUNE was wrecked the next year, through the folly of her captain and sailing master in trying to enter Halifax, Nova Scotia without a pilot. The THAMES, however, had quite an extensive service after she was restored to the Royal Navy.

In 1797 Byam Martin was given the 38-gun frigate TAMAR, and sent to the West Indies to join the squadron under Rear-Admiral Henry Harvey in the PRINCE OF WALES, 98, with Captain John Harvey as flag captain. (The Harvey family supplied more officers to the Royal Navy than any other at this time, and never a bad one; they, like everybody else, used family interest to the utmost.) The squadron was based on Port Royal, Martinique, which had been taken from the French, and the first objective was Trinidad. The protecting Spanish squadron, four ships of the line and a frigate, were found at anchor in Chagua-rama Bay, in a strong position covered by the fortified island of Gaspar Grande. Although he had one ship of the line more than the Spaniards, Harvey also had the responsibility of a fleet of transports with a small army under the famous Lieutenant-General Sir Ralph Abercrombie; evening was coming on, and Harvey decided that nothing was to be lost by waiting until morning. Nor was it: during the night the Spaniards set all their ships on fire except one, and abandoned them, along with the batteries on the island; no doubt they mistook some of the transports for ships of war, and concluded that they were faced with an overwhelming force. The remaining ship, the *San Damiso*, was boarded from the boats of the British ships and taken out without resistance. On the same day the troops were landed near Port of Spain, the capital, which was entered un-opposed, and the following day the Spanish governor sur-rendered the whole island. The total casualties on both sides was one British Army lieutenant wounded.

The next island attempted was Puerto Rico, where the squadron anchored off Boca de Congregos. They were hampered by the lack of detailed charts of that reef-lined shore, but eventually a passage was discovered which allowed sloops or smaller to reach the shore, where the army was disembarked about fifteen miles east of San Juan, not without some opposition. From here they had to advance along the narrow peninsula on the tip of which stood the town, against the strong fortifications which had been erected, and under fire from both sides by light gun-boats; while even the lighter ships of the squadron could not, on account of the reefs, get within a distance to give supporting fire. After ten or twelve days spent in trying everything which might occur to so able a General, Sir Ralph withdrew and re-embarked, having suffered a heavy loss of 225 killed, wounded and missing.

While all this was excellent experience, and service per-formed to the satisfaction of his superior officers, there was not much honour and glory to be won as a frigate attending on a line-of-battle squadron whose task was convoying small armies about the West Indies; and Byam Martin was no doubt delighted when his next command, in 1798, was a practically independent one, cruising about in the chops of the Channel looking out for French vessels going to Ireland or, more rarely, going home. In spite of the requirements of the Egyptian expedition under General Buonaparte, the Directory still looked to Ireland as the weak spot in British defence, as was indeed the case; but as in every case in which France tried to stir up rebellion, the aid they sent was too little and too late. The idea in this case was to arm and organise the Irish peasantry (who had good reason to rebel), and support them with a brigade of four or five thousand regular troops, again under General Humbert; a smaller scheme than that of December 1796, but for that reason more feasible. Everything happened, but at the wrong time. In May, Father Murphy had thirty thousand armed peasants assembled; but there was no backbone of French regulars, and they were cut to pieces by General Lake's troops. The first part of the French expedition did not sail from Roche-fort until the 6th of August, with General Humbert and about 1,200 men, whom they put on shore in the Bay of Killala and left to their own devices. After about a fortnight of desultory skirmishing, the remnant surrendered at Ballinamuck to General Lake, on 8th September. On the 15th the rest of the army sailed from Brest, at least 3,000 strong, in a 74 and eight frigates, too late for their friends in Ireland, but just in good time for the equinoctial gales. They were sighted by the frigates as they left

Brest, and shadowed all the way to the north-west coast of Ireland, while a squadron was being collected to deal with them; this they did so effectively that the 74 and three frigates surrendered in Donegal Bay, while the other five saved themselves for the time by scattering, not a single soldier having been landed.

Captain Byam Martin's frigate was the FISGARD, formerly the French *Résistance*, captured off Brest after the odd expedition to Fishguard (Chapter 4). She was at the top of the 38-gun class, mounting thirty-eight long 18-pounders on the main battery, and eight carronades, 32-pounders, on quarter-deck and forecastle. At 1,182 tons she was one of the largest British frigates, well able to carry her armament and her complement of 284 men, a well-trained crew with a keen and efficient young captain.

It was at 8 a.m. on the 20th of October 1798 that the look-out hailed the deck with the long-hoped-for report — a strange sail to the westward headed directly for Brest, about a hundred miles away, with a fine steady wind from west by south-west. The FISGARD kept on close-hauled for half an hour, then tacked in chase, with the wind nicely on her quarter. The chase was the *Immortalité*, smaller than the FISGARD but slightly more heavily armed, having twenty-four long 24-pounders on her main battery, and fourteen long 8-pounders and four carronades, 36-pounders, on her forecastle and quarter-deck. In addition to her normal complement of 330 men, she had on board 250 soldiers whom she had been unable to land in Ireland.

At 11 a.m. the *Immortalité* hoisted her colours and began firing her long 8-pounder stern-chasers, to which the FISGARD could make no effective return, having only carronades on her forecastle, with the result that when she did come up with her antagonist, she was badly knocked about in the rigging, so much so that after a short engagement she had to fall back to make repairs. On this, the *Immortalité* hoisted all sail and made off on the fair wind. It is easy to imagine the scene of furious activity on the deck of the FISGARD as they saw their enemy escaping; they re-rigged almost the whole ship in three-quarters of an hour, a feat only possible for the very best of crews, most skilfully commanded. By 1.30 p.m. she was again level with the *Immortalité*, keeping wide during the chase to avoid that battery of stern-chasers, and then converging, but keeping far enough away to be out of range of aimed musketry from the 250 soldiers. Now ensued a most furious cannonade, both sides standing to their guns with the utmost resolution. The FISGARD received some of her opponent's heavy 24-pound shot between wind and water, and at 2 p.m. the carpenter reported six feet of water in the hold. He was ordered to keep plugging and pumping, and the cannonade went on for another hour with undiminished fury. By this time the hull of the *Immortalité* was in a sinking condition, her mizzen-mast gone by the board, and the rest of her masts very badly damaged; moreover, her gallant Captain Legrand and the first lieutenant were both killed, as also General Monge of the Army; she now hauled down her colours and surrendered.

The FISGARD had thirty-six killed and wounded, and her hull so damaged that after all possible repairs she had to keep one pump going continually all the way to Plymouth. The *Immortalité* had 115 killed and wounded, including the officers mentioned. This was a classic example of a combat between two ships well matched in force, meeting on the high seas with plenty of sea-room and no other ship in sight the whole day. The hard-fought fight was equally honourable to both combatants, but of course the laurels go to the victor. The IMMORTALITE was taken into the Royal Navy under her own name, but after the hammering she had taken from the FISGARD she was reckoned not strong enough to remount 24-pounders, which were replaced by 18s.

This was the last of Byam Martin's exploits as a frigate captain; henceforth he commanded ships of the line during the rest of the wars, always with credit and success. He became Admiral of the Fleet in 1849, and died, full of years and honours, in 1854.

The East Indies station was the command that gave the widest powers and discretion to the C-in-C, because of the great distance. To send a despatch from Fort St George to London by the usual convoy, with long stops at the Cape of Good Hope and St Helena, took about six months, so that a reply could not be looked for inside a year; and unless the despatch from Admiralty was very peremptory, another year might well elapse before the

C-in-C had to alter his plans. In fact this scarcely ever happened; the C-in-C was always a proved and trusted officer, Admiralty gave him a broad picture of what was expected, and left the details to him; that he would promote his relatives was taken for granted, within reasonable limits. Thus when Rear-Admiral Peter Rainier as C-in-C, East Indies station, made an expedition under his own command to take Amboyna, it is not surprising to find James Sprat Rainier in command of the 16-gun ship-sloop SWIFT, in February 1796; nor is it surprising that in 1799 he was a post captain in command of the two-decker 50-gun ship CENTURION, in the Mediterranean; but on the renewal of the war in 1803 he was back on the East Indies station, in the same ship. He never commanded a frigate.

Now Vice-Admiral, Rainier had his nephew and godson, Midshipman Peter Rainier, sent out to the East Indies, and in very little more than a year made him post captain in the 36-gun 18-pounder frigate CAROLINE; quick promotion, but it had to be quick, for Rear-Admiral Sir Edward Pellew was already on his way to relieve Rainier, and he had with him his son, Fleetwood Pellew, whom he had already had made a commander at seventeen. He might possibly not have observed those qualities in young Rainier which his uncle did, but now that Peter junior was a post captain there was nothing to be done about it. In fact, Pellew did very well by Rainier's protégé, and sent him out on very promising cruises.

On the 18th of October 1806 the CAROLINE captured a small 14-gun Dutch brig, off the north coast of Java; and learned from the prisoners that there was a Dutch 36-gun 12-pounder frigate, the *Maria-Riggersbergen*, in the roadstead at Batavia (now Djakarta). Captain Rainier at once followed up this information, and found not only the frigate but three other ships, two of 14 guns and one of 18, as well as more than thirty gun-boats close inshore. Captain Rainier prepared to anchor by the stern, with a spring on the cable, and sailed boldly in; as soon as the CAROLINE was within shot the *Maria-Riggersbergen* opened fire, but the CAROLINE remained quite silent until within forty yards, when she loosed her broadside with devastating effect. The Dutch ship fought back bravely, and had the three smaller ships and the mass of gun-boats come boldly forward, they would have had a superiority of three to one against the CAROLINE; but their efforts were very half-hearted, and within half an hour the *Maria-Riggersbergen* hauled down her colours and the CAROLINE took possession. The CAROLINE was undermanned, having sent away 57 men in various prizes; of the 204 remaining she had 21 killed or wounded, plus 4 Dutch prisoners, and scarcely any damage to the hull or rigging. The Dutch frigate, out of a complement of 270, lost 50 killed or wounded, and had extensive but tolerable damage.

Sir Edward Pellew took the frigate into the Royal Navy, under the more pronounceable name of JAVA. On the East Indies station a ship was a ship, hard to replace, but had she been at Portsmouth she would not have been taken into full service, being fairly old and not in good condition. The following year, under Captain George Pigot, she was escorting in the Indian Ocean the BLENHEIM, 74, wearing the flag of Vice-Admiral Sir Thomas Troubridge, Bart., that most renowned of Nelson's paladins. What actually happened will never be known, for both ships disappeared without a trace. No doubt they had met the full force of a typhoon, which might conceivably have overwhelmed them both without a boat or spar breaking away. It cannot have been very far from the place where the new 12,000 ton liner *Waratah*, fitted with radio, disappeared without signal or trace in 1898.

In January 1807 the CAROLINE, and her young captain, had a stroke of luck such as every man in the Navy liked to dream about. They captured the Spanish *San Raphael*, with trifling resistance, and found her so richly laden that her prize-money came to nearly £170,000. The twenty-two-year-old captain had more than £50,000, while the C-in-C, Pellew, thousands of miles away, had half that sum; still, there was cut-and-come-again left, and the most ordinary seaman had about £200, enough to set him up in a cosy pub on shore, while the lieutenants would have more than £5,000 apiece. The timing was lucky too; had the capture taken place eighteen months later, the CAROLINE would have found, on reaching port, that Spain was now Britain's gallant ally and there was no prize-money forthcoming.

Rear-Admiral Sir Edward Pellew had lost no time in making

his son Fleetwood Pellew, age twenty, a post captain in the 32-gun 12-pounder PSYCHE; he now sent the two young captains out together on a long-range reconnaissance. It was known that there were two Dutch ships of the line, 68 guns each, somewhere on the Java coast. At a time when a very few warships were controlling vast areas of ocean, two powerful warships were of such importance that it was imperative to discover their whereabouts and condition. Accordingly the CAROLINE and the PSYCHE sailed from Fort St George in June 1807, and at the end of August reached the eastern end of Java. Here they were able to ascertain that the two Dutch line-ships were the *Pluto* and the *Revolutie,* that they were laid up in Gressik at the mouth of the Sourabaya river, unfit to go to sea and probably in too poor a condition to be repairable.

This meant that there was most probably no ship in the area which could be a match for either of the frigates separately; accordingly they parted, the CAROLINE sailing back by the south side of Java and the PSYCHE by the northern. When off Samarang, about 200 miles west of Sourabaya, shipping was observed in the roadstead towards evening, and the PSYCHE anchored offshore for the night. At dawn she stood into the harbour and found a small 8-gun schooner and a merchant brig, which were seized and towed out by the boats of the frigate, under Lieutenant Kersteman. Now three more vessels appearing to be warships were seen in the offing; Captain Fleetwood Pellew therefore destroyed his prizes, not wishing to weaken his crew by detaching prize-crews. On making sail in pursuit of the strangers, they made off to the westward, but finding that the frigate was quickly overtaking them they ran themselves on shore. In this position they opened fire on the frigate, trusting to the shallows to keep her at a distance, while they could probably deal with the boats if sent in. The PSYCHE, however, ghosted in until she anchored with scarcely half a yard of water beneath her keel; from here she fired broadsides at each of the three in turn, and in about an hour all three struck their colours. They were the *Resolutie,* an armed merchantman of 700 tons, the 24-gun corvette *Scipio,* and the 12-gun brig *Ceres.* They had very little damage and the only casualty was the Captain of the *Scipio* killed; the PSYCHE had no damage or casualties. By working hard all through the night, the crew of the PSYCHE got all three prizes floated off, and brought them to Madras.

It may seem strange that such great ship-builders as the Dutch should allow their two best ships to fall into hopeless disrepair, and that such determined fighters should so tamely surrender their ships; whereas in the first war the Dutch were considered the toughest of opponents, and Camperdown was by far the most desperately contested battle of the wars. The fact is that their hearts were no longer in it. When the Batavian Republic was in alliance with the French Republic they fought with a right good will; but when the Kingdom of Holland was a vassal state of the French Empire, with a Louis Buonaparte on the throne, their enthusiasm evaporated. In all war it is essential that men 'should know what they fight for, and like what they know'.

Before long Sir Edward promoted his son to the command of the 38-gun 18-pounder frigate PHAETON, in which ship he remained on the station after his father returned to take over the Mediterranean command on the death of Admiral Collingwood. In this ship he served in the powerful fleet under Rear-Admiral Stopford which, along with 10,000 troops, finally took all Java in 1811. The naval force of four line-of-battle ships, fourteen frigates, and many smaller craft, was so great that there was no resistance by sea; but Captain Fleetwood Pellew saw some service on land, in command of about a hundred men.

Unlike Byam Martin, neither Rainier nor Pellew further distinguished themselves. Rainier commanded several ships at different times, but was never involved in any famous action. Pellew had great difficulty in getting a command at all. Although certainly a brave and efficient officer, he had acquired such an unfortunate reputation for brutality towards his crew that it was difficult to get anybody to serve under him, and he was always having near-mutinies, which were sometimes quite serious. After he had been on the beach for many years, having attained flag rank by simple survival, he was given command of the squadron which went out in 1842 to take over Hong Kong. Even here he managed to have a mutiny by refusing to allow shore leave to the crews, owing, he alleged, to the bad and dangerous climate. The ship which took home his despatches brought back another admiral to relieve him.

10

The Last Viking

Excepting Nelson, no naval officer impressed himself so much upon his times, as a hero of romance, as Captain Lord Cochrane. Certainly he had every advantage. Eldest son of the Scottish Earl of Dundonald, he was very tall, immensely strong, and of a most imposing presence, even as a very young man. He had every good quality of the warrior, leaving nothing to chance but accepting ascertained risks, absolutely without fear but retaining his cool head in the midst of the fiercest combat. He trained his men in the same strict discipline that he trained himself, and they loved him. He was strictly impartial: for example, it was absolutely necessary that every man should roll up his hammock very tightly before stowing it in the hammock nettings above the bulwarks; Cochrane had an iron hoop made, and every hammock, when rolled, had to pass through the hoop, or else. There was no room for the whim of a boatswain's mate; either the hammock passed the hoop or it didn't. When he came to the command of ships, he had never the least difficulty in getting together a crew, the only trouble being in selecting from the over-numerous volunteers. In his official letters, he never mentioned his own part, but lavished praise on his officers and men, who no doubt deserved it because they had absorbed his own high spirit, as had Nelson's officers.

Nevertheless, he had the defects of his qualities. He could not see any injustice or abuse without attacking it with the same headlong ardour that he did the French; but alas! the shining knight was unhorsed by the windmills. The whole Establishment of the time—religious, civil, Army or Navy, was completely based on the great principles of patronage and corruption, and woe betide the solitary stormer of those bastions! Cochrane himself was quite illegally enrolled on the books of the various ships commanded by his uncle, from the time he was five years old until he actually went on board a warship for the first time at the age of eighteen; this to give him a sufficient 'sea-time' to qualify him to sit the examination for lieutenant. This sort of cheating and exercise of influence was absolutely necessary if a young man was to get his foot on the captain's ladder when young enough to give him a chance of becoming at least a rear-admiral before he was too old for active service, but it was a bad way to officer a navy.

In December 1801 Cochrane was made a post captain, and might reasonably expect command of a frigate. He had the right connections and a splendid record; in his last cruise, in a very small brig, he had terrorised the Mediterranean coast of Spain, capturing 50 ships, 122 guns and 534 prisoners, and conducted the most brilliant single-ship encounter in naval history. When he was made post, he urged the claim of his first lieutenant to be promoted commander for this last exploit; when refused, he returned again, pressing his point in terms which were certainly undiplomatic, and which the First Sea Lord, Earl St Vincent, took as personally insulting. The grim old admiral never forgave; there was no ship for Cochrane to command; the most brilliant of the young captains was on the beach.

On the resumption of war after the brief Peace of Amiens, in 1803, Cochrane again offered his services, and was given the ARAB, an old coal boat which had been fitted with just enough guns to qualify as a post-ship, and detailed for coastal duties in the Channel, west of Beachy Head, as part of the protection against Napoleon's army gathered at Boulogne for the invasion. Not much of a command for an active officer, but the country was in quite a fever of apprehension (with some cause), for if Napoleon had set down in Kent the army which he later led to Austerlitz, there was very little in Britain to match that superbly equipped and trained force. The only problem was getting them to Kent, and St Vincent spoke for the Navy when he told the House of Lords, 'I do not say the French cannot come, but I do say they cannot come by water.'

In May 1804 the Addington Cabinet fell, and Pitt became Prime Minister, with his friend Henry Dundas, now made Viscount Melville, as First Lord of the Admiralty. This active Scotsman introduced a great programme of naval expansion, in which he was unlikely to overlook another active Scotsman. Cochrane got his frigate, the 32-gun PALLAS, 667 tons, newly built of fir instead of oak, with a main battery of twenty-six long 12-pounders and twelve carronades, 24-pounders, on her quarter-deck and forecastle. No doubt many captains junior to Cochrane commanded much more powerful ships; still, it was a frigate, fast by reason of its light structure, and fitted for its intended role of raiding commerce and inshore patrol. Moreover, he was given a very desirable commission; to proceed under Admiralty letter to the vicinity of the Azores, and cruise there for enemy merchantmen, which meant that all the prize-money would fall to the ship's company, without deductions for distant admirals or other senior officers. After a certain time in this employment, he was to proceed to the Biscay coast of France and put himself under the orders of Vice-Admiral Thornborough, commanding in that area.

The Azores cruise was highly profitable, and after seeing his prizes safely into Gibraltar, Cochrane went to the Biscay station. Hanging about off the Gironde, the estuary which leads up to Bordeaux, he found out that the entrance was guarded by two 14-gun brig-corvettes, taking turn about up-river and down-river, the estuary being further defended by land batteries on both shores. Cochrane could see no good reason why he should not have at least one of those brigs, and on the evening of 5th April 1806 he sent in all the boats of the frigate, under the command of his first lieutenant, John Hansell, and piloted by his sailing master James Sutherland, the other boats being commanded by three midshipmen; the PALLAS anchored to await their return, and to prevent any interference from outside. Even with the help of the tide it was a long pull of twenty miles for the men, but by 3 a.m. on the morning of the 6th they were alongside, and boarded her in great style. There was no surprise, for the brig was fully prepared, but nothing could resist the men Cochrane had trained, and in a few minutes the brig, the *Tapageuse*, was their prize. They now looked to the other brig, further up-stream, but the tide had turned and there were not enough men to look after the *Tapageuse*, whose crew out-numbered the PALLAS boatmen, and attack her consort also; so, at first light they made sail outwards. Immediately the shore guards gathered what was happening, the batteries opened fire on the TAPAGEUSE, and the other brig made sail in pursuit, coming within gunshot and engaging in a desultory exchange of long bowls for about an hour, when the sight of the three masts of the PALLAS persuaded them to desist. The whole loss in this engagement, a class-room demonstration of 'cutting out by boats' was three men wounded.

The PALLAS had not been swinging idly at her anchor. At dawn she was under way, having seen three ships approaching, which were in fact the two 20-gun ship-corvettes *Garonne* and *Gloire*, and the 16-gun brig-corvette *Malicieuse*. Between them those ships mounted 56 guns to the 38 of the PALLAS, but they showed no desire to engage. The PALLAS ran all three of them ashore, where they were all dismasted by the shock of striking, and lay, apparently, complete wrecks. Had they been well handled, they could very well have given a good account of themselves, especially as so many men of the PALLAS were away in the boats; this of course they could not know, but what they probably did know was the name of the frigate, and who commanded her, and the terror of his name. Having seen the three Frenchmen ashore, the PALLAS returned to her station in good time to receive her boats and their prize.

After re-uniting with Vice-Admiral Thornborough's squadron, the PALLAS was detached on 25th April 1806 to reconnoitre the Aix roads, between the Île d'Oleron and the mainland at Rochefort, the heavily fortified Île d'Aix lying in the centre of the northern end of the roadstead, about 46°N 1°10′W. Standing boldly in, Lord Cochrane observed one three-decker and four two-decked line-of-battle ships, five frigates, a ship-corvette and three brig-corvettes. Not being in any particular hurry, Cochrane hung about for a while in the roadstead, in case there might be any more information, and to see what might turn up. Signals were seen from the three-decker; and one frigate, the 40-gun *Minerve*, with the three brig-corvettes, weighed and got under way to drive the PALLAS away. Not wishing to hurry, Cochrane waited for the French ships, and, as they approached exchanged several broadsides with them, without, apparently, any damage or casualties. There now were visible the 32-gun 12-pounder frigate IRIS, the 16-gun ship-sloop HAZARD, and a cutter; so that Captain Collet of the *Minerve* judged it prudent to take his little squadron under the batteries of Île d'Aix. As he showed no signs of coming out, and as it was inadvisable to engage the whole French fleet in the roads, Cochrane rejoined his squadron to make his report.

Napoleon had instituted a system of coastal signal stations, all within easy view of each other, and also communicating with Paris; by this means every movement of the British inshore cruisers was almost instantly known all along the coast, and this knowledge saved many merchant ships which must otherwise have been snapped up, whereas they simply remained in a fortified anchorage until the coast was clear. These signal posts were quite large structures, with barracks and other buildings, guarded by from fifty to a hundred militia. Having a few days to spare, Cochrane decided to make a break in the line, by destroying half a dozen neighbouring stations; this was done by landing parties, who chased away the militia, took off the flags and burned the masts and buildings. For men trained by Cochrane, this was a straightforward job in five cases, but the sixth was more complicated. At L'Aiguillon, on the Breton Strait between the Île de Ré and the mainland, the signal station was guarded to seaward by a battery of three 32-pounder guns firing explosive shells, and at the time a small French convoy was lying under the protection of the battery, which had a garrison of fifty regulars. Cochrane led a night attack in person, which was successful. The battery was stormed, the guns spiked, the shells thrown into the sea, the emplacements demolished, the buildings and gun-carriages burnt. Next, the signal station was razed like the others, but there was one disappointment: the convoy, which they had expected to capture, had got up the river Lay into safety.

It was now known that the commanding officer of the French squadron in Aix roads was Vice-Admiral Allemand, and it was thought wise to keep a close eye on so able an officer. Accordingly, on the 12th May 1806 the PALLAS again approached, accompanied by the INDEFATIGABLE, 44 guns, Captain John Rodd, and the KINGFISHER, 16 guns, Commander Seymour. The INDEFATIGABLE, Pellew's old ship, was twice the size and power of the PALLAS, but Cochrane was senior to Rodd. Two frigates and three brigs came out to meet them. There was very little sea-room for eight ships, shoals were numerous, and the wind fell light and variable, so that there was every chance of running aground or being becalmed under one of the batteries. The British squadron withdrew, doubtless reflecting that there would be another day.

It came two days later, the 14th May, when the PALLAS, alone, worked her way in against a fair breeze from south by west, which ensured a good retreat if necessary. The *Minerve* and the three brig-corvettes were again ordered out, but this time the *Minerve* came along in great style, flying before the fresh wind with every stitch set, even to studding-sails and royals, determined to bring the PALLAS to action and eliminate this nuisance once for all; this was not impossible by any means, since she was 1,100 tons to the 667 tons of the PALLAS, and had more than twice her weight of broadside. Lord Cochrane, who had shortened sail to topsails only, set his main topsail aback and lay-to until the *Minerve* came within short range, when he gave her such a broadside as effectually shortened her sail for her.

There ensued a battle unique in naval annals, such as could only be fought by a captain of complete intrepidity and consummate skill, with an enthusiastically devoted ship's company. He was engaged with a ship of twice the power, along with three brigs which had between them more guns than he had; he was always within range of at least one of the shore batteries, on the island of Aix or on the coast; and the battle was fought in a confined strait, further encumbered with many hidden shoals. His tactics were to engage the *Minerve*, and at the same time to keep close to her in such a position that the nearest shore battery could not fire without danger of hitting their own ship; at the same time to fight off the three brigs, with their fourteen 8-pounders apiece, who came swarming in; and, still at the same time, to keep in mind the positions of the shoals and sound continually, for a touch on the ground would be instant

disaster. With all those conflicting calls for immediate attention, it was only one of the great captains who could continuously issue his orders, completely imperturbable, amid the
thunder of the guns and the scream of the shot.

After two hours of this extraordinary combat, the fire of the
Minerve perceptibly slackened, and Cochrane determined to
board her, for an immediate decision; this was essential, for the
look-out reported that two more frigates in the roadstead were
hoisting sail. As the PALLAS approached, the fire of the *Minerve*
ceased altogether; there seemed to be no preparation to repel
boarders, for there was nobody to be seen on deck but Captain
Collet and a few officers on the quarter-deck. As the ships came
alongside, at some speed, a surge threw them together with
great force; and the difference was seen between the light fir
timbers of the PALLAS and the stout Adriatic oak of the *Minerve*,
which took no injury by the collision. The PALLAS lost her jib-
boom, fore-topmast, fore and main topsail yards, all her forward
rigging, and all the ship-furniture of her side forward, including
her cat-head and bower-anchor, by which Cochrane had intended
to hook her on to the *Minerve*. There was no question now of
re-engaging, for the two fresh frigates were on their way.
Setting what sail she could, the PALLAS made outwards to the
offing, where she met the KINGFISHER, sloop, which took her in
tow. Cochrane, having fought against fearful odds to within a
few minutes of victory, was defeated by the cheeseparing
economies of his own government.

Casualties were low for such an engagement. PALLAS had one
Marine killed, one midshipman and four ratings wounded. Her
damages were such that she had to return to Portsmouth for
extensive repair. The *Minerve*, with a much larger crew (330
against 214) reported seven killed and fourteen wounded. She
had her fore-yard shot away, and much minor damage, easily
repaired in Rochefort. She was certainly at sea on 25th September of the same year, for on that day she was captured, along
with three other frigates, by a powerful squadron of six line-of-
battle ships under Commodore Sir Samuel Hood, who lost his
right arm in the engagement. The French frigates put up a
determined resistance against such overwhelming odds, and
enabled the *Themis*, 36, and two brigs to escape. The *Minerve*,

at last, struck her colours to the MONARCH, 74, and was taken into the Royal Navy under the name of ALCESTE; she will be heard of again.

Cochrane's official letters on those actions were, as usual with him, very terse, describing the engagements very briefly and mentioning many of his officers, without any hint of his own conduct; Vice-Admiral Thornbury, in his despatch, did Cochrane full justice, commending him to the attention of their lordships; but when Cochrane came home no attention whatever was paid to him. His friend Lord Melville had left the Admiralty, to be succeeded by Lord Barham, who in turn was followed by Charles Grey, created Lord Howick, merely a politician and quite new in the office, very unlikely to do anything against the advice of the Establishment at the Admiralty, which persisted in the view that no amount of courage and skill could help an officer who had dared to question the justice of omniscient Admiralty. Although nineteen frigates were added to the Royal Navy during the year 1806, there was none for its best frigate captain.

Unwilling to rust on the beach, Cochrane now got himself elected Member of Parliament for Honiton, in October 1806. In our days, when a back-bench Member of Parliament is merely 'a welfare officer for his constituents',* it is difficult to understand the immense influence wielded by every member who could speak to the point, even if he represented 'a grassy mound in an unpeopled plain' or 'three niches in a wall'.† Feeling that Lord Cochrane's heavy guns would be better directed against the French than against themselves, the Lords of the Admiralty ('their feelings matter not') posted him to the IMPERIEUSE, 38-gun 18-pounder frigate, with orders to join Commodore Keats' squadron in the south of the French Biscay coast.

On the way down the familiar Biscay shore, Cochrane thought he would like to look into the Basin d'Arcachon, about seventy miles south of the entrance to the Gironde estuary. There was, however, a strong fort on Cap Ferret, the point of the peninsula

* The late Sir James Henderson Stewart, Bt., M.P., in personal conversation with the author.

† Lord John Russel, House of Commons, March 1st 1831, introducing a Reform Bill.

which entirely protects the land-locked basin. To clear the way, Cochrane sent all his boats ashore, under Lieutenant David Mapleton, to assault the fort, which looked large and formidable. The men of the IMPERIEUSE, however, stormed the fort and chased away its garrison; then they spiked all the guns, four 36-pounders, two 6-pounder field guns, and a 13-inch mortar for throwing explosive shells. They burned the military stores, platforms and gun-carriages, and used the gunpowder to blow up the buildings. The road into the basin was now open, but it does not appear that there was any valuable prize there. Cochrane generally laid his plans so well, and they were carried out with such *élan* that his casualties were generally light; on this occasion there were none whatever. This beautiful little action took place on 6th January 1807.

Cochrane was not long with Commodore Keats' squadron, for Parliament was prorogued on 27th April, and dissolved, with a view to a general election. Cochrane went home, gave up his seat for Honiton, and got himself elected as one of the two members for the City of Westminster. This was unique among constituencies at that time; there was no bribery, and almost every householder was a voter. In those days of pocket boroughs and open bribery, Westminster alone represented *vox populi* — and it was heard. The new Parliament met at the end of May 1807, and on 10th July Cochrane tabled a motion about the scandalous abuses in the Navy, couched in terms which his friends thought injudicious. The motion was never heard in the House. Cochrane was immediately ordered to reassume command of the IMPERIEUSE, proceed to the Mediterranean, and put himself under the orders of Vice-Admiral Lord Collingwood.

Whether Collingwood did not want such a firebrand under his direct command, or whether he thought the service suited to Cochrane's experience and resource, at any rate he detached him with orders to harass the coasts of France and Spain, from Toulon westward as far as Barcelona. This Cochrane pitched into with enthusiasm, first destroying the signal stations which reported his movements, then the batteries under which shipping could lie in safety, and then snapping up prizes all along the coast and sending them in to Minorca. There were few nights without a boating party, and the enemy had to devote more and more troops to guarding the coast and the lines of communication.

In May 1808 there was a change: the population of Spain rose with one accord against the French garrisons which had been allowed into Spain by the treachery of Godoy. The juntas sent deputations to England to ask for help. Help was promised, and the first step was to announce to the Navy that Britain was now at peace with Spain, and that all possible assistance was to be given to the ships and armies of the juntas. Cochrane's role was not much affected, but more complicated; before, he had only to fire at anything that moved; now he had to be selective. However, the disciplined armies which France was now pouring into Spain were readily distinguishable from the guerrillas.

A French army was besieging the frontier fortress of Gerona, and as part of the operation seized a castle and established an outpost on the coastal part of the road between Gerona and Barcelona, thus cutting off supplies to the besieged town. On the 31st July 1808 Lord Cochrane landed with his Marines, stormed the castle and demolished it with all its outworks, taking seventy-one prisoners. He gave all their arms to the guerrillas, but judged it more humane to take the prisoners off in the IMPERIEUSE.

To facilitate the movement of his armies into Spain, Napoleon had erected a chain of signal stations, not with flags as on the west coast but with semaphores after the British pattern, the advantage being that they did not depend upon the wind to spread the flags. Cochrane was cruising off the coast of Languedoc, and towards the end of September recommenced his attacks on the signal stations. He landed, with a large part of his men, at Frontignan, surprised and demolished a chain of six signal posts, with all their buildings, a shore battery, and a tower on the shore of the Etange de Thau. This was a most daring enterprise, for it was carried out against garrison forces more than double his own in aggregate, within twenty-five miles of the military centre of Montpellier, and ten miles from the highway down which a hundred thousand men were marching for Spain. It deprived them not only of their communications but of their supplies, for without information the coasting vessels which accompanied the armies scarcely dared venture from harbour, and those which did were promptly snapped up by the IMPERIEUSE. His movements were so swift that the French never knew where to expect him, and his attacks were delivered with such impetuosity that no equal force could stand against him. Eventually, the French had to station ten thousand men along the coast which he menaced, so that the mere terror of his name was as effective as a minor fortress.

The fortress and harbour of Rosas, only twenty miles south of the French border, was stoutly defended by the Spaniards, aided from time to time by two British 74s and two bomb-vessels. On the 7th November 1808 the French occupied the town of Rosas, and began siege operations against the citadel and the detached Fort Trinidad, also erecting batteries to drive away the ships. In this they were partly successful, for by the 24th November the 74s had withdrawn the Marines they had landed, and sailed away, leaving the two bomb-vessels, LUCIFER and METEOR, to carry on shelling the French trenches. On the 24th the IMPERIEUSE came into the bay; it was impossible to get to the citadel, but Fort Trinidad was open to seaward, and Cochrane went ashore himself to ascertain the position. The garrison, only eighty strong, was ready to surrender, but decided to hold out, since Cochrane himself undertook to take part in the defence, with fifty seamen and thirty Marines. The Spaniards were astonished at the energy of the Englishmen, and especially admired Cochrane's resource in filling up the breach in the wall with bags filled with earth and sand; indeed, this is possibly the first time sandbags were used as a protection against artillery and musketry. On the 30th November a force of a thousand first-class French troops made a general assault on the fort; after a determined attack and equally determined defence they were repulsed, with heavy losses including their commanding officer and all their equipment.

On the 5th of December 1808 the citadel of Rosas surrendered by capitulation, after a most creditable defence. There was now no point in defending Fort Trinidad any longer, so during the night Cochrane re-embarked, giving passage to those of the garrison who wished to leave that part of the country. He brought away the lighter stores and guns, spiked the heavy guns, and finally blew up the fort. He had delayed for ten days a

French army under Marshal St-Cyr, and he had not lost a man. As usual, his official letter was far too brief, a bare statement of facts, with high praise for all his officers engaged, among whom we may distinguish Midshipman Frederick Marryat.

In February 1809 several squadrons which were blockaded on the west coast of France managed to evade the blockade in bad weather, and gathered together in the Aix roads, under the command of Rear-Admiral Willaumez, who was superseded by Vice-Admiral Allemand. His fleet consisted of nine line-of-battle ships, a cut-down 50-gun ship, and four frigates. His flag-ship was the *Ocean*, 120 guns, one of the most powerful ships afloat. Outside, in the Basque roads, lay Admiral Lord Gambier, with eleven line-of-battle ships, including the new CALEDONIA, 120 guns, a match for the *Ocean*, with six frigates, twelve smaller warships, and a number of store and transport ships. He made excellent dispositions for the defence of his fleet, but none for attacking the enemy. Admiralty could not spare so fine a fleet to lie at anchor close to the enemy shore; neither could they permit so powerful a French fleet to remain within easy reach of the immense convoys which were supplying the British forces in Spain and Portugal: it must be destroyed. On the 19th March Admiralty sent Lord Gambier a despatch, advising him that they were sending to his aid twelve fireships, and Colonel Congreve with a supply of his rockets and men to use them; he was furthermore directed, 'to take into your consideration the possibility of making an attack upon the enemy...'. (In short, don't just sit there, *do* something.) In reply, on the 26th March, Lord Gambier wrote a long despatch emphasising the enormous difficulties, for he was a man who always saw his own troubles very clearly, but had no imagination of the difficulties of the enemy; however, he concluded that he was ready to obey any orders, 'however great the risk may be of the loss of men and ships'.

On the 19th March, the same day that the Admiralty sent the prod to Gambier, the IMPERIEUSE, with Lord Cochrane in command, anchored at Plymouth; and it says much for the Admiralty system of semaphores that within an hour he received an order to attend at Whitehall. On the 21st March he was received by

Lord Mulgrave, the First Lord, who explained the position in Aix roads and asked him to give his opinion, based on his intimate knowledge of the area, as to whether an attempt would be successful. He thought it had every prospect. Given suitable weather conditions, twelve fireships would cause the utmost confusion, if not panic, and in a confined roadstead, encumbered with shoals, several at least of the big ships must go aground; unable to manœuvre, they could be forced to surrender by a few bomb-ships, some gun-brigs with heavy carronades, and two or three frigates in deeper water. Cochrane was now asked if he himself would take command of such an attack. He refused, on the grounds that there were many officers senior to himself in Lord Gambier's fleet, and his being given such a command over their heads would cause a great deal of ill-feeling. 'The present is no time for professional etiquette,' said Lord Mulgrave, and pointed out that he was the only captain who knew the ground thoroughly, and also was confident that the attempt would succeed; on this Lord Cochrane agreed, as he would not have it thought that he would propose a hazardous attack which he would not undertake in person.

Admiralty now sent an official despatch to Lord Gambier, informing him that they had selected Captain Lord Cochrane to conduct (under Lord Gambier's directions) the attack by fireships and other vessels on the enemy in Aix roads. This despatch was carried by Cochrane himself, who delivered it in person on 3rd April 1809. The social effect was as he expected, although he could not know that Rear-Admiral the Hon. Robert Stopford, second-in-command of the fleet, had proposed just such an attack, had offered to command it himself, and had been turned down by Lord Gambier. Now a young captain had somehow got himself an Admiralty instruction to Gambier to give him the command that Stopford had been refused. However, orders were orders, and the work at once commenced of fitting out fireships, explosion vessels and light rocket-carriers.

Unknown to the British, the fleet assembled in the Aix roads had been intended for the relief of the West Indian island of Martinique, which was hard pressed by a strong fleet under Rear-Admiral Sir Alexander Cochrane, uncle of Captain Lord Cochrane, and an army of ten thousand men under Lieutenant-

General Beckwith. However, the news came through that the island had surrendered on the 24th February, and Vice-Admiral Allemand, having no further orders, took all proper steps to make his position in Aix roads secure. He knew the position well: it was very different from the secure harbour of Brest; an open roadstead, beset with reefs and encumbered with shoals; very open to an attack by fireships, or an attack *à la Aboukir*, had there been a Nelson in command in the blockading fleet. Against the latter possibility, he moored his ships in two parallel lines almost a mile in length, with a distance of rather more than two ships' lengths between each ship, and the two lines staggered, so that each ship was opposite the corresponding space in the other line. This ensured that any ship could engage without danger of firing on one of her consorts. The frigates formed a third line. This excellent disposition ensured that if an enemy fleet entered the roadstead in line ahead — and no other formation was possible — each ship as it advanced would come under the fire of two ships without the danger of their firing into each other. Against bomb vessels he had the heavy shore batteries, which could sink a bomb-ketch with a single hit, also his frigates and brigs. Against fireships, he laid down a great boom, composed of enormous cables more than 30 inches in diameter, secured by five-ton anchors and floated by numerous buoys. This boom was half a mile in length, and completely closed off the channel leading from the Basque roads to the Aix roads. He further ordered that all the boats of the fleet were to patrol the boom from dusk till dawn to drive away any British boats, and to be prepared to board fireships and steer them to shore at a safe distance from the fleet. The ships of the line were ordered to strike all their upper masts and sails, as they were to fight at anchor; but the frigates and smaller vessels were to be in a state of instant readiness to sail as requisite. For a fleet blockaded in an open roadstead by a superior fleet those orders could not be improved upon, and show that Vice-Admiral Allemand was a most able and resourceful officer.

Lord Cochrane's dispositions were made so completely and prudently that he refuted for ever the charge made by his ill-wishers that he was a mere berserker, rushing upon the foe without heed or preparation. His own ship, the IMPERIEUSE, was to anchor just out of gun-shot of the French fleet, with the explosion vessels beside her. Three frigates, AIGLE, UNICORN and PALLAS, were to anchor a little further out, with the fireships. The ETNA, his only bomb-ship, was stationed near the Île d'Aix, to bombard the batteries when they opened fire, and the INDEFATIGABLE, 44-gun frigate, and FOXHOUND, 18-gun sloop, were detailed to cover her. A schooner and two cutters, which had been fitted for discharging Congreve rockets, were stationed near the IMPERIEUSE, to move in with the fireships. A frigate and four smaller vessels were to appear to attempt to pass into the road by the east side of the Île d'Aix. Two small 10-gun sloops, REDPOLE and LYRA, were sent in to show lights, screened from the enemy, to guide in the fireships. The fireships were well prepared, as three French coasters laden with tar and resin had recently been captured, and leading them was the MEDIATOR, Captain James Woolridge, a 32-gun frigate which had been partly disarmed to act as an armed storeship; Captain Cochrane had specially asked for her, and Admiral Gambier agreed, with some reluctance. It has been alleged against Cochrane that he did not know about the great boom, thus showing a defect in his reconnaissance; but it is far more probable that he did know, and kept the knowledge to himself, in case Gambier, with his well-known caution, should call the whole action off. Otherwise, why did he ask for the MEDIATOR, when a much smaller and cheaper ship would have served just as well as a fireship? It was because only a frigate had weight enough to break the boom, and Captain Woolridge was a man after his own heart, to whom he could confide the secret.

The explosion vessels were most formidable. Their bottoms were strengthened with logs jammed together to form a solid floor; on this were placed a large number of casks, holding altogether 1,500 barrels of gunpowder, roped together and tamped down to increase the force of the explosion; on top were hundreds of mortar shells and thousands of hand grenades, with fuses, the idea being that the explosion would ignite the fuses as well as throwing the projectiles far and wide.

The operation began at 8.30 p.m. on the evening of 11th April 1809, with a strong wind from the north-west, and the tide with the fireships, the MEDIATOR leading. Lord Cochrane naturally took the leading explosion vessel, with Lieutenant Bissell and four volunteers. This is the most dangerous of all naval operations: to take a ship crammed with explosives into a fortified harbour against a powerful fleet fully prepared for the attack. A single hit on the terrible cargo, and not a fragment of the crew would be available for burial. Fireships were quite often used, particularly in the seventeenth century, but the explosion vessel was very rare indeed. (It has, however, been used twice in this century, when Lieutenant Sandford thrust his submarine under the mole at Zeebrugge, and in the second war when Captain Beattie rammed the CAMPBELLTOWN into the dock-gates of St Nazaire. Never were Victoria Crosses better earned.)

In this case the explosion vessels were not very successful. One of them appears to have been swept away prematurely, and although her crew were on board either they did not light the fuse or the fuse failed. The other two both lighted their fuses, Captain Cochrane about ten minutes later than the other, and took to their boats in very rough sea conditions. Unfortunately, both vessels were stopped by the boom, which had not yet been broken by the MEDIATOR, and the effect of their terrific explosions was largely moral. Some of the fireships were ignited far too soon, and ran ashore before reaching the boom; but when Captain Woolridge broke the boom there were six other fireships, which, taking their time from the MEDIATOR, did not start their fires until they were past the boom, and the wind and tide were bound to bring the fireships right amongst the French fleet.

Few battles go precisely to plan; the boom had delayed the explosion vessels and the fireships, but now, as the blazing ships bore down on the French fleet, the rough weather made it impossible for the boats of the fleet to carry out their assigned task of boarding the fireships and towing them ashore. Moreover, who could tell that there were not more explosion vessels behind the sheet of flame which the gale blew in front of the advancing fireships? It would be an exaggeration to say that there was panic on board the French ships, but there was certainly a well-founded alarm. Every ship except one, the *Foudroyant*, which was in the rearmost of the lines, either cut or

The Last Viking

slipped her cables in order to get some steerage-way to avoid the desperate peril. Of those, one, the *Cassard*, anchored again about a quarter of a mile ahead of the *Foudroyant*; every one of the rest went on shore, and that at the top of the tide. Cochrane regained the IMPERIEUSE on the falling tide, stood out a little into deeper water, and re-anchored where he could observe the whole of the Aix road. He was tolerably content; his scheme had worked; all that was now necessary was for a few of the ships of the line to sail in and finish the job on the next tide.

This did not happen.

As soon as it was light enough Cochrane began making signals by semaphore to the CALEDONIA, as follows:

4.48 a.m. Half the fleet can destroy the enemy; seven on shore.
6.40 a.m. Eleven on shore.
7.40 a.m. Only two afloat.
9.30 a.m. Enemy preparing to heave off.

This last signal stirred even Lord Gambier into some kind of action, and at 9.35 a.m. he signalled the fleet to weigh, but delayed the execution of the order by calling a conference of all captains on board the CALEDONIA. This took more than an hour, after which the fleet got under way, but at 11.30 a.m. re-anchored three miles north of the Île d'Aix, and six miles from the grounded French fleet. By this time the IMPERIEUSE had gone in to her former station abeam the south end of the island. Admiral Gambier now sent into the roads his only bomb-ketch, the ETNA, covered by three small gun-brigs, with orders to take position for bombarding the vessels aground. Captain Bligh of the VALIANT, 74, was ordered to take under his command the BELLONA and REVENGE, 74s, and also the frigates and smaller ships, and to anchor them where they could move in if necessary; this squadron anchored about half-way between the fleet and the IMPERIEUSE.

The French had not been idle during the low tide period. The two battleships still afloat had got up their topmasts, which had been taken down by general order. All those on shore had carried out, by boat, anchors which were laid well out, with the intention of kedging off at the top of the next tide. They put overboard most of their water, which they could replace, and many guns, which they might hope to retrieve. As the tide rose, the ships which had been badly heeled over began to rise unharmed, largely due to Vice-Admiral Allemand's foresight in having their upper masts struck down, for if they had heeled so far over with their top- and top-gallant-masts rigged they must either have cut them away or else filled before they could right themselves. At 12.45 p.m. the *Foudroyant* and *Cassard* made sail and steered for the Charente river, but grounded on the mud bar at the entrance. Three more of the stranded ships managed to kedge off, but also stuck on the mud-bar; and the great *Ocean* seemed to be moving.

Nothing could be more exasperating to a man like Cochrane than to witness the enemy escaping into safety, after all his exertions, simply because of the inertia of his admiral. By 1 p.m. all that had gone in were the bomb-ketch and three little brigs, and now Cochrane, without orders, weighed anchor; but to conceal the fact for a little he kept the ship's head still up, and drifted in with the tide stern first. The nearest French ships were the *Calcutta*, 50, a captured East India ship, and the *Aquilon* and *Varsovie*, 74s, all three on the rocky Palles shoal. Cochrane engaged the *Calcutta*, at the same time signalling for help. For very shame Gambier could not leave him unsupported, and at 2 p.m. ordered in the INDEFATIGABLE, and later the whole of the advanced squadron. All those ships concentrated on the three French ships which were hard and fast on the Palles, and made no serious attempt on those which were getting out of the mud and making for the safety of the river. The stranded vessels shortly surrendered; the *Calcutta* was set on fire by a midshipman sent to accept her surrender, and the other two were fired by Captain Bligh's orders, shortly after 3 a.m. on the morning of the 13th April; the *Tonnerre*, hopelessly on the rocks further south, was fired by her own men, before they took to their boats.

At 6.30 a.m. Captain Bligh led all the heavy ships out of the Aix roads, leaving Cochrane in command of the small craft. As the INDEFATIGABLE passed, Cochrane hailed Captain Rodd, to suggest that they should attack the *Ocean*, one on either quarter; Rodd prudently replied that he was under Captain Bligh's orders. Half an hour later came along the PALLAS,

Cochrane's old command, with Captain George Seymour, the same who, in the KINGFISHER, had towed out the PALLAS after the action with the *Minerve*, and who, fifty years later, as Admiral Sir George Seymour, was to be a pall-bearer at his comrade's funeral in Westminster Abbey. He now hailed Cochrane, 'Shall I go or stay?' 'Stay by all means, if you have no orders to the contrary.' The PALLAS and all the small ships immediately anchored near the IMPERIEUSE, to wait until the tide served. By 11 a.m. the smaller ships came within range of the *Ocean*, *Regulus* and *Indienne*, still on the mud at the mouth of the river, the BEAGLE, 18-gun brig-sloop, Captain Wool-combe, taking the brunt, as she was armed with 32-pounder carronades. The two frigates were unable to get within decisive range, and after battering away for five or six hours the flotilla was forced to retire on the falling tide, at 4 p.m.

About noon, while the action was in progress, Cochrane received a letter from Lord Gambier, politely and praisefully phrased, but directing him to rejoin the flag-ship. Cochrane replied that he could destroy the ships on shore, which he hoped his lordship would approve. At 9 a.m. the admiral signalled to Cochrane to communicate with Captain Wolfe of the AIGLE, who was ordered to supersede Cochrane in the command inside the roads. At noon the AIGLE joined the IMPERIEUSE, and Captain Wolfe handed over the definite order, on which the IMPERIEUSE joined the CALEDONIA in the Basque roads; and next day, the 15th April, sailed for home, with Captain Sir Harry Neale, Captain of the Fleet, and Lord Gambier's despatches. Meanwhile the fleet lay in Basque roads for another fortnight watching the French getting their ships up the river without much interference from the British.

Lord Gambier's despatches did full justice to Lord Cochrane's exploits, and he was created a Knight of the Bath for his services. He was, however, obsessed with the idea that he had, from mere spite and jealousy, been prevented from achieving, with a few frigates, a victory comparable to that of the Nile. There can be no doubt of Gambier's courage after his handling of the DEFENCE on the glorious first of June; but he was a deep-sea sailor, and distrusted the shoals and tides inshore. His flag-ship, the CALEDONIA, was Britain's newest and best battleship; what if he had lost her by an error in the timing of the tide? And no doubt there were plenty of jealous officers to suggest that it was as well to send this firebrand captain home, on honourable terms, before he managed again to get the deep-water fleet involved among the shoals. But Cochrane took his recall as a personal affront and launched against Gambier a political assault, in which he found more dangerous and treacherous waters than he ever met on the Biscay shore. We may leave him here, for he never commanded a frigate again; the last word lies with Napoleon. 'Cochrane could not only have destroyed all the ships,' he said on St Helena, 'but he might and would have taken them out, had your admiral supported him as he ought to have done …The French admiral was an *imbécile*, but yours was just as bad. I assure you, if Cochrane had been supported, he would have taken every one of the ships.'

Few historians have disagreed with the verdict of the greatest of all the great captains.

11

Prize Money

Spanish gold! There was little other gold in Europe from 1500 to 1850. Thereafter the discoveries in Australia, in California, later in Alaska, and lastly in South Africa have quite eclipsed Latin America as the source of gold, although three-quarters of the world's silver still comes from former Spanish possessions in America. A little gold was brought from the west coast of Africa, whence our guinea, but this was a drop in a bucket compared with the treasure which flowed across the Atlantic. It has been estimated that between 1500 and 1820 there were 17,000 voyages of treasure ships from America to Spain, carrying £4,000,000,000 sterling at sovereign value, five times as much in present paper. Naturally, everybody wanted to get in on an act like this, but the Spanish colonies were very firmly closed against all nations. Unabashed pirates such as Drake could get away with a lot, but the only legal method was to pick a quarrel with the Spanish government and declare war. By a curious coincidence, every time Britain has been reluctantly dragged into hostilities with Spain, there have been Spanish treasure ships at sea. Cromwell's war on Spain had no possible justification; his speech of 17th September 1656 to Parliament explaining it is the most confused and confusing of all his turgid orations, so different from his actions; but when, the next month, General-at-Sea Blake sent thirty-eight wagon-loads of gold and silver from Portsmouth to the Tower, the reason for the war was plain to all men, and they had a day of national thanksgiving. The War of Jenkin's Ear, begun in 1739, had no possible political justification, but one was provided by Commodore Anson when he took the Manila galleon, the *Nostra Signora de Cabadonga*, and brought the CENTURION into Portsmouth on 15th June 1744 to send thirty-two wagons of treasure to the Tower. When, near the end of the Seven Years War, Britain declared war on Spain in January 1762 for no clearly discernible reason, it so happened that the Spanish treasure-frigate *Hermione* was at sea, and was swiftly picked up by two British frigates, which divided between them an all-time record in prize money.

This popular pastime was regulated by an Act of 1708, which laid down the proportions into which the value of the prize was to be divided. There were certain Droits of the Crown, but these were kept in reserve; in general, the full value of the prize, ship and cargo, went to the captors, as follows: the captain had three-eighths, of which he gave one to the flag officer under whom he served; the other officers, down to sergeant of Marines, had three-eighths, in three categories which ensured that the more senior had the bigger share; and the remaining two-eighths went to the rest of the crew, again shared according to seniority. Nor was this all: in the case of warships captured or destroyed, Admiralty paid head-money at the rate of £5 per head of the enemy crew at the commencement of the engagement. This was to encourage doubtful captains to engage warships rather than seek the easier and more lucrative merchant prizes; moreover, a successful engagement with a warship meant probable promotion, which never rewarded captors of merchantmen.

It is, fortunately, no part of our business to clarify the political reasons why Spain, ally of Britain in 1795, should become the ally of France and declare war on Britain on 2nd October 1796; but the timing was certainly injudicious, for Spanish treasure ships were at sea, and the frigates were at sea too, and within a fortnight made their pounce.

On the 15th of October, about 150 miles west of Vigo, the 38-gun frigate NAIAD, Captain William Pierrepont, at 8 p.m. discovered in the dusk two large sails and went in chase; by midnight they were ascertained to be Spanish, and frigates of some force, now steering to the south-east under all sail, the wind being dead aft. They were in fact the 34-gun frigates *Santa Brigida*, Captain Pillon, and *Thetis*, Captain de Mendoza, from Vera Cruz with treasure, and ordered for any port in Spain which they could make. A British 38-gun frigate had no reason to avoid combat with two Spanish 34s, especially if they were suspected of bearing treasure, and the NAIAD continued in pursuit under all possible sail. At 3.30 in the morning of the 16th another large sail was descried to the south-west, which came up and made herself known to be the ETHALION, 38 guns, Captain James Young. At dawn two more frigates appeared and joined in the chase, both 32-gun 12-pounders, the ALCMENE, Captain Henry Digby, and the TRITON, Captain John Gore. Of the four, Captain Pierrepont was the S.N.O.

The chase continued through the morning, the *Thetis* leading the *Santa Brigida*, and the ETHALION, the best sailer, leading the British line. At 7 a.m. the two Spanish ships separated, on which Captain Pierrepont ordered the ETHALION to pass the rear Spaniard and chase the *Thetis*, which was done, although Captain Young could not forbear giving the *Santa Brigida* a broadside in passing, at 9 a.m. By 11.30 a.m. the ETHALION came up with the *Thetis*; after a desultory running fight they came alongside, and after two full broadsides the *Thetis* hauled down her colours, having had one man killed and nine wounded, while the ETHALION had no casualties whatever.

The *Santa Brigida* was a very good sailer, and her captain evidently had a good knowledge of the dangerous coast he was now approaching. Making south, he rounded Cape Finisterre very close to the rocks, so close that the TRITON, first in pursuit, touched the rocks at seven knots, at 5 a.m. on the 17th. She got off, and by 7 a.m. was able to open fire on the *Santa Brigida*, which now threw overboard her anchors and boats, to aid her sailing; but the ALCMENE came up between her and the port of Muros, for which she was making. The *Santa Brigida* now tried to throw off her pursuers by elaborate manœuvres among the rocks of Commarurto in the entrance of Ria de Muros, but the NAIAD now came up and, surrounded by three powerful opponents, the *Santa Brigida* had no option but to surrender. Captain Don Antonio Pillon had shown the utmost courage and tenacity during a chase of thirty-two hours, and superb seamanship in attempts to gain port. His loss was 2 killed and 8 wounded, the British ships 1 killed and 10 wounded.

The result of the odds of at least four to two could readily be predicted; what made it interesting was the loot. Besides a cargo of valuable commodities such as cochineal and indigo, the two ships had between them about a thousand boxes each containing 3,000 silver dollars, besides odd bags and kegs and some gold. There can have been few literate persons in the squadron who were not doing pleasing little sums during the short voyage to Plymouth, where they arrived on the 21st November. The treasure was conveyed in sixty-three wagons to the citadel of Plymouth, and thence to London. The prize-money was divided thus:

Each Captain	£40,730
Each Lieutenant	5,091
Warrant-Officers	2,468
Midshipmen, etc.	791
Each Seaman and Marine	182

One has to consider that the rate of pay per annum did not exceed £150 for a frigate captain, £75 for a lieutenant, and £12 for an ordinary seaman. A captain would have to serve for 250 years to earn the money he picked up in a couple of easy days; and even the humblest seaman could set himself up in a cosy pub. It was very wise of Admiralty to allot these astounding prizes; it was like the football pools and the lotteries: I know that the chance is remote, but all the same, people have in fact won such prizes, and why should the next one not be me? Honour and glory are excellent things, but so are silver and gold; and if all are to be had in the same engagement, let us go heartily about it!

The next really big prize had some dubious aspects. Spain was at peace with Britain, but had entered into a special relationship with France, which included among other advantages an annual subsidy of about three million sterling, more than a third of the whole Spanish revenues. The British government received information that an armament was being prepared at Ferrol, and that French troops had crossed the border and were marching to Ferrol; an attack on Britain was projected, and waited only for the arrival of the next treasure fleet. The British government now resolved to cut off the subsidy at its source, and detain the treasure on the seas. This was really an act of war without war being declared, which in those gentlemanly days was considered highly immoral. However, the decision was taken, and orders were sent to Cornwallis, off Brest, Sir Alexander Cochrane, off Ferrol, and Nelson, off Toulon, each to detach two good frigates to cruise off Cadiz and intercept the treasure fleet, and detain them until the pleasure of the British government should be known; but to refrain from any act of hostility unless the enemy, or friend, began a combat.

Four of the detailed frigates assembled off Cape Santa Maria, the southernmost point of Portugal, and commenced their patrol, the ships being INDEFATIGABLE, 44, Captain Graham Moore, MEDUSA, 32, 18-pounders, Captain Gore, AMPHION, 32, 18-pounders, Captain Sutton, and LIVELY, 38, Captain Hammond. On 5th October 1804, being about 30 miles south-west of the cape and 100 miles west of Cadiz, they sighted the expected squadron, which consisted of the 40-gun frigate *Medea*, with Rear-Admiral Don Joseph Bustamente, and the 34-gun frigates *Fama*, *Clara*, and *Mercedes*. On the approach of the British squadron, the Spaniards formed for battle in line ahead, *Fama*, *Medea*, *Mercedes*, *Clara*, on which the British adopted the same formation, MEDUSA, INDEFATIGABLE, AMPHION and LIVELY, thus giving the biggest ship to the INDEFATIGABLE, a very powerful frigate, as we have seen. The two squadrons continued for some time side by side, about thirty yards apart, when Captain Moore hailed the *Medea* to shorten sail; no reply was given, so a shot was fired across her bows, and she complied. Lieutenant Arscott was now sent on board her, to inform the rear-admiral what were the orders of the British squadron, and to urge him to comply without making necessary the use of force. The boat did not return for some time, and Captain Moore made a signal for her to return, and fired another shot ahead of the *Medea*. Lieutenant Arscott now returned with a negative reply, on which Moore fired another gun ahead of the *Medea*, and bore down on her weather bow. At once the *Mercedes* fired into the AMPHION, and the *Medea* fired into the INDEFATIGABLE;

whereon that ship made the order for battle and a hot engagement commenced.

Within ten minutes the *Mercedes* blew up alongside the AMPHION, with a tremendous explosion which blew her to fragments with all in her, except about forty men who were rescued from the forecastle which broke off and floated for a time. A few minutes after, the *Fama* struck her colours, but when the MEDUSA ceased fire she rehoisted them and made off, with the MEDUSA in hot pursuit. About twenty minutes after the commencement, the *Medea*, which had been suffering from the 24-pounder broadsides of the INDEFATIGABLE, found the AMPHION coming up on her other bow, and struck her colours. Five minutes later the *Clara* also struck, thus releasing the LIVELY, a very fast ship, to go in pursuit of the *Fama*, which she overtook at the same time as the MEDUSA; now the *Fama* hauled down her colours and was taken in possession. The whole action was over by 1.15 p.m.

The British casualties were very small: 2 killed and 4 wounded in the LIVELY, 3 wounded in the AMPHION by fragments from the explosion of the *Mercedes*, none in the other ships. In the Spanish ships there were more: *Medea*, 2 killed and 10 wounded; *Fama*, 11 killed and 50 wounded; *Clara*, 7 killed and 20 wounded; and *Mercedes*, 240 killed. It is clear that the Spaniards fought with the greatest courage against a much more powerful squadron, especially after the loss of the *Mercedes*, and made every endeavour to carry out their orders and get into Cadiz. The *Fama* was criticised for making off after striking, but we are not fully aware of all the circumstances, and her casualty list shows that whatever the reason it was not cowardice.

There was one particularly unfortunate episode of this battle. A Captain Alvear of the Spanish Navy had spent thirty years in Montevideo, during which time he had acquired a modest fortune of £30,000, a wife, four daughters and five sons; and having decided to return to Spain, he embarked with his all on the *Mercedes*, for quick and safe transport. When the British squadron approached he and his eldest son transferred to the *Medea*, possibly at the request of the rear-admiral, as they were both fluent in English. From this ship he witnessed the explosion which at once annihilated his nine family and the fortune on which he had hoped to support them. Nothing could possibly make up for the loss of his family, except the coincidence whereby one son remained to him; but it is pleasing to record that, in an age when it was possible for politicians to be gentlemen, the British government restored to him the whole of his pecuniary loss.

The prize was very rich; having sailed from Montevideo, it carried the produce of the southern part of South America. There were sealskins, seal oil, vicuna wool, bars of tin and copper, and dollars and gold ingots to the amount of two millions sterling.* However, in stepped the Droits of the Crown afore-mentioned. Undoubtedly there had been an action fought and plenty of blood shed, under the orders of the government, which surely constituted warfare; but war had not been declared, and government chose to regard it as a police action in time of peace; hence the Droits of the Crown swallowed most of the loot. However, the squadron was given a quarter of a million as a sop, and as the captains would have about £15,000 apiece, they would be able to soak their sop in Madeira. Had the action taken place the following January, after the formal declaration of war between the two powers, this would have been the richest prize ever.

There are a number of other instances of prize-money scattered throughout this book. In general, the system went on the time-honoured principle of giving to him that hath. Almost every admiral commanding a station became a rich man, with the exception, perhaps, of Nelson, who received great emoluments but had rather an expensive way of life; when he died, he was paying £500 a year in interest on borrowed money. But at least half a dozen of his coevals made between two and three hundred thousand pounds, worth a million in today's paper, and it was reckoned that a tour of duty as C-in-C of either the East or the West Indies was worth £100,000. These sums, too, represented only an eighth of what was collected by the other officers and men

With so much money around loose, there were bound to be

* A number of historiographers, following James, have put the amount at one million; I prefer Alison, who was a Member of Parliament, read Captain Moore's despatches, and took part in the debates on the matter.

pickings. It was usual for officers to appoint agents to look after their prize interests, and many of those agents became very rich men. Within the prize system itself there was plenty of peculation, against which Lord Cochrane raged in vain. One safeguard was that as permanent paid officers of every prize court were two, one called proctor and one called marshal, who were supposed to be some sort of check on each other. When in June 1810 Lord Cochrane paid a visit to the prize court at Malta, to inquire about the money for the prizes he had taken years ago, he found that in that court the marshal and the proctor were one and the same person, named Jackson. One half of him held consultations with the other half, at a fee, and one half attested the other's signature, also at a fee. Cochrane expressed himself so freely about the corruption inside and outside the court that the two halves of Jackson agreed to have him arrested for insulting the court, and ordered the deputy marshal, named Chapman, to take him in custody. Cochrane refused arrest, on the grounds that Chapman was illegally appointed, being already deputy auctioneer! The appointed auctioneer lived in London and had no other activity than collecting his fees. Afraid to act, Chapman followed Cochrane about Malta for several days, but at length resigned his deputy marshal office, another was appointed more legally, and Cochrane was put in prison. Here he refused to supply himself with provisions, and the dual Jackson, who began to wish he had not been so high-handed, gave him an open order on the best hotel; Cochrane made full use of this, and entertained the Naval officers on the station to long, sumptuous and well-lubricated dinners in the prison. On 2nd March he was taken to court, which could not determine what to try him for and begged him to go on bail, which he refused. Eventually a comic-opera escape from the prison was arranged, and the gig of the EAGLE put him on board a packet-ship bound for England, where he arrived before the officials of double-duty Jackson had finished searching Malta for him. He made several motions in the House of Commons on those corruptions, all which motions were negatived without a division.

The fact is that at that period peculation and corruption were accepted as something regrettable, but just to be accepted, in the same way as we regard the fearful slaughter on the highways today. In both cases, it is felt that one can't do a thing about it, the reason being the same in both cases: the strength of the vested interests involved. Government grossly under-paid all its employees, and expected them to make it up to themselves, by fees legal or illegal, and in the case of the Navy, by prize-money. It was an intrinsic part of the Naval structure, very popular with the officers and men, and cost the government nothing. It was impossible to dispense with it, and if there were always dirty fingers in the dish, that was just one of those things which one finds everywhere.

12

Squadron Action

It is difficult to understand general European strategy at the beginning of the nineteenth century without fully realising what an important European power was the Ottoman Empire. It included almost the whole of modern Yugoslavia, half of Rumania, and the whole of Bulgaria and Greece. Belgrade and Bucharest were Moslem cities. Turkey in Europe was more extensive and populous than any western European state, and beyond lay a vast ramshackle empire including all Asia Minor, Arabia, Egypt, and indeterminate border regions. Not long before, historically speaking, under strong leadership the Turks had been thundering at the gates of Vienna, and had been turned back from the complete domination of the Mediterranean at Lepanto. True, generations of weak rule had weakened the Ottoman Empire; but if a resolute organiser were to make his way to its throne, it would once again be one of the great powers.

By the provisions of the Peace of Tilsit, Napoleon took the province of Illyria, which stretches from Trieste for more than three hundred miles down the coast of the Adriatic Sea. Instead of handing it over to some satellite ruler, Napoleon incorporated the province as an integral part of metropolitan France, under his direct rule. He now had a French province which had two hundred miles of frontier with the Ottoman Empire. With his mind always a tiger-spring ahead, he could visualise building up a great army in Illyria; given security in the rest of Europe, in one campaign Constantinople would be his. Meanwhile, he had to keep the Adriatic open for his supply ships, and for this purpose a large number of frigates were stationed there, mostly based on Ancona, while the shipyards of Venice were urged into production, especially of 74-gun ships.

The British frigates were based chiefly on Malta and Sicily, but managed a forward base in the Adriatic by capturing the island of Lissa (now Vis). This is a small island, about ten miles by five miles, with an excellent harbour in Port St George, and several other good anchorages. Batteries were erected and provided with plenty of guns and stores, but the garrison was never sufficient for a point of such importance, which has always been held to be the key to the Adriatic. With this base for refuge in need, the small British vessels had a wonderful time in the Adriatic, capturing cargo ships at sea or cutting them out in harbour. It was not possible to blockade all the fine harbours, but they captured a large percentage of all the shipping that stirred.

The French could not leave such a thorn alone, and made repeated attempts to recapture the island. In October 1810, in the absence of any British warship, a squadron under Commodore Dubourdieu actually landed a considerable body of troops, and had possession of the island for several hours, but withdrew on hearing news of the approach of a British squadron. The following spring a more determined attack was ordered; Commodore Dubourdieu now had four 40-gun frigates, the *Favorite* (flag), *Corona*, *Danae* and *Flore*, two 32-gun frigates, the *Bellona* and *Carolina*, a 16-gun brig *Mercure*, a 10-gun schooner, the 6-gun xebec, and two gun-boats; also a battalion of infantry under Colonel Gifflenga, to form the garrison of the island after capture; a force of about 300 guns and 2,500 men, all told. This powerful squadron sailed from Ancona towards evening on 11th March 1811, and hove-to off the north shore of Lissa shortly after midnight the following day. There they were reported at 3 a.m. on the 13th March to the defending British squadron. This consisted of the 32-gun frigate (18-pounders) AMPHION, Captain William Hoste (S.N.O.), 38-gun frigate ACTIVE, Captain James Gordon, 32-gun frigate CERBERUS, Captain Henry Whitby, and the 22-gun ship VOLAGE, Captain Phipps Hornby; a total force of about 150 guns and 900 men, rather worse odds than one to two.

Admiralty could not spare many 74s for the Adriatic operations, and few large frigates; to make up for this, they sent some of their very best officers with good crews, to make up for too few and too light ships. Captain William Hoste, in command of the squadron, had the inestimable advantage of having been reared on the quarter-deck under Nelson himself, who took an interest in the promising youth and helped forward his promotion. Since coming to the Adriatic, both he and the other frigate captains (who were not always under his command, being detached from time to time) had been very active in their inshore duties, capturing many prizes, and also engaged in the less remunerative work of correcting charts, a tedious but, in this case at least, a rewarding occupation.

At dawn the French squadron could be plainly descried, about two miles to windward, the wind fair at NNW. Their strength could also be clearly understood; but under Nelson's midshipman there could be no question of 'fight or flee?' He formed his squadron in close line ahead, himself leading in the AMPHION, followed by the ACTIVE as the most powerful ship, the VOLAGE as the weakest, while the CERBERUS brought up the rear. Meanwhile the French formed in two divisions, each line consisting of three frigates and some smaller ships, so that each division was more powerful than the whole British squadron. Having the weather-gauge, they bore down on the compact squadron, in the hope, no doubt, of breaking the line. Hoste now made a signal 'remember Nelson!' and the loud cheers with which this was greeted in all the ships told the captain that all his men were with him.

Commodore Dubordieu in the *Favorite* was leading the windward division, and decided that the close and steady formation of the British line would be hard to break; he therefore stood ahead, meaning to cross the bows of the AMPHION with his division, and thus get the British squadron within the cross-fire of both of his divisions. The heavy fire of the two leading ships made this a difficult manœuvre, and he decided to board the AMPHION, when his great superiority of numbers must tell. Accordingly he assembled a large boarding-party on the forecastle, and approached the quarter-deck of the AMPHION; but that ship had on her quarter-deck a 5½-inch howitzer, loaded

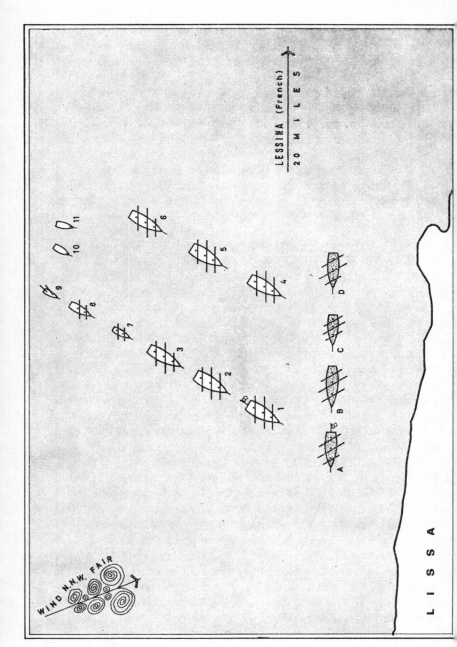

with 750 musket-balls, which was discharged with accuracy at a range of about ten yards. The destruction was fearful; there fell the commodore, the captain, and most of the senior officers, so that the command devolved upon Colonel Gifflenga, with a junior sea officer to work the ship. The *Favorite* gave up the attempt to board, and kept on working forward of the AMPHION, which was just what Hoste wanted, for he had corrected his charts. At the right moment — the last possible moment — he signalled for all his ships to wear about simultaneously, and when the *Favorite*, ahead, also wore, she ran upon the rocks in a hopeless condition, so near had Hoste led her to the shore. About 200 of her men escaped to shore, armed, having set fire to the ship, which blew up with a great explosion about 4 p.m.

While wearing, the CERBERUS had her rudder damaged by a shot, and could not get round so handily as the VOLAGE, which now became the leading ship and the AMPHION the rear. The *Flore*, the second ship in the weather division, now was able to carry out the manœuvre which the Commodore had tried so disastrously; she crossed the stern of the AMPHION and came up on her leeward side, while the *Bellona* approached on the other, so that the AMPHION was caught between the fires of two ships, one of them equal to and the other larger than herself. In such a position, any captain would have been justified in surrendering; but Captain Hoste was not any captain: he had walked Nelson's quarter-deck. He could trust his seamen to work the ship through any manœuvre, however complicated, amid the storm of round-shot and musket-balls that came from almost every direction. With superb seamanship, the AMPHION made more sail, moved ahead, suddenly turned right across the bows

Battle of Lissa: The Approach

British ships in line ahead: AMPHION (flag) 32 guns, A; ACTIVE, 38 guns, B; VOLAGE, sloop, 22 guns, C; CERBERUS, 32 guns, D

French ships in two divisions: Windward division, *Favorite* (flag) 40 guns, 1; *Flore*, 40 guns, 2; *Bellona*, 32 guns, 3; *Mercure*, brig, 16 guns, 7; 6-gun xebec, 8; 10-gun schooner, 9
   Leeward division, *Danae*, 40 guns, 4; *Corona*, 40 guns, 5; *Carolina*, 32 guns, 6; 2 gunboats, 10 and 11

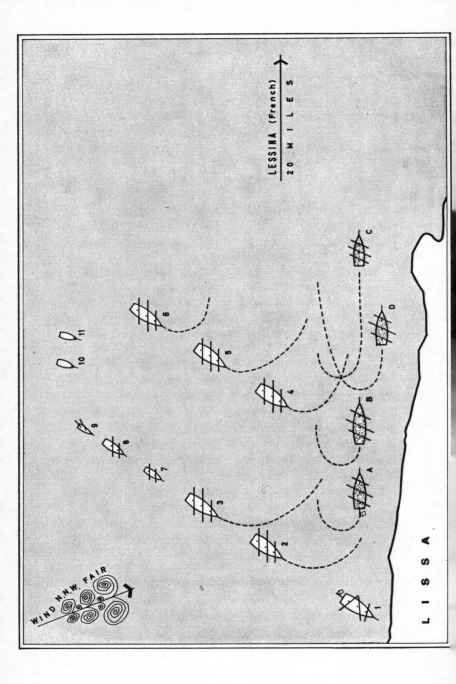

WIND N.N.W. FAIR

LESSINA (French)

20 MILES

LISSA

of the *Flore*, wore again, into a position where her whole larboard broadside could bear on the starboard bow of the *Flore*, while that ship completely screened her from the fire of the *Bellona*. From this favourable position the AMPHION opened such a fire that in a few minutes the *Flore* struck her colours. Meanwhile the *Bellona* had passed the stern of the *Flore*, and now re-engaged the AMPHION; but again by superior seamanship the AMPHION was enabled to get a position on the *Bellona*'s bow from which she could rake the ship with very little reply, and after a few broadsides the *Bellona* too struck her colours.

The AMPHION now made a signal for a general chase, and sent a party to take possession of her prizes; the *Bellona* was duly taken over; but seeing the shortage of boats in the AMPHION, the *Flore* now made sail and escaped, much to the chagrin of all on board the victor, which was too much cut about in the rigging to give chase.

While all this was going on, the head of the line was being attacked by the three frigates of the lee division. The 40-gun *Danae* came close alongside the little VOLAGE, which, however, was armed with 32-pounder carronades, at that range quite as effective as the long 18s of the frigate, which made haste to lengthen the range. Meanwhile the CERBERUS was closely engaged by the *Corona* and, at a much greater distance, the *Carolina*. Both the VOLAGE and the CERBERUS were in serious trouble, when up came the ACTIVE, which the French frigates had tended to avoid; on her approach the three French frigates made off to the eastward under all sail, chased by the ACTIVE, which came up with the *Corona*, the largest of the three, about 12.30 p.m., and fought her for two hours, when she too surrendered. The *Carolina* and *Danae* escaped to the protection of

Battle of Lissa: The critical Manoeuvre

Hoste orders his ships to wear right about simultaneously. The *Favorite*, which has been trying to head him, runs ashore and is wrecked. The *Flore* and the *Bellona* wear to attack the AMPHION. The *Danae* and the *Corona* wear to attack the new leading ships, while the *Carolina* shows no great eagerness to engage. The CERBERUS, having a shot in her rudder, does not get about very handily, and drops astern of the little VOLAGE, which becomes the leading ship of the squadron.

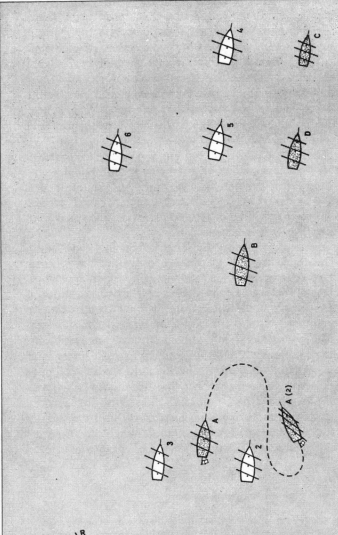

WIND N.N.W. FAIR

the batteries of Lesina, where they were joined by the *Flore*, which had surrendered and then escaped (not at all the done thing). The small craft scattered and all got into some port or other.

The British ships were all more or less knocked about in rigging and hull, but nothing that fishing, splicing and patching could not make good temporarily. The losses were heavy, a total of 45 killed and 145 wounded among the four ships; yet less than might have been expected in so desperate an attack. The French losses are not precisely ascertained, but have been estimated at about 700, with some probability, apart from prisoners. The 200 men who got ashore from the *Favorite* marched boldly to Port St George, where they hoped to seize shipping enough to carry them to Lesina, only twenty miles away; but they were prevented by two young midshipmen, James Lew and Robert Kingston, who had been left there in charge of some prizes, and who now assumed command of all the ships in the port, under threat of what Captain Hoste would do when he returned. What he did do was to send a flag of truce to Lesina to demand that the *Flore* be given up, as she had surrendered. The reply was as might be expected, and indeed no French captain's life would be worth a rap if he gave up a valuable ship on a point of honour; Napoleon had much more use for the ship.

Of the two prizes which were brought away, the *Corona*, which had been built the year before at Venice, was taken into the Royal Navy under the name of DAEDALUS, while the *Bellona* was bought in for a troopship (for which there was great demand) under the name of DOVER. This was a neat bit of prize-money, and in addition the four captains had a gold medal apiece, and all four first lieutenants were made commanders.

Battle of Lissa: The Crisis of the Battle

AMPHION is engaged by both *Flore* and *Bellona*, one on each side; but by a masterly move Hoste disengages himself and takes a position on the starboard bow of the *Flore*, which now covers him from the *Bellona*; the *Flore* shortly surrenders. The CERBERUS and the VOLAGE are heavily engaged at great odds with the *Corona* and the *Danae*, with the *Caroline* in the offing. The ACTIVE is pushing up under all sail to assist.

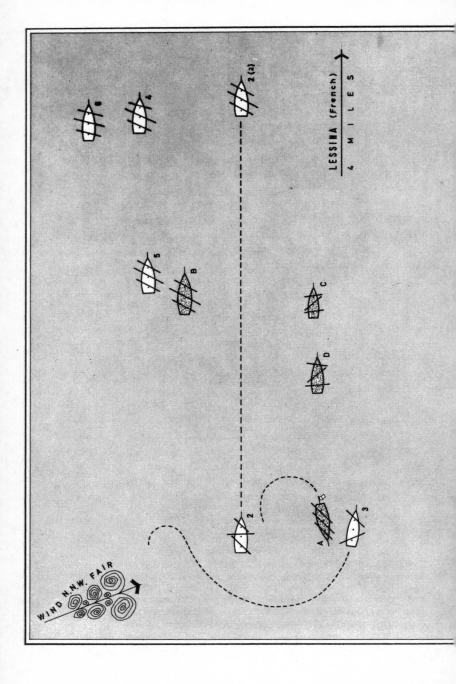

At a later date Captain Hoste was knighted. Indeed, they were worthy of every honour the country could bestow. Seldom in naval history has a squadron attacked another of more than twice its force, and so completely defeated it. It was only done by courage, skill and seamanship, and was a proof, if any were needed, of how well Hoste and his brother captains had trained their men and gained their complete confidence.

Note: In this chapter all the enemy ships are referred to as French; in fact the *Bellona*, *Carolina* and *Corona*, and some small ships, were Venetian, and fought under that flag, in a manner which would have done it credit in the greatest days of the Republic. In particular, Captain Pasqualigo of the *Corona* elicited the warm admiration of his opponents; he 'ennobled an already noble name'.

'I came home in the squadron with the prizes in 1811, and recollect to have heard Sir William Hoste, and the other officers engaged in that glorious conflict, speak in the highest terms of Pasqualigo's behaviour.' — *Lord Byron, in a note in an appendix to* 'The Doge of Venice'.

Battle of Lissa: The End of the Battle

Flore (2) has surrendered, but improperly sets sail again and makes off (2 (2)). *Bellona* has come around the stern of the *Flore*, but by another feat of seamanship Hoste engages her in an advantageous position and she surrenders. The ACTIVE is heavily engaged with the *Corona*, which will shortly surrender after a very honourable resistance. The other frigates are making off for Lessina; the small ships have scattered to make what port they can. The VOLAGE and the CERBERUS are licking their wounds.

13

The Big Frigates

Lord Palmerston once said, 'Only three people have ever really understood the Schleswig-Holstein business: the Prince Consort, who is dead; a German Professor, who has gone mad; and I, who have forgotten all about it.' Much the same might be said about the reasons why the United States of America declared war upon Great Britain on 18th June 1812. There had been grumblings for at least four years, but nothing which could not have been settled by negotiation; in fact, *was*, and twice, settled by negotiation; but on one occasion the British and on the other the American government refused to ratify what their envoys had agreed. The ostensible reason was the British blockade of Europe, proclaimed by Orders in Council; but these had been rescinded *before* hostilities actually commenced. Historians and commentators have advanced their simplifications of the complex motivations of an emerging nation, with which fortunately we have nothing to do —

> '*But one thing I'm sure*
> *That at Sheriffmuir*
> *A battle there was that I saw, man!*'

Apart from the *why*, the *when* of the American declaration of war is hard to understand. True, the news they had from Europe was of Napoleon's conference at Dresden, with almost all the sovereigns in western Europe tributary to his imperial power, while he reviewed an army of five hundred thousand men, superbly equipped. This may have seemed a good wagon to jump on, and they could not have known that within three days of the declaration of war, Wellington was to cross the Aguedo on the way to Salamanca, Vittoria and Toulouse; and within nine days Napoleon was to cross the Niemen, on the way to Moscow, Leipzig and Elba. But what they certainly did know was that the whole Navy of the United States consisted of 8 frigates and 12 sloops, of which 20, only 17 were available for sea service; and they also knew that Britain had 584 ships at sea in full commission, of which 102 were line-of-battle ships and 124 were frigates, with an immediate reserve of 18 battleships and 15 frigates. Moreover, the area of responsibility had diminished, since there were now no French or allied bases in all the seas of the world. The fleet with which Rear-Admiral Stopford had recently taken Java, with four line-of-battle ships and fourteen frigates, was at least three times stronger than the whole American Navy; nothing was easier than to call them home, and desire them to eat up the American Navy as they came by; but of course this did not happen.

The Royal Navy was suffering from a severe attack of superiority complex, resulting, not unnaturally, from almost twenty-two years of almost complete victories. The Navy of the United States consisted of only a few frigates: good enough, we have plenty of frigates on the West Indies and Halifax stations, let them deal with the situation. This was exactly the spirit with which, in 1914, Admiralty, with Winston Churchill as First Lord of the Admiralty and Jacky Fisher as First Sea Lord, sent out Rear-Admiral Craddock to Coronel with a mixed rag-bag of ships, manned mostly by reservists, to meet the crack cruiser squadron of the German Navy. It was the qualitative factor which they overlooked, and it was very difficult to tell them anything. In 1910–14, any Briton who dared to hint that the ships of the German Navy were better constructed, and their gunnery practice of a better standard, than the Royal Navy, was instantly branded as a traitor. In the same way, when Doctor Gregory, a well-known citizen of Edinburgh, said in 1808, 'The Americans are building long 46-gun frigates, which really carry 56 or 60 guns; when our 44s come to meet them, you will hear something new some of these days', of course nobody paid the least attention; what could a physician know about naval matters?

In fact the big American frigates were superior to any other frigate afloat, in two essentials; the ships themselves, and their crews.

The United States had in the great forests an endless supply of the finest ship-building timbers in the world. Northern white oak is only very slightly inferior to the Adriatic oak, while the pine and spruce for masts and spars was at least equal to the best the Baltic could produce. There was plenty of it, no need to scrimp, and only the selected best went into an American warship. To further ensure this, every American ship had an experienced captain standing by her during the whole course of her construction, a thing previously unknown, although now of course standard practice in all navies. Thus all American warships of whatever size were built of the very best materials, by skilled shipwrights, under strict and expert supervision. Class for class, they had no superior.

But the Americans were not content with class for class; they had to have something altogether superior to anything of the same nominal classification.

In 1794 it was decided to construct two 74-gun line-of-battle ships, and these were laid down; but due to changes in the political situation it was decided to finish them as frigates, but retaining, except for the extra gun-deck, the construction and sail-power of the 74. These were launched in 1797, as the *United States* and the *Constitution*, and rated as 44-gun frigates; in 1798 two more 44-gun frigates were built as frigates from the beginning, and therefore of slightly lighter construction and better sailing capacity, but still far bigger and more powerful than any other frigate in the world: the *President*, built at New York, and the *Philadelphia*, built at that city. All four 44-gun frigates actually mounted a main battery of thirty long 24-pounders, eighteen carronades, 42-pounders, on the quarter-deck, and on the forecastle six similar carronades and two long 24-pounders, a total of 56 guns, with a broadside of 768 pounds. By American measure they were all about 1,444 tons, but by British measure they were 1,533 tons. With their great length* and sail-power, they were the fastest warships in the world.

* It is generally understood that the speed of a sailing vessel is limited by its water-line length, maximum speed under similar conditions varying as the square

Not only were the big frigates larger and more powerful than anything they need meet, they were far better manned. While Britain was raking the gaols to make up the 'quota', the Americans were rejecting all but skilled seamen of first-class physique. The reason, of course, was the small number of ships compared to the seamen available. The north-east states of the Union produced a race of bold and hardy seamen, manning a very large merchant marine, many of whom were unemployed as the British blockade tightened. The western states produced the most highly skilled riflemen in the world, and these constituted the Marines. Lastly, the ranks were supplemented by a large number of trained seamen, deserters from the Royal Navy. There were something like 5,000 deserters every year, of which about half were Able Seamen. During the Peace of Amiens, about 70,000 men were dismissed, or liable to be dismissed, from the Royal Navy, and many took service with the United States Navy, which was at that time engaged in naval operations against the Barbary States. It is highly probable that every large American frigate had a hundred British seamen aboard. When war was declared, some of these asked to be released from their service, but many did not. In action, these could be relied upon to the death, for it was death for them anyhow if they were captured.

One of the four big frigates was lost in the Mediterranean in 1804. The *Philadelphia*, Captain Bainbridge, had chased a ship which escaped into the harbour of Tripoli; but, in beating out, the *Philadelphia* ran on a rock, not marked on her charts. All efforts were made to float her off, anchors cut away, guns thrown overboard, without effect; and on the approach of some Tripolitan gun-boats the *Philadelphia* surrendered without resistance. In about two days the captors managed to float her, and took her into Tripoli harbour. Lieutenant Stephen Decatur, now first heard of, proposed to Commodore Preble to go into the harbour and burn her, which the Commodore at first thought too risky, but at length approved. On the 18th February

---

root of the L.W.L. Thus if a ship of 100 feet long does 10 knots, one of 144 feet should do 12 knots. There are of course some thousands of other considerations in the design of sailing ships.

Lieutenant Decatur, with seventy volunteers in a captured ketch, entered the harbour, boarded the *Philadelphia*, and after a sharp engagement captured her. She was immediately set on fire, and the boarding party made good their escape, having only four wounded.

There are some odd aspects of this story; if the *Philadelphia* could be captured by 70 small-arms men, how could she not have been defended by 300? And, having captured her, why was no attempt made to bring her out? A good deal may be put down to inexperience, but it would superficially appear that more might have been done to preserve what, after all, was more than an eighth of the whole American Navy of that date.

In those days of slow communication, it was very difficult for ships at sea to be informed of a declaration of war; the side which was going to declare war could give advance information to commanding officers, but the ships on the receiving end had to depend on unofficial rumours and otherwise wait until actually attacked. Thus when war was declared on the 18th of June 1812, a strong squadron was able to sail from New York on the 21st, the object being the Jamaica convoy, which had not the least idea of hostilities, and was making a leisurely course for Britain; a hundred richly laden merchantmen under the protection of a frigate and a brig; easy meat for the American squadron, which consisted of two of the big frigates, a 36-gun frigate and two brigs. However, when they were still some hundreds of miles west of the convoy, they came upon a solitary British frigate, and the whole squadron altered course to pursue her, the leading ship being the big frigate *President*, Commodore Rodgers.

The British frigate was the BELVIDERA, 36 guns, 18-pounders, Captain Richard Byron. He must have had some grave suspicions, for when the whole squadron approached him, quite unnecessarily if only for greeting and information, he stood away to the NE by E, about as close as he could haul to the wind which was at NW. Finding the squadron gaining on him, Captain Byron cleared for action, and shifted two long 18-pounders so as to fire through the sternports in his cabin, as well as bringing two 32-pounder carronades to the stern of the quarter-deck. All guns were loaded, but not primed, so that there should be no accidental shot on his part. The wind veered to WSW and decreased, so that by 4.20 the *President* was able to open fire with her bow-guns, three hits causing damage and casualties. The BELVIDERA returned fire with her well-prepared stern-chasers, the Captain and the First Lieutenant Sykes personally pointing the quarter-deck carronades, while Lieutenants Bruce and Campbell did the same for the 18-pounders in the cabin. Within a few minutes one of the *President's* forward 24-pounders burst, a most serious accident, killing and wounding sixteen men, including the commodore, who had gone forward. The damage to the decks and side was severe, and put her chase-guns out of action for a considerable time.

Thus deprived of her forecastle armament, the *President* began yawing from side to side to allow her main battery guns to bear; and as this would allow the BELVIDERA to make away, the fire was directed mainly at the rigging, which was considerably damaged; however, as only the four stern-chasers could fire, the crew were set to replacing and splicing the rigging and fishing damaged spars. It requires no common steadiness and discipline to go aloft about this work with the shot of heavy broadsides screaming past the ears. The *President*, however, was gaining, and Captain Byron now ordered four anchors to be cut away, on which the BELVIDERA began to get ahead. The 36-gun frigate *Congress*, Captain Smith, now took up the chase about 6.30 p.m., and appeared to be gaining, although her shot was falling short. Captain Byron now threw overboard four of his boats and fourteen tons of water, and by 8 p.m. was two miles ahead of any pursuer; now the business was to fish the damaged main topmast, a difficult and risky job with the spar in position and the ship under way. However, it was done, and at 11 p.m. Captain Byron, now three miles ahead, altered his course to ESE, boomed out studding sails, and went ahead at such a rate that by midnight the American squadron gave up the chase.

This was a very neat little engagement, and reflects the greatest credit on Captain Byron and the ship's company of the BELVIDERA; but as they had been engaged in running away, they received no acknowledgement whatever from their government. Nevertheless, they had scored a notable victory, the saving of the Jamaica convoy. By keeping the whole American squadron hotly engaged from dawn to midnight of a long summer's day, in the wrong direction, and inflicting such injuries on the *President* that took another day to repair, they had ensured the convoy's escape. 'Lose not an hour', said Napoleon; and the big frigates had lost forty-eight.

On the 19th of August 1812 the *Constitution*, Captain Isaac Hull, about 500 miles south of Newfoundland, came up with the GUERRIERE, Captain Dacres, on her way to Halifax for a much-needed refit. This was a 38-gun 18-pounder frigate, a powerful vessel, but under-manned and in poor condition; she had been struck by lightning, which had damaged her mainmast and bowsprit, and her hull was leaky. She was no match for the big frigate, being 1,092 tons to 1,533, a much lighter broadside, and only 244 men against 460. However, when Captain Dacres descried the enemy frigate he shortened sail to allow her to come up, and at 5 p.m. opened fire, all her shot falling short.

Ten minutes later the *Constitution* opened up with a broadside so effective that the GUERRIERE began dodging about, in the hope of upsetting the aim of the American gunners; but in fact it had a far worse effect on the British. After half an hour of fairly long-range firing, Captain Hull decided to bring on a decisive action, and closed in. At about 6 p.m. the mizzen-mast of the GUERRIERE was shot away; it fell right aft, knocking a large hole in the ship's counter in which some of the rigging stuck, difficult to cut away, while the mast kept dragging astern like a sea-anchor. The *Constitution*, handled with great skill, now ranged athwart the bows of her opponent, raking her with tremendous broadsides to which she could only reply with a few bow-guns. Shortly the two ships fell foul, the bowsprit of the GUERRIERE tangling in the starboard mizzen-rigging of the *Constitution*. Captain Hull now decided on boarding, and his men assembled on the quarter-deck, while Captain Dacres went forward to the forecastle with his determined force to repel them. The Marines on both sides kept up a sharp and deadly fire at very close range. The officers were naturally the most conspicuous targets. The leaders of the two American boarding parties, the first lieutenant and the lieutenant of Marines, were both shot down, which caused some delay in preparation; and the sailing master was wounded. On the GUERRIERE, Captain

Dacres was severely wounded in the back, but refused to leave the deck, while the sailing master and a master's mate were also wounded.

Now the GUERRIERE got her bowsprit free, and was able to get a good position across the stern of the *Constitution*, firing a broadside at so short a range that the burning wads set fire to the captain's cabin. But now the foremast came down, taking the mainmast with it, so that the GUERRIERE lay quite dismasted, while the *Constitution* ranged ahead to make some repairs to the rigging. Without masts to steady her, the GUERRIERE was rolling enough to dip her main deck guns in the sea, and there was grave danger of their breaking loose. Captain Dacres set a division to secure the guns, another to clear the decks of wreckage, and another to set a sail on the sprit-sail yard, which warships still carried but seldom used. However, as soon as the wind filled this little sail, the yard carried away. The *Constitution* now came up, and the GUERRIERE hauled down her colours from the stump of the mizzen-mast.

The casualties in the GUERRIERE were terribly severe, 78 killed and wounded, as against 14 in the *Constitution*. The ship was a shattered wreck, so much so that next morning the prize master hailed that she was sinking. The prisoners and prize crew were taken on board the *Constitution*, the wreck of the *Guerriere* was fired, and shortly blew up. Captain Hull repaired the slight damages to the *Constitution*, and on 30th August arrived at Boston to a hero's welcome, the thanks of the government, and a present of $50,000.

The *United States* was one of the big frigates which had been laid down as a 74-gun ship, and her construction was even more massive than usual for that heavy class; she sailed a little slower than the others, and was nicknamed 'The Wagon', hence, doubtless, the term 'battle wagon' for a more modern battleship. Provisioned for a long voyage, with an ample crew of picked seamen, and commanded by the fine officer Commodore Stephen Decatur, she was cruising in the Atlantic with no doubt the hope of intercepting some of the convoys from India. When about five hundred miles south of the Azores, at dawn on 12th October 1812, a sail was descried about twelve miles to windward, headed on a parallel track, both ships being as close-hauled as possible on a fresh wind from the SSE. This was a fine new 38-gun frigate, the MACEDONIAN, Captain John Surman Carden, rather under-manned as usual, with only 262 men and the extraordinary proportion of 35 boys; but a crew in good heart with excellent officers.

Immediately on sighting, the MACEDONIAN boomed out studding sails and bore away in pursuit. At first Commodore Decatur took her for a 74, no doubt deceived by the vast spread of canvas, and therefore wore away also, to get the wind more on the quarter, as he had, very properly, no intention of engaging a line-of-battle ship so far from any possibility of support. As the MACEDONIAN came closer, her single deck of guns became visible, and the *United States* put about and advanced to meet her, at the same time hoisting her colours, the broad pendant showing her to be commanded by a commodore and therefore one of the new '44s'. This caused no hesitation on the MACEDONIAN, for they had had no news for some time, had not heard of the GUERRIERE, did not know the power of these new big frigates, but were quite sure that a British 38-gun ship could capture any size of frigate afloat.

Being asked his opinion, Lieutenant Hope thought it would be best to continue the present course, which would bring her very close across the bows of the enemy, in the hopes of raking her; a good manœuvre, but dangerous if the enemy were clever enough. Captain Carden preferred to keep the advantage of the weather-gauge, which he already had, and hauled closer to the wind. As the two ships passed in opposite directions, the *United States* fired a broadside, without any effect, the range being too great for accuracy. Having got himself into the position he wanted, Captain Carden now put about and followed the *United States*, coming up on her windward quarter about 9.20 a.m., when the cannonade commenced. The first exchange brought down a small spar of the *United States*, but took the mizzen top-mast of the MACEDONIAN, letting her driver-gaff fall; so that the *United States* had now the advantage in sailing, and continued with the MACEDONIAN on her quarter, at a fairly long range, where the 24-pounders of the American were much more effective than the 18s of the British. Particular aim was taken at the carronades on the forecastle and quarter-deck, which were all dismounted and the bulwark shattered on the engaged side, before Commodore Decatur closed the range to a decisive distance.

Shortly after 11 a.m. the MACEDONIAN was a wreck; mizzen-mast gone, main and fore top-masts gone; nevertheless they set the only remaining sail on the foremast, to make enough way to come against the *United States* and try boarding her; however at that moment the fore-brace was shot away, and the sail swung round. The *United States* now passed the bows of the MACEDONIAN, without firing a shot, and stood away. The crew of the MACEDONIAN began cheering this surprising deliverance, but in fact the *United States* went off a little way to refill cartridges, having fired seventy broadsides in the action, using up all her ready cartridges. By noon, having filled a sufficiency and repaired some rigging, she tacked around and took up a position athwart the stern of the helpless MACEDONIAN; and the colours had to come down.

In this stout defence, the casualties of the MACEDONIAN were very heavy, amounting to 104 killed and wounded, as against 12 killed and wounded in the *United States*, which was also very little damaged, whereas the MACEDONIAN had more than 100 shot in her hull. Indeed, the two ships had to lie together for a fortnight until the *Macedonian* could be made fit to sail, and it was the 4th of December before they sighted Long Island. It is quite remarkable that during this long period, two weeks lying-to and five weeks passage, the two ships were never sighted by any British vessel. The *Macedonian* was purchased into the US Navy, with prize-money of $200,000 to the crew; along with the thanks of both Houses, a gold medal to the commodore and silver ones to the officers. These were well deserved; with hindsight, it is clear that the action could have no other ending, but this was by no means so clear before. Some bloodthirsty historians have criticised Decatur for not closing immediately, but in that case the 32-pounder carronades of the British ship would have been very effective; he was quite right to put them out of action before he closed. He won a complete victory with minimum loss, which should be the aim of every commander. There was every possibility that some British warship might come up, while there was no possibility whatever of American support. Had he fought a close action immediately and incurred severe damage, he would have been in a very poor position. His action at Tripoli had sufficiently shown the dashing lieutenant; this one showed the clear-headed and cautious commodore.

The government of the United States now decided to put a strong squadron into the Pacific, commanded by Commodore William Bainbridge, in the *Constitution*, along with the *Essex*, frigate, and the 18-gun *Hornet*. They were to sail from different ports and meet at Salvador (Bahia) in Brazil, not a good arrangement. The *Essex* sailed from the Delaware River on 27th October 1812, and the other two from Boston on the 30th, arriving off Salvador towards the end of December, where they found no sign of the *Essex*. The commodore ordered the *Hornet* into the port to make inquiries, while he took the *Constitution* about thirty miles off the coast.

The *Renommée* had been captured in an action off Madagascar by the ASTREA, Captain Schomberg, in February 1811, taken into the Royal Navy at Portsmouth and renamed JAVA, the former ship of that name having been lost (p. 95). On 17th August 1812 Captain Lambert, a brave and efficient officer, was commissioned to her, with orders to fit her out in order to convey to Bombay the new Governor, Lieutenant-General Hislop, with his suite, and also stores, largely copper, for ships which were building at Bombay. With the resources of Portsmouth the ship was quickly got ready; but to get a crew was a very different matter. With 140,000 seamen and Marines at sea, the barrel had been scraped clean. Officers and senior petty officers were easy, and 50 Marines were provided, 18 of them raw recruits, but good material. The 23 boys were easily found. 60 Irish landmen were put on board, along with 50 seamen suspected of mutinous intentions, from a sloop at Spithead. At length 292 out of 300 were got together. Captain Lambert naturally remonstrated about the poor quality and inexperience of his crew, but was laughingly assured that a voyage to Bombay and back, under his captaincy, would make sailors of them all; and besides, the chance of meeting an enemy was now very remote. At length, he was allowed to take eight real seamen, volunteers, from the RODNEY. He now had his complement, of whom, excluding the officers, less than fifty had ever been in action. Eventually he sailed on the 12th of November, having 397 people on board, including the Governor, his suite and servants; and having two East India merchantmen under his convoy.

As is well known, long before this period the study of winds and currents had shown that the best route to India was to make Madeira, then keep west of the Canaries and Cape Verde Islands and then S by SW almost to the coast of Brazil, then S by SE until latitude 35° South, and there pick up the great westerly wind which circles the world in 35° to 55° South; returning, the route is fairly near the African coast all the way, although it was usual, after touching at St Helena and sighting Ascension, to stand well to the westward for the Azores. Following this course, the JAVA touched at Madeira, where the officers and the Governor's suite laid in a stock of the native product. On Christmas Eve, being at the nearest point to Brazil on the well-known route, Captain Lambert had a report that water was short; the Governor and his suite had brought such an immensity of luggage that it was impossible to get at the water casks until the upper load was taken out of the ship. Captain Lambert then decided to put into Salvador to adjust cargo and take on water, but the two East Indiamen, feeling no need of further convoy, kept on their way. He was left with the WILLIAM, an American merchant ship he had captured on the way, putting into her a master's mate and nineteen seamen, whom he could ill spare.

On the 28th December, for the first time on the voyage, Captain Lambert ordered six broadsides of blank cartridge to be fired; for the majority of the crew it was the first time they had served a gun on ship-board. Next day, the 29th, at 2 a.m., the *Constitution* was seen, lying hove-to, a bad sign in those waters, where all shipping should be going about its business. Captain Lambert therefore parted with the WILLIAM, ordering her to go into Salvador while he examined the stranger, which was now seen to be making sail. In fact, it was supposed on board the *Constitution* that the JAVA was the expected *Essex*, and they kept approaching until, at about four miles away, the JAVA made the private recognition signals for British, Spanish or Portuguese ships, without reply; and the *Constitution* made the American one, without reply, and then wore ship away from the JAVA.

The JAVA was under a press of sail, and went in pursuit, definitely gaining in the chase; but the wind coming up quite strongly from the north-east, and the sea rising, she heeled so much that she had to take in her royals. On this, at 1.40 p.m., the *Constitution* also shortened sail, and hoisted her colours; the JAVA did the same, and they approached under the usual sail for fighting in moderate weather, top and top-gallant sails, one jib and the driver.

The action commenced at 2.10 p.m., with the *Constitution* firing a broadside at half a mile range, falling short; then, as the JAVA came close, another which whistled overhead; then the JAVA, ranging alongside within a few yards, gave a most effective broadside, which carried away the wheel, killed four men and wounded several more. The *Constitution* fired a third broadside, and under cover of the smoke wore away to lengthen the range. The JAVA followed, more broadsides were exchanged, and the *Constitution* again wore away. This time the JAVA passed close under her stern, in a most advantageous position for raking, but only one shot was fired; probably the inexperienced crew had not reloaded in time. The *Constitution* now had the weather-gauge, but this did not suit her tactics, so she made sail to leeward, giving the JAVA again the opportunity of crossing her stern, and this time giving her quite a raking broadside.

It was now 3 p.m., and the JAVA, with her raw crew, had given a very good account of herself; had for fifty minutes sustained the fire of an enormously superior opponent, and given as good as she got. Now, however, Commodore Bainbridge decided to close, and came alongside within forty yards, when the rapid fire of his well-served guns began to tell; the JAVA's rigging was cut to pieces, her masts badly damaged, and men were dropping every minute. Captain Lambert saw his serious disadvantage, and determined on boarding in a desperate attempt to save his ship; before the JAVA could be laid aboard of the enemy, however, the foremast came down with a terrific crash, smashing in the forecastle and blocking most of the deck. The *Constitution* now attained a commanding position on the JAVA's quarter, and poured in a tremendous fire of all arms, to which scarcely any reply could be given. At 3.30 p.m. Captain Lambert was mortally wounded by a musket-ball, and the command devolved upon Lieutenant Henry Ducie Chads, who was himself wounded but kept the deck. Still the pitiless fire continued; at 4 p.m. the mizzen-mast went, and from this or some other cause the ships fell away a little and lay broadside to broadside; immediately the men at the guns of the JAVA opened fire again, with the best broadsides they had given yet, although the flame from the guns was igniting the wreckage that hung overside. The *Constitution* now drew ahead to repair damages, and the crew of the JAVA cheered wildly, thinking she was retreating.

They were now set to work furiously, to get some sail on the wreck; a sail was rigged between the stump of the foremast and the remains of the bowsprit; a spare top-gallant mast was fished to the same stump, with a studding-sail set on it; the mainmast could not stand in the heavy rolling, so it was cut away, and in the strong wind the JAVA began to make headway. Now, however, the *Constitution* began to come down, but the JAVA's men reloaded her guns with ball and grape-shot, and returned the fire defiantly. By 6 p.m. she had seventeen guns out of action, no spars left standing, all her boats destroyed, pumps disabled and the hull a mere piece of wreckage; when Lieutenant Chads ordered the colours to be hauled down. The raw, botched-together crew of the JAVA had acquitted themselves like veteran heroes; they had sustained a fight against fearful odds for four hours; they had 124 casualties killed and wounded; but they were ready to fight on when their commander put an end to the slaughter. Lieutenant Chads,* though wounded, remained on deck throughout the action; Boatswain Humble had his hand shot off, went below to have a tourniquet on the stump, and returned to the deck. 'I had my orders from Lieutenant Chads,' he explained simply, 'to cheer up the men with my pipe.'

The *Constitution* had 34 casualties killed and wounded, according to Commodore Bainbridge's account; but the British officers on board as prisoners estimated 52. She had several shot through her hull and masts, and of her eight boats only

* In 1824, Captain Henry Ducie Chads commanded the Irrawaddy flotilla during the Burmese War.

one could take the water. In this only boat Lieutenant Parker, first of the *Constitution*, boarded the *Java* and took possession; but had to send a message to the commodore that the ship was in a sinking condition and could not be salvaged. He was now ordered to remove all the prisoners and their baggage to the *Constitution*, and then set the *Java* on fire. With only one boat, the transfer was a tedious business, taking up the whole of the next day; but on the morning of the 31st January the *Java* was fired, and blew up about 3 p.m.

The officers of the *Constitution* have been criticised for the pressure brought to bear on the seamen prisoners to induce them to enter the American Navy; however, only three did so, believed to be Irish Roman Catholics, who had little cause to adhere faithfully to the British government. As the *Java* was about to blow up, one of these deserters informed the commodore that a large part of her cargo was gold bars, which he himself had helped to stow; Bainbridge's chagrin at this information may well be imagined, but after having enjoyed the ameliorations of the position for some time, the British officer prisoners were able to assure him that the precious metal was in fact copper.

Part of the prize was a very splendid service of silver, suited for the pomp and dignity of a Governor of Bombay; this Commodore Bainbridge ordered to be restored to Lieutenant-General Hislop, who returned the compliment with a present of a handsome sword. Captain Lambert died on the 4th January 1813, and was buried with full honours in Fort St Pedor, attended by the Governor of the fort, the Conde' dos Arcos. The American officers did not think it suitable to attend, but the commodore wrote to Lieutenant-General Hislop:

Commodore Bainbridge has learned, with real sorrow, the death of Captain Lambert. Though a political enemy, he could not but greatly respect him for the brave defence he made with his ship; and Commodore Bainbridge takes this occasion to observe, in justice to Lieutenant Chads, who fought the JAVA after Captain Lambert was wounded, that he did everything for the defence of that ship that a brave and skilful officer could do, and that further resistance would have been a wanton effusion of human blood.

On the 6th of January 1813 Commodore Bainbridge decided that the damages to the *Constitution* were beyond local repair to fit her for a voyage round the Horn, and returned to Boston, where he was naturally received with rapture, a gold medal, the thanks of Congress supplemented with $50,000, silver medals for all the officers and a triumphal procession.

Commodore Bainbridge has been criticised (by a *very* partial British historian) for delaying the action so long, and indeed appearing to evade it; but it must be considered that he was at any moment expecting his consort the *Hornet* to come up, and at any hour the *Essex*. Before this formidable squadron it might be expected that the JAVA would surrender without further resistance, and allow him to resume his Pacific cruise; which, by engaging, he was forced to abandon. Indeed, it has to be observed that all these tactical victories of the big frigates were in fact strategical defeats; they had to abandon their main objective in every case. By running away from the *President* and consorts, the BELVIDERA saved the Jamaica convoy. By fighting the *United States*, the MACEDONIAN, although surrendered, caused that powerful ship to leave the track of the East India convoy and return to her home port; and by fighting the *Constitution* to the death, the JAVA turned her back from the Pacific, where her presence might have had very serious consequences. These defeats must be aligned with the defeat of the JERVIS BAY, Captain Fogarty Fegen, V.C., by the *Scheer*, Captain Krancke, on 5th November 1940. In all those cases the convoys were saved; the warships were lost: they had carried out their orders.

> *Go tell the Spartans, you that pass us by,*
> *Obedient to their orders, here we lie.*
> SIMONIDES, EPITAPH AT THERMOPYLAE.
> Author's trans.

14

Challenge Encounter

In England there was great dismay at the success of the big frigates in combat with British frigates of nominally nearly equal force; but Admiralty did not allow itself to attach too much importance to what was in fact a side-show. The whole American Navy was only a light squadron, compared with the powerful fleets which Napoleon had in the Scheldt, at Brest, at Rochefort, and at Toulon; the blockade of those fleets was recognised as the first business of the Royal Navy. It has been suggested that if Vice-Admiral Sir Edward Pellew, Bart., had been detached from Toulon with the lighter half of his fleet, the whole American business would have been settled in a few months. This is probably true, but the French fleet in Toulon was at least ten times more formidable than the whole American Navy, consisting of 21 ships of the line, 6 of them three-deckers, 3 of 130 guns each, plus 10 large frigates and all supporting craft, and several more building. To keep this immense force corked up in harbour was infinitely more important than odd frigate actions on the other side of the Atlantic.

Nevertheless, some action was taken. Three of the small class of 74-gun ships were cut down and lightened by having their quarter-decks and forecastles removed. Two new large and light ships were built of pitch pine, of about 1,560 tons, with powerful batteries. Any of these five was quite equal to any of the three big frigates; but in addition there were ordered twenty-six more large frigates, of the 36- and 38-gun classes, to be built of pine for speed and cheapness. The captains of frigates on the Halifax and Jamaica stations were ordered not to engage in single-ship actions with any of the big frigates, an order which almost caused a mutiny in one ship which ran away accordingly. The only thing Admiralty could not do was to provide them with good crews of seasoned sailors, and it must have been galling for the excellent officers of the new ships to man them with what was available, while in the Mediterranean there were twelve thousand fully trained prime seamen, hanging about hoping and praying that Vice-Admiral the Comte Emeriau would really come out and fight.

One ship that had no man-power problems was the 38-gun frigate SHANNON, Captain Philip Bowes Vere Broke, who took command on 14th September 1806 of a crew dragged aboard by the usual means; but by his skill as a seaman and a gunner, and by his outstanding personality as a leader of men, he shaped them into one of the best crews that ever trod a deck. Discipline was firm and impartial; sail drill and gunnery were more important than paint and polish; Broke spent his own money for extra powder, and gave a pound of tobacco to every gun that hit the mark. Seven years he spent in training his men, and by that time every man knew exactly what he was required to do, and how to do it; he had done it often before.

In 1813, on the Halifax station, Captain Broke found himself the senior captain, under Rear-Admiral Sawyer. There was a bit of two-and-fro squadron demonstrations, but eventually Broke found an objective in May 1813, the *Chesapeake*, completing repairs in Boston Harbour. She was a frigate of equal or slightly greater force than the SHANNON, well manned, and commanded by Captain Lawrence, who had earlier had a successful cruise in command of the *Hornet*, sloop. The *Constitution* was also in the harbour, but having an extensive repair and alteration, so that she was not to be ready for sea for some months. Broke had with him the TENEDOS, 38-gun frigate, Captain Hyde Parker; Broke now took some supplies out of the TENEDOS, and sent her away, with orders not to come within reach of Boston before 14th June, as it was obvious that the *Chesapeake* could not be expected to come out to fight two to one.

Thinking that the *Chesapeake* was somewhat tardy, Broke now sent in a formal written challenge to Lawrence, by a captured

American merchantman, Captain Slocum, surely an ancestor of Captain Joshua Slocum, the first single-handed circumnavigator.

'As the *Chesapeake* appears now ready for sea, I request you will do me the favour to meet the SHANNON with her, ship to ship, to try the fortune of our respective flags.' He goes on to detail precisely the armament and complement of his ship, and promises that there will be no interruption by any British ship, concluding with a request for a speedy reply. As a matter of fact, Captain Lawrence was just as ready for a meeting as Broke, but he had to get permission from Commodore Bainbridge, who had had to get permission from Washington, which was forthcoming; and Lawrence did not ever receive this faintly medieval invitation to come out and be killed. This is probably the very last formal challenge between warships. Before Slocum reached the shore, the *Chesapeake* was making sail, and shortly after noon was seen standing out from the harbour under easy sail, accompanied by a perfect regatta of small craft filled with spectators, including, it is believed, two commodores and some other officers. The wind was light from west by north, and the SHANNON now stood away from the shore, not wishing to engage surrounded by all those boats, which would certainly be a nuisance and possibly might conceal a menace. The *Chesapeake* followed under all sail, which she shortened at 4.50 p.m. At 5.30 the SHANNON shortened sail to battle rig, Boston lighthouse then being about twenty miles to the westward. *Chesapeake* now came up, and having the weather-gauge could either engage on the weather side, or pass under the SHANNON's stern, rake her with a broadside and then engage on the lee side. Captain Broke had provided for both possibilities; the *Chesapeake* chose to keep the weather side, and came along quite slowly at a range of about fifty yards.

This was the moment the SHANNON had been training for, through seven years. A.B. William Mindham, gun-captain of the aftermost starboard 18-pounder, knew his orders; to wait until his gun could bear on the second gunport from forward of the enemy; at 5.50 p.m. he fired the first shot of the action, hitting his objective with two round shot and a keg of musket balls. Now the rest of the guns fired in succession as they came to bear, and as the *Chesapeake* passed, the 32-pounder carronades on the quarter-deck of the SHANNON swept her quarter-deck with grape-shot as well as round-shot. The *Chesapeake* now fired her broadside, which was answered; and as the *Chesapeake* was running too far ahead, her main-top sail was backed, to take the way off her. Unfortunately the men at the wheel were all killed or wounded by the fire from the SHANNON's quarter-deck, so that the *Chesapeake* continued to swing into the wind, losing all way, thus presenting her quarter-deck and quarter to the raking fire of the SHANNON, to which little reply could be given. The *Chesapeake* now began to drift astern, and fell on board the SHANNON, with the larboard corner of her stern against the starboard side of the SHANNON, a little forward of the mainmast. This check swung the *Chesapeake* more into the wind, and her foresail began to take up, although damaged, and she moved ahead slowly, rubbing along the SHANNON's hull, until she hooked on to the SHANNON's small bower-anchor.

Captain Broke now ordered the ships to be lashed together, First Lieutenant Watts to get together the quarter-deck men for boarding, and the main deck boarders to be ordered up, while he himself ran forward to take command of the forecastle boarders, whose leader, midshipman Samwell, was mortally wounded. The lashing together of the ships was done by Mr Stevens, the SHANNON's veteran boatswain, who had fought in the battle of the Sainte's Passage thirty-two years before, 'when Rodney beat the Comte de Grasse'. Mr Stevens was assailed by the defenders as he worked, and his left arm was hacked off by repeated cutlass-strokes, but he finished his job with his right hand before he was shot down by musketry.*

Captain Broke now stepped over the gangway railing, around the foremast rigging, on to the muzzle of the *Chesapeake*'s aftermost quarter-deck carronade, and threw himself over the bulwark, followed immediately by the forecastle party of about twenty men. They found the quarter-deck clear of all except dead and wounded, but about thirty men on the gangways. A fierce charge drove these back to the forecastle, where after a

---

* Parallels almost as precise are to be found in Cynaegeirus after Marathon, under Miltiades and Caius Acilius, in the battle off Marseilles, under Julius Caesar. Such devotion to duty is seldom to be found except among the followers of the great captains.

brief struggle some (no doubt British deserters) jumped over the bows into the sea, while the others laid down their arms and surrendered. Meanwhile the enemy tried to regain the quarter-deck by coming up the main hatch; but First Lieutenant Watt was already there, with the quarter-deck boarders and a division of the Marines, who were followed by the main deck boarders and more Marines. Lieutenant Watt was shot through the foot while boarding, but remained in command on the *Chesapeake*'s quarter-deck. The shot came from the American Marines in the main and mizzen tops, and it was the duty of the small parties in the SHANNON's tops to deal with this. Midshipman William Smith, in the fore-top, observed that the main-yard of the *Chesapeake* was in contact with the fore-yard over which was his fighting-top. Waiting until the Marines opposite had fired a volley and were reloading, he swarmed along both yards with his four men and cleared the *Chesapeake*'s top with the cutlass. The *Chesapeake*'s mizzen-top was silenced and cleared by Midshipman Cosnahan, from the main-top of the SHANNON; a good shot, he kept his four men loading muskets, enabling him to keep up a rapid and accurate fire which killed or wounded all the American Marines in the mizzen-top; they used rifles, which at that time took three times as long to load as a musket, which was as accurate at twenty yards.

Boatswain Stevens' tackle held; but the quarter-deck gallery of the *Chesapeake*, to which he had made fast, now fetched away, and the two ships began slowly to drift apart. On the forecastle of the *Chesapeake* Captain Broke, setting a single sentry over the prisoners, directed the rest of his boarders to return to the quarter-deck where fierce fighting was engaged. While casting his captain's eye round the ship, he was alerted by a shout from the sentry. The prisoners had picked up their weapons and resumed fighting, the first casualty being the sentry, immediately after he had warned his captain. Broke was now attacked by several men: he parried a thrust from a pike, and wounded the pikeman; but was stunned by a blow from the butt-end of a musket, and cut down by a blow from a cutlass; this assailant was in the act of swinging his cutlass to finish off the wounded captain, when, with a rush and a roar, the main deck boarders charged along the gangways. William Mindham, that accurate gun-captain, cut down and killed Broke's adversary, while the rest of the main deck boarders cleared the forecastle in one furious assault. No quarter was given, as was indeed justified by the laws of war, but it is doubtful if the seamen stopped to debate the legal point; their blood was up, and they had seen their captain fall.

Midshipman Smith, who had just cleared the main-top, came down to the deck and helped A.B. Mindham to get Broke to his feet. While they were bandaging his head as best they could, Mindham cried: 'There, Sir, there goes the old Ensign up over the Yankee colours!' Immediately Captain Broke was helped to the quarter-deck, where he was seated on a carronade-slide, in command of the CHESAPEAKE.

An unfortunate accident, however, had marred the changing of the colours, Lieutenant Watt himself hauled down the American flag, and hauled them up again, with, as he thought, the British ensign above it. He had been better to have left the job to a signal rating, for he had somehow got the toggles mixed and the colours went up with the Ensign underneath. The ships had by this time drifted about a hundred yards apart, and the quarter-deck gunners of the SHANNON, seeing through the smoke these colours, judged that the ship had been retaken and fired a broadside, which killed their own first lieutenant and four of their shipmates. Their chagrin and regret may be imagined, but they were doing their duty in the circumstances. After the colours were hoisted correctly, some Americans in the hold of the ship fired up, killing a Marine; Lieutenant Falkiner, third of the SHANNON, ordered his men to fire into the hold, which they did with effect. Captain Broke ordered Lieutenant Falkiner to cease fire, and to ask the men in the hold if they surrendered; no quarter if they wanted to carry on the fight. They surrendered and all fighting ceased. The ship was not formally surrendered, for there was not a single commissioned officer left on his feet to offer his sword. The SHANNON's jolly-boat came alongside with reinforcements just as Captain Broke fainted from loss of blood, and the jolly-boat took him back to the SHANNON.

This was one of the shortest actions of the wars. From the first gun until the changing of the colours only fifteen minutes elapsed — roughly, eleven for the cannonade and four for the boarding action. It was also one of the fiercest — in that quarter of an hour 229 men had been struck down, many never to rise. The SHANNON had 24 killed and 59 wounded, some mortally; but the *Chesapeake* had 47 killed and 99 wounded, 14 mortally. Her casualties included all her commissioned officers; captain and first lieutenant mortally wounded, second and third lieutenants wounded, fourth lieutenant killed, lieutenant of Marines killed.

Lieutenant Provo Wallis, second of the SHANNON, now took command of her, while the third, Lieutenant Falkiner, took the CHESAPEAKE; on the 6th of June 1813, they arrived at Halifax to great acclamation. Captain Lawrence died during the voyage, and was buried at Halifax with full military honours of his rank; Lieutenant Ludlow died after arrival, and was similarly buried; but a cartel later was given the remains for burial in their own country. Both Lieutenants Wallis and Falkiner were promoted to be commanders, and Wallis was commissioned to take the CHESAPEAKE to Portsmouth.

This battle excited the greatest excitement in Britain, and with good cause. The history of the naval war with America had up till now been an unbroken succession of defeats, which might be explained away but were undoubted defeats; was the sceptre of the seas slipping from the hand of Britannia? Now, in a straight fight between ships of equal force the British had been decisively successful. There were, too, touches about it which stirred the imagination, touches reminiscent of the days of chivalry. The formal challenge — the heroic devotion of the boatswain — the Captain leading the first wave of boarders — the Captain engaged single-handed in a three-to-one close combat — the young midshipman storming the enemy fighting-top along the yard-arms — the fierce combat on the enemy deck: here were all the elements of romance.

Captain Broke was made a Baronet for this engagement, but owing to his wounds and the war ending he did not serve again, dying fairly young as a rear-admiral. Very different was the later career of his second lieutenant. Provo Wallis was not made post captain, which he might have expected after commanding a frigate, if only for a few weeks; but he got post rank in 1819. Now all he had to do was to survive, and he had emerged unscathed from his only engagement so that there were no old wounds to worry about. He kept on steadily up the captains' ladder, and then up the admirals' ladder; until in 1877 he became Admiral of the Fleet, and moreover enjoyed that rank and pay for nearly fifteen years, dying in 1892, age 100. He was an institution, especially as he retained all his faculties and replied with his own hand to all the congratulations on his hundredth birthday. To a nation proud of its fleet, equal to all the navies in the world together; in those days of twelve-inch armour, steam propulsion, and 81-ton guns; here was a man who could tell how he had fought ship to ship under sail in the wooden walls, eighty years before.

15

South Pacific

Somewhat elated by the early successes of their big frigates, the government of the U.S.A. decided to put a squadron into the South Pacific, where no American warship had formerly made an appearance. The ships chosen were the *Constitution*, one of the extra-large frigates, the *Hornet*, a sloop, and the *Essex*, a small frigate of 867 tons, but with a very powerful close-range battery, having forty carronades, 32-pounders, and six long 12-pounders. Sailing from different ports, the three were to rendezvous off Salvador (Bahia) on the coast of Brazil. While waiting around there, the *Constitution* met the British frigate JAVA, and after a fierce fight captured and sank her; but was so much damaged that she had to return to a home port for repairs, accompanied by the *Hornet* (Chapter 13). When the *Essex* arrived and found no consorts, Captain David Porter decided to make the cruise alone, and arrived at Valparaiso on the 14th of March 1813, having captured by the way a British packet-ship out of which he took £11,000 in coin. Here he refitted the *Essex* after the stormy passage round Cape Horn, took in provisions and water, and set off to cruise in the whaling-grounds of the South Seas.

On receiving this intelligence Admiralty sent in pursuit the 36-gun 18-pounder frigate PHOEBE, Captain James Hillyard, who had been doing good service in the Indian Ocean, along with the 18-gun ship-sloop CHERUB, Commander Thomas Tucker. At first sight it seems quite ludicrous to send two ships to find one ship in the vast emptiness of the great South Seas; but the task was not as impossible as might appear. If the *Essex* were going to prey on the whale-fishing, which was probable, she must keep in the vicinity where the whale-ships were accustomed to go, for water, provisions and careening; and the eastern South Pacific has very few such places; it is the only stretch of water in the world where it is possible to be more than a thousand miles from the very nearest scrap of land.

After rounding the Horn Captain Hillyard made for Juan Fernandez, where he got no news; then to Guayaquil on the Ecuador coast—still no news; then to the Galapagos Islands, where he learned that the *Essex* had been there in October with some captured whale-ships, one of which, the ATLANTIC, he had renamed the *Essex Junior* and armed with twenty guns. Where now? It was probable that Captain Porter would try to sell his prizes on the coast of South America, for the chances of getting them home through the blockade were remote. Captain Hillyard therefore went to Lima, where he waited two months without any news.

Actually at that time the *Essex* was at Nuka Hiva, one of the Marquesas islands, nearly five thousand miles away, where Porter remained until 12th December 1813, cleaning ships and dealing with his twelve captures. One of these he had armed as described, and manned with a crew of ninety-five men; two he gave over to the prisoners, having taken the oil into the other prizes. One he armed with sixteen guns, and sent her off to the U.S.A. with two others, all fully laden; they were all captured by the frigates in the Atlantic. Three were burnt at sea. One was taken by the CHERUB, and one was seized by her prize crew and taken to Sydney Harbour. This leaves one not accounted for, possibly sold in Chile, possibly lost at sea.

The *Essex* and the *Essex Junior* with two of the prizes now sailed for Valparaiso, where they arrived in January 1814, hoping to sell their prizes. It is possible that the *Montezuma*, the one not accounted for, was sold on this occasion, but there were no bidders for the *Hector*, the other one; rumours of a British force on the coast made it a perilous speculation. In fact Captain Hillyard had tired of waiting in Lima for news, and coasted south; rounding the point of the harbour of Valparaiso, he found what he had been seeking for the last nine months.

The rules about belligerent ships in neutral waters were less well defined in those days, and were further complicated by the fact that Chile, as a Spanish colony, was now an ally of Britain in the war against France, but neutral in the American war on Britain. As usual, much depended on what force was available. Both sides, therefore, called their men to quarters, without, however, clearing for action. The PHOEBE came in very close to the *Essex*, and, according to a letter written a little later by a midshipman who was on the quarter-deck at the time, Captain Hillyard hailed Captain Porter to ask if he was well (they were old acquaintances). Captain Porter returned the compliment, but added, 'If the PHOEBE touches the *Essex* there will be serious consequences.' 'Upon my honour, I do not mean to touch you, I respect the neutrality of the port, and only came alongside to inquire after your health.' Captain Porter replied, 'Excuse me, Captain Hillyard, in calling my boarders', to which Hillyard replied, 'I thought you knew me better, Sir, than to think I would break my word—you have no occasion to be so much alarmed.' 'I am *not* alarmed, Sir—stand by, my boys!' On this the crew of the *Essex* manned her side and rigging, fully armed to repel boarders; the PHOEBE did the same, and passing on in this state of readiness came to anchor quite close. In the same way the CHERUB anchored almost alongside the *Essex Junior*, and the crews spent most of the night shouting insults at each other.

At 8 a.m. next morning, along with the usual colours the *Essex* hoisted a large white flag at the fore top-gallant masthead, bearing the motto 'Free Trade and Sailors' Rights'. It was known that a number of British sailors out of the captured whalers had been persuaded to enter into American service in the *Essex* on some such grounds, 'sailors' rights' being interpreted as meaning rum without ration. The PHOEBE now prepared and hoisted a counter-blast, 'God and country, British sailors' best Rights, Traitors offend both'. While these childish demonstrations were going on, the PHOEBE and CHERUB were taking in provisions, wood and water; when this was completed they stood out to cruise about in the bay, while the Americans remained moored in the anchorage.

The PHOEBE, in addition to her main battery of twenty-six

long 18-pounders, carried fourteen carronades, 32-pounders, and four long 9-pounders on her quarter-deck and forecastle. She was thus somewhat lighter in weight of broadside than the *Essex*, with the vital difference that almost the whole of the battery of the *Essex* was in carronades. She had therefore little chance against the PHOEBE, which in open sea conditions could keep out of carronade range and hammer the *Essex* into surrender with her long 18s. At close quarters it would be different, but the CHERUB carried eighteen carronades, 32-pounders, as well as six 18-pounder carronades and two long 6s, so that in 32-pounder carronades the *Essex* was out-gunned by two, and there were still the twenty-six 18-pounders in the PHOEBE. The *Essex Junior* was not constructed as a warship and had only ten each 18-pounder carronades and 6-pounder long guns; quite hopeless against the CHERUB. The plan therefore was to get away rather than fight in such circumstances. The usual wind in that area being from the south, Captain Porter decided to try to decoy the British ships to the northern coast of the shore, slip out himself and let them chase him, fighting if he must, to give the *Essex Junior* a fair chance of escape. In case both got away, the rendezvous was fixed for Nuka Hiva.

Some weeks passed in futile manœuvres. On the 25th February Captain Porter had his prize the *Hector* towed out of port and burnt. On the night of the 27th of March Captain Porter sent a small party to the north shore of the bay to burn blue-lights and shoot off rockets, to attract the British ships in that direction. This was partially successful, but at daylight the PHOEBE was still too close to the mouth of the port for an attempt at escape. A strong wind began to blow from the SSE and increased so much that the *Essex* dragged her starboard anchor. Seizing the opportunity, Captain Porter ordered the other cable to be cut and sail made. The *Essex* reached the mouth of the harbour well to windward of her opponents exactly as Captain Porter had planned, but just as she emerged to the open sea a still stronger squall carried away her main topmast, and with it all hope of escape. The *Essex* bore up, and after running before the wind for some time came to an anchor in a small bay. Between 3.30 and 4 p.m. the PHOEBE crossed the stern of the *Essex*, at a greater distance than was intended, and gave some raking broadsides, while the CHERUB also opened fire. The *Essex* replied with three of her long 12-pounders, which the crew had managed to run out of her stern-ports. After half an hour of this long-range firing, the British ships were too near the shore and had to wear away for sea-room. They had by no means had the best of this brief encounter. The PHOEBE had a 12-pound shot through her hull well below the waterline, and was much damaged in the rigging, as was also the CHERUB. After about an hour the wind fell almost to a calm, and the PHOEBE once more approached the *Essex*, this time much closer. After about twenty minutes of fierce cannonade the *Essex* cut her cable and tried to run on shore, but a sudden squall from off the mountains (a 'williwaw') drove her right back again; she again anchored about three-quarters of a mile off shore, but this left her in a hopeless position, with her stern exposed to the fire of both the British ships' broadsides.

The *Essex* had gone into action with many ensigns flying, but the cannonade had left only one, which she now hauled down; 'but,' says our midshipman, 'kept *Free Trade*, etc. flying, so we gave her several more broadsides before she sent a man up to haul this flag down, but a shot took him, flag and all, just as he was in the act of striking it and so put an end to the business.'

Now was seen the extraordinary sight of about a hundred men leaping from the deck of the *Essex* into the sea. These were the British seamen who had been induced to join the *Essex* out of the captured whalers, and who now realised the full meaning of the word 'traitors' on the flag the PHOEBE was still flying. The non-swimmers crowded into the only boat the *Essex* had left, in such numbers that the boat swamped and left them struggling hopelessly in the water. Of the rest, about 40 reached the shore, about 30 drowned, and 16 were taken from the water by the boats of the British ships.

'I was in the 1st boat that boarded her,' wrote our midshipman. 'Nothing was to be seen all over her decks but dead, wounded and dying—we threw 63 overboard that were dead and there were several wounded that it would have been a mercy to do the same to…One poor fellow, who had his thigh shot off, managed to crawl to a port and tumble himself into the water which put an end to his misery. There were 44 amputations performed that night…Captain Porter was in tears when he went on board the PHOEBE to give up his sword and he told Captain Hillyard that there were 15 of his brave fellows killed after she struck.'

The loss sustained by the *Essex* has been the subject of much controversy. Captain Porter gives it as 58 killed and mortally wounded, 39 severely and 27 slightly wounded. This tallies not badly with the account given by our young eyewitness, and is quite consonant with the expectable loss of a heavily manned ship which had been exposed stern-on to broadsides from a total of 33 guns and carronades, 18-pounders and over, for two hours. The official letter of Captain Hillyard says 'The defence of the *Essex*...did honour to her brave defenders, and most fully evinced the courage of Captain Porter, and those under his command. Her colours were not struck until the loss in killed and wounded was so awfully great, and her shattered condition so seriously bad, as to render further resistance unavailing.' Well, there is the testimony of three who were there; but respectable historians, who were not there, have reduced the loss figures to less than half, for reasons it is difficult to follow; and indeed if the first boat-load of British to take over the ship began by throwing the dead overboard, an accurate count is not to be expected.

The loss of the PHOEBE was 4 killed and 7 wounded, and of the CHERUB 1 killed and 3 wounded. Captain Hillyard has been criticised (mostly by American writers) for taking too long and fighting at a fair distance; but if he had thrown away the only advantage his ship had, and had fought within point-blank car-ronade range of the forty 32-pounders of the *Essex*, he would have deserved to be cashiered. A good captain will take every fair advantage open to him, and will save his men as far as he possibly can.

16

Shipwreck

After the general settlement of Europe after Waterloo, the British government determined to send an Embassy to the Emperor of China, to inform him officially of the events and settlement, to profess the friendship of the British Crown, and to convey to him a very splendid service of silver. For this important office the choice fell on Lord Amherst, a very able peer, who was later to be Governor of Canada and later still Governor-General of India. He was naturally consulted about the transport he wished, and he asked for the frigate ALCESTE, commanded by his friend Captain Murray Maxwell.

The ALCESTE and her captain had already distinguished themselves in the wars, chiefly in the Adriatic, where one action may have changed the course of history. The ALCESTE, along with the ACTIVE, Captain James Gordon, and the 36-gun UNITÉ, Captain Edwin Chamberlayne, was lying at Lissa when they were informed of a French squadron, almost identical, sailing northwards. The British immediately chased, and after a fierce encounter captured two of the French frigates, the third making its escape. This was a splendid feat of war, but what made it more interesting was the fact that the captured frigates were laden with more than two hundred guns, with the carriages and all necessary stores, bound for Trieste. This action took place on 28th November 1811, and the news of it may have made Napoleon realise that he could never build up Illyria as a springboard against Turkey. After all, he deployed only 250 guns at Waterloo, so the loss of 200 was indeed serious. Thus it may well be that Murray Maxwell's minor victory may have been the last factor that made Napoleon abandon at that time his designs on Constantinople, and go to Moscow instead.

As well as being one of the finest 38-gun frigates in the Royal Navy, assiduous in all duties and terrible in action, the ALCESTE was a happy ship. One who served in her, on the lower deck, described her as the happiest home he ever had. Murray Maxwell was the ideal captain; his personality was such that his whole crew hero-worshipped him; he had no need to use the lash; the mere idea of displeasing him was sufficient discipline. The men admired him for his seamanship and skill, and his complete intrepidity in battle; and they loved him for his impartiality and his firm and kindly command. There could be no better choice of a ship for a long, hazardous and important voyage than the ALCESTE.

The outward voyage was accomplished without particular incident, and the ALCESTE lay at Whampoa, the usual anchorage for Canton, while the Ambassador and his suite carried out their duties at the Imperial Court. They were received with the usual ceremonies, but did not make the impression they expected. The Celestial Emperor indicated that he had little interest in the squabbles of distant barbarians, and declined the present of plate, on the grounds that he had no use for it, using only gold or jade himself. *Timeo Danaos et dona ferentes* was his view, and a very sound one in his case. The Embassy returned to Canton, having accomplished as much of their mission as they could, only embarrassed about what to do with the service of plate. Obviously the Prince Regent could not receive it back again. In the long run, after various vicissitudes, it was sold by auction at Calcutta, and purchased by a Mr Hawkins, who had accumulated a vast fortune, no doubt honestly, as Agent at Bareilly for the Governor-General, and he produced it when he entertained General Lord Combermore, the Commander-in-Chief, and his suite during his Excellency's Simla progress in December 1828.

The ALCESTE sailed from Whampoa on the 21st of January 1817, having on board 257 persons, including the Ambassador and his suite, so that she would appear to be somewhat undermanned. No doubt before leaving England some guns had been put ashore, to make more accommodation room, so that fewer hands would be required. The course was through the South China Seas, for the Sunda Strait between Sumatra and Java, whence there is a clear run, with mostly favourable winds, to Cape Town.

The South China Sea is the most dangerous water in all the oceans. Even today there is a great area, about 100,000 square miles, west of Palawan, which has never been surveyed; some reefs and rocks round the perimeter have been marked, the rest called 'The Dangerous Area' and left at that. From Bangkok to Java is 1,500 miles, nowhere deeper than 40 fathoms, and in those shallow waters the frequent typhoons can whip up a fearsome short steep sea. Moreover, from the shallows rise hundreds of shoals, islands and sunken reefs, many of which are so steep-to that the sounding-line, and even the echo-sounder, can give no warning of their proximity.

Having chosen the season with care, the ALCESTE had favourable winds throughout the passage, and twenty-eight days out was approaching the last hazard before the Sunda Straits. Nowadays ships use the Gaspar Strait, between the small island of Liat and the large island of Belitung; but at that time the known channel was the Bangka Strait, between the large island of Bangka and the west coast of Liat. It may be assumed that every precaution was taken, and certainly the sounding-line was kept going continuously throughout the passage, but she struck with terrific force upon a sunken and uncharted reef, where she stuck fast.

Everyone on board was as cool as the captain, who ordered the sails to be furled and the best bower anchor let go, to prevent the ship slipping off the reef until the state of damage could be ascertained. Mr Cheffy, the carpenter, now reported that the water was coming in much faster than all the pumps could cope with, that the damage to the hull underwater was beyond repair, and if she came off into deep water she would immediately sink; in fact, she was a total loss.

The captain's first care was for the Ambassador, the King's Representative. An island was seen about three miles away. The barge and cutter were put under command of the First Lieutenant, Hopper, who was ordered to convey the Ambassador and suite to the island, and land them there if it seemed safe.

They made the island, which appeared to be uninhabited but heavily forested; they had to coast for three more miles before they found an opening in the mangroves, and were able to land their passengers, after which they returned to the ship. Meanwhile the remaining boats had been hoisted out, and a large raft constructed, on which were placed the articles too large to be stowed in the boats. All that could be reached in the way of food, water, arms and tools was stowed in the boats, which made for the landing-place with the whole ship's company, towing the raft. On landing, a space was cleared under the nearest trees, where all the castaways bivouacked for the night.

In the morning, on taking stock, it was found that the most immediate shortage was water; one small cask, and a jar in the barge, was the whole stock. Parties were now sent out in various directions, but returned having found no water. After a council, it was decided that the first lieutenant should convey Lord Amherst and his suite to Batavia (now Djkarta) in Java, which lay a little more than two hundred miles to the southward, using the same boats which had brought them ashore. Given fair weather, the voyage should be easily done in four days; but of course the weather might not stay fair. On arrival, Lord Amherst was immediately to send a relief ship. There was very little prospect of sighting a passing vessel, as the Company's ships which used the Sunda Strait continued eastward for Java and the Spice Islands, while those bound for China sailed from Calcutta using the Singapore Strait 350 miles to the north. For food they had a side of mutton, a ham, a tongue, twenty pounds of coarse biscuit and a few pounds of fine; and for drink a seven-gallon jar each of water, beer, and spruce beer, and thirty bottles of wine. For four days this was a pint of liquid per man per day, a very meagre allowance when it is considered that all their provisions were either salt meat or dry biscuit, and they were in latitude 3° south of the equator. However, the men left behind were in worse case; so the boats rowed out well clear of all the rocks, and then made sail and were soon below the horizon.

The party on the island numbered two hundred men and boys, and one woman, turned up, as usual, from nowhere. The water-cask saved from the ship would afford one pint per head for two days only, while it must be at the very best nine days before relief could arrive. Water was the first consideration. The Captain made a quick survey to decide a likely spot, and set a party to digging a well. Another party was sent on board the wreck, to get by what means they could as much provision and arms they might reach. Captain Maxwell decided to remove the bivouac to the top of a small hill, for better air and for defence, and he set a party to cut a path and to clear away the undergrowth at the top. A sort of cave near the top formed a cool larder, where the provisions were stowed, and a Marine guard posted. In short, everything was done to prepare for an indefinite stay on the island.

The great interest was the well, where digging went on continuously. At eleven at night the diggers were twenty feet down, where they came across a layer of clay, into which there appeared to be a slight seepage. A little after midnight a bottle of muddy water was brought to the captain, who pronounced it to be fresh. This caused such a rush to the well that the captain posted a guard to allow the diggers to get on with their work, at the same time proclaiming that no water would be served out until there was an equal ration for everybody. At that moment there commenced a heavy fall of rain, which was collected as well as possible in sails and sheets, and gave everybody at least a mouthful, while the well-diggers completed their work by sinking a cask into the clay and lining the shaft with wood. Before noon the next day, the 20th February, every man had a pint of fresh water, tasting slightly of coconut, and the well was filling at a rate which promised at least two pints a day. The most dreaded of all calamities was averted.

At dawn next day the party on board the wreck found themselves surrounded by several Malay proas, some with swivels mounted in their bows, filled with about eighty Malays, well armed with spears and krises. As the wreck-party had no weapon of any kind, all they could do was to get into their boat and pull for the shore, pursued by the Malays. This was observed from the shore, and two boats with armed parties pushed out, on which the Malays gave over and returned to the wreck. Shortly a look-out reported that two proas were landing armed men at a point about two miles from the encampment.

It was at once assumed that they intended to attack, as it was well known that when these sea-Dyaks took a ship they invariably murdered everybody on board, and indeed some tribes were suspected of cannibalism, not improbable in those protein-starved rain-forest islands. Captain Maxwell therefore ordered all other activity to cease, and to prepare for defence.

A party under Mr Cheffy, the carpenter, felled the remaining trees on the hill-top and made an open stockade around the area. The boys were set to cutting saplings and branches and weaving them into the uprights, making a tolerable breastwork which would give some protection and certainly prevent a rush assault. Stock was taken of weapons; the Marines had thirty muskets and bayonets, but only seventy-five ball cartridges amongst them. The gunner, however, had drawn the charges from the quarter-deck carronades before leaving the ship, so that there was about a hundred pounds of loose coarse powder and some horns of fine for the pans; broken bottles supplied the place of shot. Spear-shafts were made from branches and saplings, and knives, chisels and ship-nails were fixed to the ends; when these ran out, sharpening the end of the shaft and hardening it in the fire made a good enough weapon for a stout arm. There were about a dozen cutlasses. When the breastwork was complete, and all hands mustered, every man had some sort of weapon and the determination to use it.

A scouting party now returned, and reported that the pirates had not actually landed on the island, but on some off-lying rocks, which they were using as a depository for their plunder from the wreck. Every precaution was nevertheless taken against a night attack. Parties were set to guard the boats and the well, and inside the stockade the men were arranged in their divisions, each with a place allotted in the event of an alarm.

Next morning, the 22nd February, some Malay boats approached the landing-place, and an officer went out to them, waving a green bough; they made no response to this overture, however, but returned to the rock. Captain Maxwell perceived that the pirates were now in two separated bodies, and ordered Second Lieutenant Hay (the first having gone to Batavia) to take three boats and a well-armed boarding party and attempt to regain possession of the wreck. As the boats approached, those on the rock threw their plunder into their proas and made sail away. There were two large proas at the ship, and these also made off; but first they set fire to the ship so efficiently that the boats were unable to board her, and returned to shore. This was no calamity, however, for Captain Maxwell had already made up his mind to burn her, so that when the upperworks and decks were destroyed it would be possible for stores to float up from below. What the Malays chiefly wanted were nails and copper and any kind of metalwork, which was of no interest to the castaways, so that if contact had been made some sort of accommodation might have been arranged, but this was not possible with such ferocious and suspicious savages. The ship burned all night, the flames lighting the shore, casting odd shadows, so that a sentry fired on a baboon which failed to answer his challenge. This was quite a good exercise, however, for instantly after the shot every man was at his station.

In the morning, while the captain took the Service, two boats were sent to the smouldering wreck and returned with some barrels of flour, cases of wine, and—cheers!—a cask of beer; so that everybody had a Sunday pint. The lookout reported that most of the Malays had gone no further than an islet two miles away, but some had made sail apparently for Belitung. This suggested that they had sent for reinforcements, so all efforts were made to improve the position by cutting trees and burning undergrowth outside the stockade, to strengthen the work and to clear a field of fire. At the same time every effort was made to secure more ammunition and provisions from the wreck.

Nothing more was seen of the pirates until first light on Wednesday the 26th, when two proas with canoes astern were seen stealing into the cove where the boats were moored. Lieutenant Hay, who had the night watch, immediately sallied at them with his boats, on which the Malays cut their canoes adrift and made sail away. The boat with Hay overtook one of them, which fired its swivels without hitting anything, and the boat's crew boarded; four of the pirates were killed in a short desperate struggle, five jumped overboard and were not seen again, and two were taken prisoner. The proa would have been a useful prize, but the Malays had scuttled her and she sank almost immediately.

Later that morning fourteen more proas appeared, and anchored off the islet two miles off; one appeared to be much larger than the others, and to carry some rajah or other magnate. This gave rise to some hopes of a treaty, but the next day, the 27th, the rajah was observed superintending the plundering of the wreck, which went on for the next few days. Meantime Captain Maxwell had his boats moved to another and safer cove, where two little fortlets were erected on rocks which covered the entrance. On the 1st of March fourteen more proas arrived, and during that night several more were observed, but too indistinctly to count them. Next morning, while a number surrounded the wreck, twenty of the largest vessels approached the landing place, and anchored in a line about a cable from the shore; firing their swivels, beating gongs, and altogether making a most belligerent display. They did not yet attempt a landing, but it seemed certain that they were only waiting for nightfall.

At divisions that evening Captain Maxwell made his men a speech. 'My lads, you must all have observed the great increase in the enemy's force, and the threatening posture they have assumed. I have reason to believe they will attack us this night. I do not wish to conceal our real state, because I do not think there is a man here who is afraid to face any sort of danger. We are in a position to defend ourselves against regular troops, far less a set of naked savages, with their spears and krises. It is true they have swivels in their boats, but they cannot act here. I have not observed that they have any muskets, but if they have, so have we. When we were first thrown on shore we could only muster seventy-five ball cartridges—we have now sixteen hundred. They cannot send up, I believe, more than five hundred men; but with two hundred such as now stand around me, I do not fear a thousand—nor fifteen hundred of them. The pikemen standing firm, we shall give them such a volley of musketry as they will be little prepared for; and when they are thrown into confusion, we will sally out, chase them into the water, and ten to one but we secure their vessels. Let every man be on the alert, and should these barbarians this night attempt our hill, I trust we shall convince them that they are dealing with Britons.'

The loud cheers with which this harangue was received may have had a deterrent effect on the pirates, for the expected attack was not made. They retained their position, however, and next morning, 3rd March, it was observed that ten more proas had joined during the night. The situation now began to look gloomy; the relief ship was long overdue, and the feeling was that the boats with Lord Amherst must have come to grief; provisions were running down, while the strength of the enemy was continually growing. In such circumstances, it appeared that the only thing was to make a night attack with the four boats, capture some proas, man them also and try to capture more, so as to get enough shipping to take the whole company to Batavia. The raft was obviously of no use, as towing it would make movement very slow, and men on it would be exposed to the fire of the swivels on the proas, whereas in the boats and captured proas they would be at least as fast as the enemy and well able to defend themselves with musketry. The general idea was for two boats to attack one proa; this would give two proas, and while the boarding parties were taking them the crews would row ashore for more.

Detailed orders for this desperate attempt were being prepared, when the look-out reported a sail at a great distance to the south. A passing squall concealed it from sight, and some thought that the look-out had mistaken the forward streamers of the squall for a sail; however, an experienced signalman was sent up with a telescope, and in about half an hour he was able to assert that it was a square-rigged vessel, either a ship or a brig, standing directly for the island. Shortly the pirates also, from their lower position, saw the approaching sail, which caused some consternation among them. Captain Maxwell now ordered almost all the company to advance under cover of the mangroves, and attack the proas by wading, the tide now being almost at the bottom of the ebb. This had been foreseen by the pirates, however, and as soon as the men emerged from the cover of the mangroves the nearest proa fired her swivel at them, without effect, and all the proas got under way and made sail with great dexterity. The Marines waded out breast-deep to fire on them, but no hits were observed; indeed, breast-deep in surging water is not the best position for using a weapon of precision, far less a smooth-bore flint-lock musket. However, the attack had the desired effect of driving the pirates away completely, for they were never seen again, although no doubt they would later return to break up the remains of the wreck.

The vessel turned out to be the TERNATE, one of the Honourable Company's armed ships, Captain Ellis, which had been despatched by Lord Amherst the day he arrived at Batavia. It was evening before the captain was able to get ashore, and he has recorded the scene within the stockade: the shelters, covered with sailcloth or with palm-leaves; the wild appearance of the men, unshaven and ragged, with their rough pikes and cutlasses in their hands, glinting in the firelight; and the perfect discipline with which they fell into their divisions on the word of command.

On arrival at Batavia, Lord Amherst chartered the Company's ship CAESAR to take the whole party to England, and after a prosperous voyage, touching at Cape Town, the ship reached St Helena on the 27th June 1817. Napoleon received the party with great courtesy, and when Lord Amherst presented Captain Maxwell, the Exile, bowing with great dignity, said (with his extraordinary memory) that the name was known to him, from the Adriatic. 'Your government must not blame you for the loss of the ALCESTE, for you have taken one of my frigates.' When they arrived in England, Captain Maxwell stood his court martial for the loss of the ALCESTE, and was honourably acquitted in the most gratifying terms, and shortly afterwards he was knighted. On the whole, Sir Murray Maxwell had no cause to regret his voyage to China and his shipwreck; he had demonstrated once more to the world the qualities of a British crew, well commanded, in striking contrast to the *Medusa* disaster the year before; he had had a rollicking adventure; and he had not lost a man.

Glossary

All terms are defined in the sense they bore during the period of the book.

ABACK: a sail is aback when the wind is pressing it against the mast.

ABOUT: to go about is to change course, especially when tacking.

ANCHOR: bower, those stowed nearest the head; best bower, then on the starboard, small bower on larboard; both same size. Sheet anchors, those stowed aft of the bowers. Stream anchor, a smaller size. Kedge anchor, usually with more than two flukes, used for dragging-off a grounded vessel.

BACK: a wind backs if its direction changes counter-clockwise.

BEATING: proceeding to windward in a series of zig-zags; tacking.

BRACES: ropes fastened to the yard-arms, for swinging them around.

BROACH-TO: to lose steerage way and lie helpless parallel to the troughs of the waves.

CAT-HEAD: a short strong beam projecting from the side of the fore-castle, to which an anchor is made fast.

CLEW: the lower corner of a square-sail, or aft corner of a fore-and-aft.

CLEW-EARRING: the loop of rope projecting from the clew of a sail, by which it is made fast to the yard.

CLOSE-HAULED: sailing as near to the wind as possible.

CRANK: unstable, liable to capsize.

DRIVER, or spanker; the largest fore-and-aft sail on a full-rigged ship, spread by boom and gaff from the mizzen mast.

FISH: to repair a mast or spar by lashing small timber around it.

HEAVE-TO: to set one or more sails aback, so as to take the way off the ship.

KNOT: a denomination of speed, signifying one nautical mile per hour.

LATEEN: a large triangular sail set on a sloping yard.

LARGE: a large wind is a favourable one, abaft the beam.

RAKE: in gunnery, to sweep the whole length of a ship with shot.

SPRING: to anchor on a spring, a rope is passed out of a stern-port, brought forward and made fast to the anchor-ring before letting go; after the anchor is fast in the ground, hauling or slackening this rope swings the ship as desired.

VEER: a wind veers when its direction changes clockwise.

WAY: a ship is under way when it is moving through the water under control.

WEIGH: to heave up the anchors.

WEAR: when a ship, having been sailing close-hauled, causes the bow to turn away from the wind so as to sail more large, she is said to wear.

Notes on the plates

Plate 1 This splendid painting by Collis is accurate in every detail. The INDEFATIGABLE, crossing the stern of the *Droits de l'Homme*, has backed her main topsail to stop her in that favourable position. The *Droits de l'Homme* is running with the wind under all possible sail in such a tempest, and is taking in one of her jibs, to ease the fore topmast, which was shortly to come down. THE AMAZON is coming up under such a press of sail which shows zeal to get into the fight rather than prudence. See page 38 et seq.

Plate 2 A spirited drawing of the chief French success of the wars. The corvette *Bayonnaise* has rammed the frigate AMBUSCADE, carrying away her mizzen mast, and the French are boarding and capturing the much larger and more powerful British ship. See page 77 et seq.

Plate 3 The SAN FIORENZE engaging the *Piémontaise* off Cape Comorin, in defence of three East India ships. This engagement is not narrated in the text, being a usual policing job for the frigates, but was a tough one; after a running fight of three days the French ship surrendered. This fine oil painting by Pocock is most accurate, except of course that all the ships are 'closed up' to make the picture.

Plate 4 The FISGARD engaging the *Immortalité*. See page 92 et seq.

Plate 5 Cutting out the *Hermione* from the fortified harbour of Puerto-Caballo in the Caribbean, by the boats of the SURPRISE, seen in the distance. This magnificent painting by Pocock is correct in every detail. Some of the boarding party can be seen aloft making sail while the battle rages furiously on the decks. See page 54 et seq.

Plate 6 SYBILLE and *Forte*. The end of the battle, as the last mast of the *Forte* comes down. See page 73 et seq.

Plate 7 Basque Roads. The IMPERIEUSE leading in the lighter vessels to attack the stranded French ships, which were, of course, not so crowded together as shown. The wreck of the *Jean Bart* is seen in the left foreground; she had stranded a month before while entering the anchorage. See page 115.

Plate 8 Basque Roads. The IMPERIEUSE, 38 guns, attacking the *Calcutta*, 50, which was shortly abandoned by her whole crew; for which the captain was afterwards tried and shot. See page 115.

Plate 9 SAN FIORENZE taking possession of the *Piémontaise*. See plate 3.

Plate 10 ALCESTE and ACTIVE capturing the *Pomone*, off Ancona. The ALCESTE engaged first, was damaged and had to turn away for repair, when the ACTIVE came up to her support. See page 168 and page 177.

Plate 11 The *Constitution* escaping from a powerful British squadron by towing and kedging during a calm. This American drawing is accurate as far as the *Constitution* is concerned, but is by no means so with the British frigates, especially the GUERRIERE. A month later the *Constitution* met the GUERRIERE alone and destroyed her. See page 144.

Plate 12 The GUERRIERE captured by the *Constitution*. She was so much wrecked that she was burned. See page 145 et seq.

Plate 13 The MACEDONIAN captured by the *United States*. Remarkably accurate depiction of the state of the MACEDONIAN just before surrender. See page 147 et seq.

Plate 14 The *Constitution* capturing the JAVA off Salvador, Brazil. The JAVA was shot to pieces and had to be burned, while the *Constitution* had to return home for repairs. See page 150 et seq.

Plate 15 The *Chesapeake* boarded by the crew of the SHANNON. This was probably the last time an important ship was carried by the cutlass. See page 157 et seq.

Plate 16 The *Essex*, left, engaged by the PHOEBE (centre) and the CHERUB, off Valparaiso. It is hard to say what part of the action this is intended to show; the *Essex* lost her main topmast in a squall before the action commenced. By the American artist Corne, who also did the engraving reproduced in Plate 11. See page 166 et seq.

Jacket illustration Squadron off Lissa. The key manœuvre which resulted eventually in Captain Hoste's amazing victory against odds of more than two to one. See page 131 et seq.

APPENDIX 2

Tonnage

Tonnage has always been a calculation, and varies very widely according to the factors used. It has been said to have been originally based on the number of tuns of wine which could be stowed, but there are doubts on this theory. At the period covered by this book, tonnage was calculated thus:

Length × breadth × ½ breadth, divided by 94.

In Britain, the measure was taken (in feet) from the outside of the stem to the outside of the sternpost, and for the breadth over the outside of the planking. In America, the length was measured inside the posts, and the breadth over the framing excluding the planking; and the divisor was 95. Thus when the *President* was captured and brought into Portsmouth, it was found that whereas by American measure she was 1,444 tons, by British measure she was 1,533. This caused a silly outcry that the Americans were trying to deceive the world about the real size of their frigates; but the methods of American surveyors were well known, and any nation could adopt any factors they pleased. The general idea was to arrive at a 'ton' of 100 cubic feet, and the American method was probably more accurate.

At present, there are in Britain four methods of estimating tonnage, which arrive at widely different results; and there are about a dozen more elsewhere. They can't all be right.

TABLES

TABLE I

Strength of the Royal Navy, 1794 compared with 1814

Rate	Guns	Average tonnage	1794				1814			
			In full commission	Reserve or repair	Relegated		In full commission	Reserve or repair	Relegated	
First 3 decks	100/120	2,500	5	1	none		7	none	2	
Second 3 decks	98	2,200	9	7	3		5	3	4	
Third 2 decks	64/80	1,750	71	24	22		87	16	80	
Fourth 2 decks	50	1,100	8	4	7		8	2	9	
Fifth 2 decks	44	900	12	3	3		2	none	1	
Fifth Frigates	32/44	900	66	3	4		121	11	45	
Sixth Frigates	28	600	22	2	4		none	none	4	
Sixth Post-ship	20/24	500	10	2	2		25	4	11	
Unrated vessels	4/18	70/450	76	3	7		360	6	46	

TABLE II

Comparative force of the frigates of the Royal Navy, 1794 compared with 1814

Rating by long guns	Average tonnage	Main battery (pounders)	1794			1814		
			In full commission	Reserve or repair	Relegated	In full commission	Reserve or repair	Relegated
44	1,400	24	none	none	none	1	none	2
40	1,260	24	none	none	none	5	none	none
40	1,150	18	none	none	none	1	2	none
38	1,050	18	11	none	none	51	6	12
36	950	18	8	none	1	48	3	10
36	930	12	10	none	3	3	none	11
32	900	18	1	none	none	3	none	4
32	750	12	36	3	3	9	none	4
28	600	12	22	2	4	none	none	4

Index

In this index, names of British warships are in SMALL CAPITALS
Names of enemy warships are in *italics*
People, places and topics are in ordinary type
Ranks are those at the time of mention
Abbreviations: Adm–Admiral: Cmdre Commodore; Cdr–Commander

The figure in brackets after the name of a ship denotes her rated number of guns; the number actually carried was usually greater

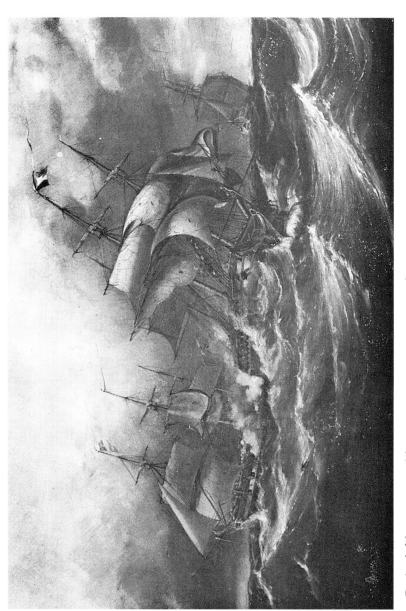

1 *Droits de l'homme* engaged by INDEFATIGABLE: AMAZON coming up

9. AMBUSCADE boarded and captured by *Bayonnaise*

3 SAN FIORENZE and *Piémontaise*

4 FISGARD and *Immortalité*

5 Boats of the SURPRISE cutting out the *Hermione*

6 SYBILLE taking the *Forte*

7 Basque Roads. IMPERIEUSE leading in

8 IMPERIEUSE and *Calcutta*

SAN FIORENZE taking possession of *Piémontaise*

10 ALCESTE and ACTIVE capturing the *Pomone*

11 *Constitution* escaping from a British squadron

12 GUERRIERE captured by *Constitution*

13 MACEDONIAN captured by *United States*

14 JAVA captured by *Constitution*

15 *Chesapeake* boarded and captured by SHANNON

16 *Essex* (left) engaged and captured by PHOEBE and CHERUB

1 A French chasse-marée chased by a brig

2 The SCOURGE and the *Sans-Culotte*

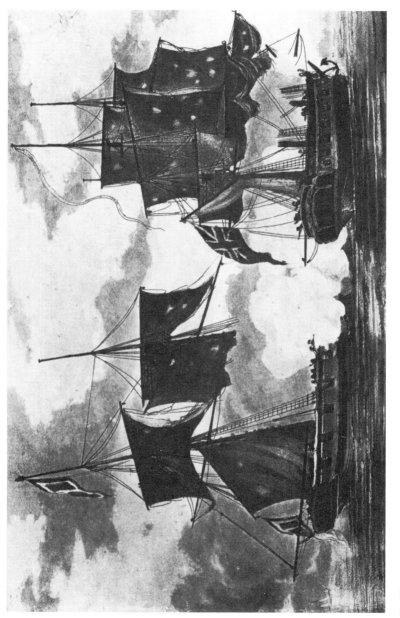

3 The ANTELOPE and the *Atalante*

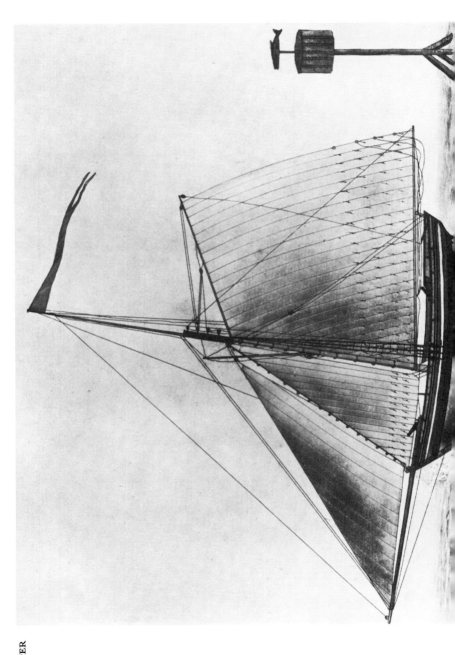

4 The VIPER

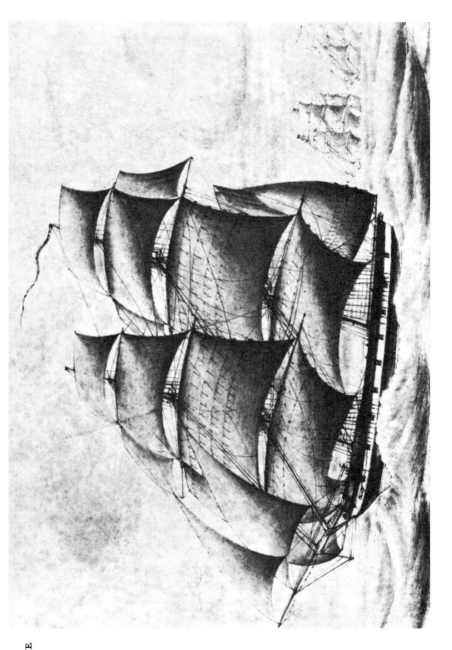

5 The
WOLVERINE

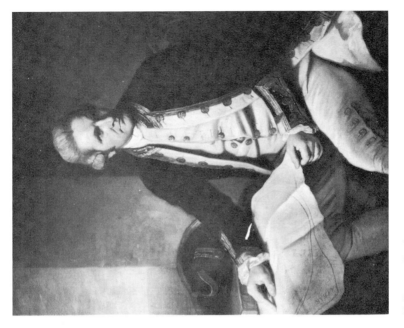

7 James Cook

6 Thomas, Lord Cochrane

8 The *Wasp* and the REINDEER

9 The *Hornet* sinking the PEACOCK

Sloops
and Brigs

*An account of the smallest vessels of the Royal Navy
during the great wars 1793 to 1815*

by James Henderson CBE

*Drawings by
Ernest E Relf*

PEN & SWORD MILITARY CLASSICS

Dedicated to the 20,000 men who served in the Light Coastal Force during the War from 1939 to 1945, of whom scarcely one in twenty was of the regular Royal Navy; who manned over 1500 ships of under 100 tons, and fought in 782 engagements; and in salutation to the complements of the 176 light craft which failed to report.

Sloops and Brigs
Contents

Plates

Notes on the plates are on pages 173 to 175

The author is indebted to the Trustees of the National Maritime Museum, Greenwich for their kind permission to publish the plates reproduced in this book

Author's Notes

To avoid any possible confusion, the name of every ship under British command is printed in SMALL CAPITALS; the names of ships of all other nations are printed in *italics*.

Dates are given fully and frequently, to avoid the annoyance of having to turn back to remind oneself. Naval accounts are very liable to be short of full dates, as the ships' logs of the period showed the day of the month, but named the month only on the 1st, and the year only on 1st January.

Facing forward in a ship, the starboard side is on the right hand; that on the left is now called port, but until well into the nineteenth century it was called larboard; the contemporary expression of larboard is used here, as there is no possibility of confusion in writing.

At that period, every officer commanding a warship, however small, was always called 'Captain' on all occasions. All sloops and lesser ships were however captained by a commander or lieutenant, who reverted to his substantive rank immediately he ceased to command the ship. A post captain, commanding a ship of 20 guns nominal or larger, was a captain for life, until he attained flag rank or committed some such fault that he was dismissed the service. He could not be reduced in rank. In this book every officer is called by his substantive rank, to avoid any confusion between the lordly captain of a 74 and the humble lieutenant who was nevertheless 'Captain' of a 70-ton schooner.

The modern yachtsman is accustomed to think of a 'sloop' as a small single-masted vessel of simple cutter rig, usually Bermuda type. At the time of which we write, however, a sloop was a full-rigged ship of 300 to 400 tons, the largest which could be commanded by an officer of less rank than post Captain.

1

The Ships

A great fleet is sailing down the Channel. Standing on Beachy Head, you can see neither the van nor the rear, for it stretches over sixty miles of sea, and with a fair wind will take a long summer's day to pass. The fleet is all small vessels, although it includes tall three-masted full-rigged ships as well as two-masted brigs and single-masted cutters. These are the little ships which Britain sent out to war against the French Republic and against Napoleon; ships too small to be 'rated', too small to be commanded by a post captain; but each with a purpose, each with a duty, and many of them to perform astounding feats of naval warfare. If you wait long enough, perhaps you will see a much smaller fleet returning; for of seven hundred ships sent out, more than three hundred failed to report.

In the earlier wars of the eighteenth century and the later seventeenth, the emphasis was on the line of battle; there was little use for a ship which could not 'lie in the line' except to carry despatches. At the great battle off the Gunfleet Sand in 1666 both the British and the Dutch deployed almost a hundred battleships apiece, three times as many as fought at Trafalgar. In the Republican and Napoleonic wars the British line of battle rarely exceeded a hundred ships altogether, and only six times in the more than twenty years of war was there a fleet engagement; the rest of the time the great ships were wearily blockading the French fleets in their various ports – fleets far too powerful to be let loose, which by their mere presence in their harbours as 'a fleet in being' immobilised the battle strength of the Royal Navy. The active part of the war was to be carried out by the smaller rated ships, the frigates, whose work I have elsewhere described, and by the light vessels, the unrated, the sloops and brigs.

This deployment of the little ships was made possible by a remarkable step in naval gunnery, the invention of the carronade. This was designed by General Robert Melville, and the first was cast at the Carron works in Scotland, near Falkirk, in 1779. This was of enormous bore, a 68-pounder, but in practice it was found that the 32-pound shot, the heaviest thrown by the long guns of the largest ships, would smash through any timber that could be built into a ship. A few 68-pounders were issued to very large ships, to be loaded with one round shot and a keg of 500 musket balls, chiefly to deter boarders; the first shot fired by VICTORY at Trafalgar was exactly this, smashing through the cabin of the *Bucentaure* with devastating effect. Ships of the line and frigates were given a few carronades for their upperworks, but most of the little ships were completely re-armed, if their construction was suitable. The enhancement of force was extraordinary. The 18-gun ship-sloop had formerly carried just that number of 6-pounders on her main deck, her upperworks being unarmed except for muskets; now she carried 18 carronades, 32-pounders, on her main deck, and six carronades, 18-pounders, on her forecastle and quarter-deck, along with two long 6-pounders as bow and stern chasers. This gave her a broadside twice as heavy as that of a 32-gun frigate of twice her tonnage.

There were of course some snags; the range of the carronade, half a mile, was only half that of a long gun; but then most actions took place inside two hundred yards. Carronades were liable to overheat, recoil too violently, over-turn, or break the tackle which fastened them to the ship's side; but all these risks could be accepted in return for a quadrupling of the fighting force of the vessel. Sloops and brigs could now undertake convoy duties, and not only beat off the French privateers which swooped out from that coast, but also pursue them among the shoals and reefs of their harbourages, where heavier vessels could not venture. They could be consort to long-gun ships; for example, when the frigate PHOEBE sailed to the South Pacific to search for the American frigate *Essex* she was accompanied by the ship-sloop CHERUB, invaluable for nosing into ill-chartered harbours, and able to account for herself in the final engagement. Many sloops were used on the East Indies station, sounding into little-known coasts in advance of the heavier ships.

The big ships of the Royal Navy were almost all built in the Royal Dockyards, which alone had the facilities for dealing with ships of 2,000 tons; but of the unrated ships few exceeded 400 tons, well within the capacity of most shipyards building merchantmen, and the majority were built by contract; as the Navy could not spare any experienced officers to 'stand by' a small ship in building, a good deal had to be left to the honesty of the contractor, which was not always impeccable. Most of the small ships for the East India station were built at Bombay, under the supervision of the Honourable Company, thus saving the long voyage round the Cape in a small vessel which could not carry water and provision for the voyage without putting in somewhere. These were mostly teak-built, a splendid sea timber, but open to one objection : in action most wounds were by splinters, and a splinter wound from teak was almost sure to go septic. For the North American station, many of the smaller ships were built in Bermuda, of the local cedar, a wood very soft but very durable; it had the advantage that shot would usually go through it without scattering deadly splinters all around.

There was an apparent anomaly connected with the introduction of the carronade : it was never included in the stated force of a warship. Thus a 36-gun frigate remained a 36, although she would in fact mount 10 carronades, doubling her weight of broadside; and an 18-gun sloop remained an 18-gun sloop, even if she were armed with 26 heavy carronades. There was reason of a sort behind this : a ship of twenty guns or over had to be commanded by a post captain, and there just wasn't room on the captains list for all the commanders of sloops as well. Moreover, the pay and privileges of most of the officers depended on the rating of their ship. The whole system was ultimately reformed, but not until after the end of the wars.

Tables are rather dreary, especially for those who compile them; but a glance at Table I will give a picture of the little-ship Navy, at the beginning and end of the wars; beginning with 52 ships and ending, after all losses, with 339 in full commission. The first class, the quarter-decked ship-sloop, only began building after the first war started, but there were 33 when the wars ended. With the formidable armament already described they were effective ships of war, and there were few squadrons which did not have at least one of them. Some, such as the ARROW and the DART, were far more powerful than rated ships commanded by post captains, but sloops they remained, and we shall hear more about them. The disadvantage of these sloops was that they could not carry provisions and water for very long voyages without calling in somewhere for supplies, thus giving away their location; so that for inter-ocean passages they were usually attached to a frigate or squadron, from which they could draw stores. The flush-decked ships could carry only their rated number of guns, and these were usually left as 6-pounder long guns.

The brig-sloop was a two-masted square-rigged vessel, so handy for all sorts of odd jobs that we begin with less than 15 and finish with more than 150. They could carry no more than their rated guns, 6-pounders in the 18-gun class and 4-pounders in the others; but quite a number were armed with 18- and 24-pound carronades. The 18-gun brig-sloops were quite as powerful as the 18-gun flush-decked ship-sloops, which they superseded, being handier in every way and requiring less crew. Their later armament was sixteen 32-pounder carronades and two long 6s as chase guns, a formidable force. The stores question limited their range, and most of the British-built brigs were used in European waters, while locally-built brigs were used on the American and East Indian stations; but they were quite capable of sailing anywhere in the world as long as they could get supplies.

The bomb-ketch was a very specialised ship, of odd appearance, like a sloop with its foremast removed and its mainmast greatly enlarged. The space between the mainmast and the bowsprit was given over to the two mortars, one 11-inch and one 13-inch, mounted on special decks stuffed up with cut lengths of old rope to lessen the effect of the recoil on the ship's timbers. The forestays of the huge mainmast were made of iron chain, because of the great flash upwards when the mortars were fired. The mortars were fixed, and the only way of using them was to moor the ship with springs on the cables, and swing the ship with these until the mortars were more or less in the line wanted. Range was adjusted by the amount of gunpowder – 'Another half-shovel, there!' The bursting charge was set off by a fuse, which could be adjusted in length; when loading, the fuse was downwards, so as to be ignited by the discharge. The idea of pitching large explosive bombs at a high angle into otherwise impregnable positions was quite a good one, but it was seldom successful. For one thing, though the 11-inch mortar was reliable enough, the 13-inch usually split after less than twenty shots. The other armament of the bomb-ketch consisted of eight guns abaft the mainmast, at first 6-pounder long guns, later 24-pounder carronades. On account of this not very formidable battery bomb-ketches were often used for convoy and other duties for which they were not designed. As they had to be very strongly built to take the kick of the mortars, after the wars were over they were used by Admiralty for Arctic exploration – HECLA, EREBUS and TERROR being the most famous.

Anything smaller than a bomb-ketch was not commanded by a Commander but by a Lieutenant, a distinction to which we shall revert later. Gun-brigs were much smaller than brig-sloops, and the only class of any importance was the 12-gun brig, of which there were 67 at the end of the wars; originally intended for 4-pounder long guns but soon mounting 18-pound carronades, with a complement of about 50 men and boys. These light vessels were mostly used on Baltic convoys, and suffered a lot of rough handling from the Danish rowing gunboats, well-armed and well-manned, equally competent in calms or squalls.

The schooners and cutters were mostly employed in carrying despatches – *avisos* the Spaniards called them. The largest class was the 10-gun cutter, of which we find 24 at the close of play. One or more were attached to every fleet, but they were not expected to take part in a fleet action – indeed, the forecastle carronades of a ship of the line would have shattered any of them into flinders. Their duty was to hang about on the fringe of the battle making observations, repeating signals, and afterwards to carry the despatches home. Thus the little schooner PICKLE, Lieutenant Lapenotiere, brought home Collingwood's despatches after Trafalgar, having taken no part in the fighting; but she was present, and the lieutenant received a hundred-guinea sword from Lloyd's Patriotic Fund, like every other captain of a ship in the action. The general idea was that these small ships, being fore-and-aft rigged, could lie at least a point nearer the wind than any square-rigged ship, and could therefore dodge any powerful interception; a theory which quite frequently worked.

The smallest class of all was the 4-gun schooner, about 75 tons, with a complement of about 20 men and boys. These were built at Bermuda of the local cedar, an excellent timber for the purpose; originally they carried 4-pounder long guns, later 12-pounder carronades. These vessels have been much decried by early naval writers as being too small for any real fighting, crank, liable to overset, bad sailers, etc; but it is impossible to believe that the expert Bermudan shipbuilders could build so badly ships of a size and type to which they were so well accustomed. Much more probably the crews and officers, trained in square-riggers, could not well handle the unfamiliar Bermudan rig; also they were liable, through ignorance, to be sent out in the hurricane season. They were intended mainly to seek out the nests of pirates which still infested the Caribbean seas, and would no doubt have been more successful if manned by Bermudans; but the canny islanders had more profitable employment elsewhere. As for size, it is worth remembering that in the Second World War the Royal Navy built more than 1,500 ships of less than 75 tons, with complements of less than 20 men, almost all RNVR or HO. Those tiny warships with their amateur crews made a notable contribution to the history of the Royal Navy.

Key to rig drawings

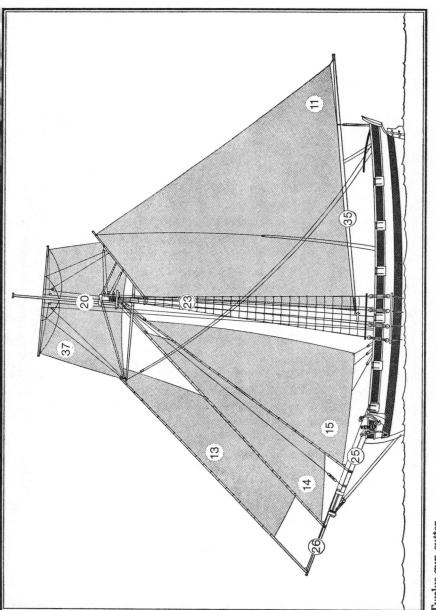

Twelve gun cutter

Eighteen gun (actual) brig-sloop

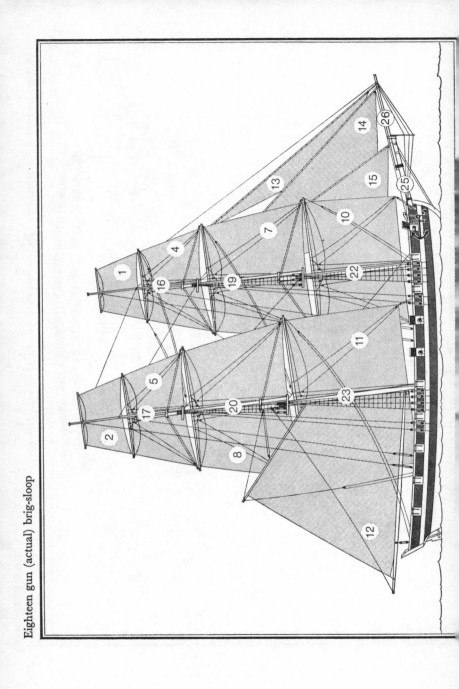

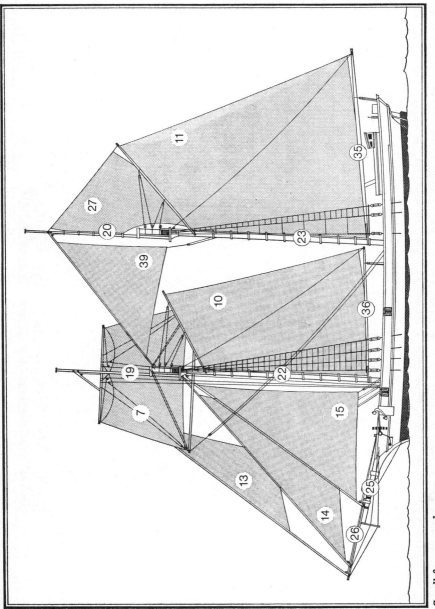

Small four-gun schooner

Eighteen gun (nominal) ship-sloop

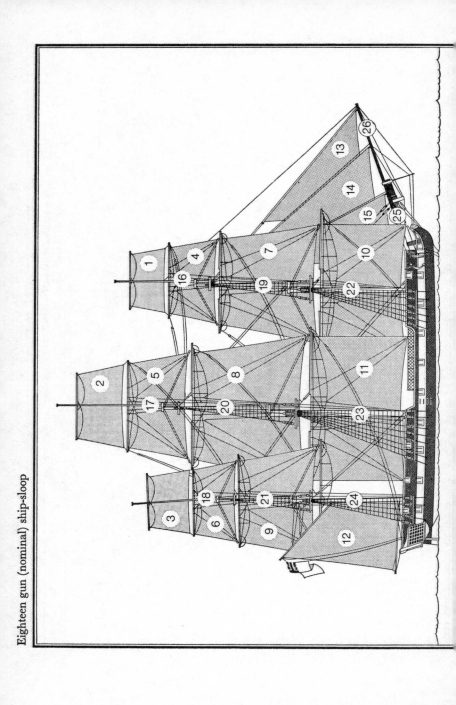

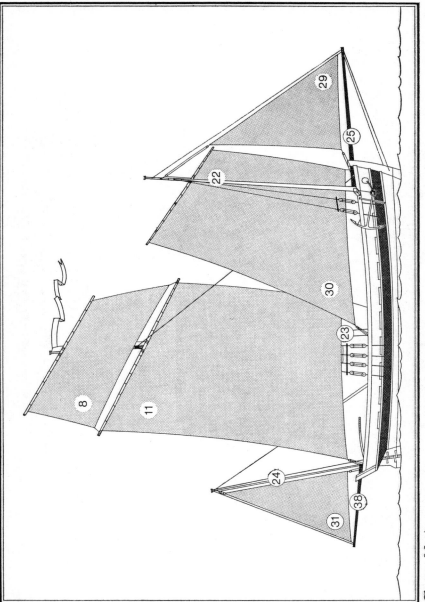

Chasse - Marée

Bark similar to WOLVERINE

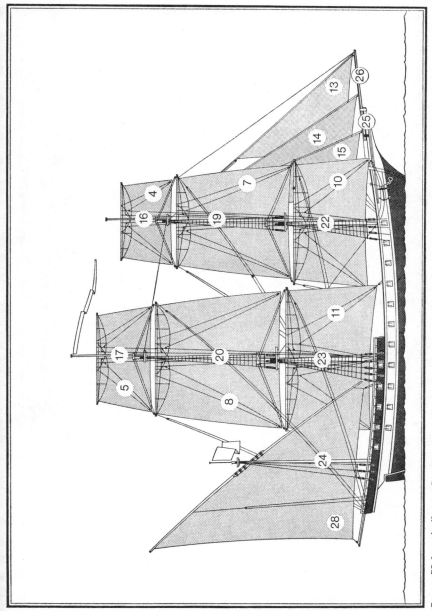

Large Xebec similar to *Gamo*

Bomb ketch similar to ACHERON

2

The Men

'There are no bad soldiers – only bad officers.' The old maxim was especially to be regarded in the case of the small ships, where a few men had to live for many months jammed together in inescapable proximity. The officer had to preserve at all times a strict and steady discipline; he had to keep his crew healthy and, if possible, happy; their morale and training high; and meanwhile he had to live almost among them, except that he had the after end of the deck and a dog-kennel of a cabin to which he could retreat. How were such officers selected?

The promotion system of the Georgian Navy was quite different from that of today; influence, then called 'interest' was essential. This is not to say that influence is not useful even in the modern Navy, where it is often necessary to choose one out of ten for a desirable posting; but there are no more post captains of eighteen years of age. Such great commanders as Pellew, Rainier and Nelson quite brazenly used their influence to have their relatives promoted post captain without any evidence whatever of their fitness for command. The reason was the system of promotion: below post captain there was no certainty whatever; once on the captains' ladder, promotion was by seniority *only*. Whether employed or on half pay, the captain went up through the captains list and through the flag officers list by survival only; only death or disgrace could knock him off the ladder. Thus if Nelson's uncle had not been Comptroller of the Navy he would not have been 'made post' at twenty, and therefore would not have been Rear-Admiral in time to have commanded the fleet at the Nile, nor Vice-Admiral in time to have been Commander-in-Chief, Mediterranean, at Trafalgar. This pressure by the influential to have their protegés pushed forward early meant of course that many able officers without such influence were kept back, and might even spend their whole naval career in the rank of midshipman; although, to the credit of Admiralty, such were usually promoted to lieutenant before retirement, so that they might have at least, for life, the half pay of that rank; there was nothing at all for midshipmen.

Sloops and brigs were too small to be commanded by a post captain; but the very smallest could be commanded only by a commissioned officer, which at that time meant a lieutenant; and for bomb-ketches and above, an appointed commander. There were two main streams from which such officers were fished : 'fortune's favourites' and 'the plodders'. The first class fell into two tributaries : those who had enough 'interest' to be brought into the flag-ship of the Commander-in-Chief of the station, which would carry eight lieutenants and up to twenty midshipmen, of approved social status; and the hero type. It became customary, after a well-fought and successful engagement, to promote the first lieutenant of each ship engaged to commander. These two sub-classes of 'fortune's favourites' were the more usual commanders of the larger sloops and brigs, not for long as a rule, because they flashed on to post rank after any kind of meritorious service. In the class-conscious society of that period, command sat more easily on the shoulders of gentlemen of good birth and breeding. The 'plodders', on the other hand, had nothing but capability and zeal to offer, and their promotion was slow. This hope deferred, which maketh the heart sick, had different effects on different men. Consider the two most famous 'plodders', who flourished a little before our period.

James Cook was well known in the Navy as the most competent hydrographer, cartographer and astronomer in the service, who had done much to make possible the taking of Quebec in 1759; but at forty years of age he was still a warrant officer, as sailing master, when in 1768 he was commissioned lieutenant in order to command the armed merchantman ENDEAVOUR on a scientific expedition to the South Seas. For his second great voyage he was promoted commander, so that he might command the sloop-of-war RESOLUTION on a similar exploration. As a reward he was made post captain in 1775 at the age of 47, and for his last voyage was in RESOLUTION with another sloop-of-war under his command. Thus the greatest of all navigators had never a larger command than a couple of 300-tonners, but this had no effect on his temper or spirits; he knew he was performing a great service, which nobody else could do so well, and it was the service that mattered. When he was murdered at Hawaii, his Lieutenant King, who continued his narrative, wrote :

> Thus fell our great and excellent commander.... How sincerely his loss was felt and lamented by those who had so long found their general security in his skill and conduct, and every consolation in their hardships in his tenderness and humanity, it is neither necessary nor possible for me to describe; much less shall I attempt to paint the horror with which we were struck, and the universal dejection and dismay which followed so dreadful and unexpected a calamity.

A notable epitaph, and from a shipmate.
The other 'plodder', for contrast, was William Bligh, who had sailed round the world with Cook and was promoted lieutenant in 1787, at the age of thirty-three, in order to command the armed transport ship BOUNTY, for a single purpose of transporting specimens of the breadfruit tree to the West Indies. He made the little ship of 215 tons an absolute hell for his crew, who, as is very well known, mutinied and turned him off in the

C

ship's launch, with the eighteen men, almost all officers or petty officers, who stood to their orders. The voyage they made, of 3,618 nautical miles to Timor, stands as one of the great sagas of the sea, and Bligh comes very well out of this; but when Government sent out a frigate to Tahiti and caught ten of the mutineers to bring home for trial, they all insisted that it was his brutal tyranny that had caused the mutiny, not the attractions of the Tahitan *vahinas*; and indeed Cook touched four or five times at Tahiti without a single desertion. It is interesting that one of the mutineers remarked that Bligh was no better born than any of themselves; they *preferred* the class system. They were all hanged, of course; but it is worth remarking that much later, when Bligh was Governor of New South Wales, he was deposed and imprisoned by the unanimous decision of the *military* officers on the station, because of his sadistic brutality. There was another William Bligh also a captain, and their naval nicknames are of interest: one was called 'Breadfruit Bligh', and the other 'Gentleman Bligh'.

Here we have two very different results of late promotion of really able men, philanthropist and misanthrope; no doubt the majority of the 'passed-overs' fell between these, concealing their disappointment and forbearing to revenge themselves on those under their command. It was with such that the smallest ships were usually officered; so many were being built that a great number of half-pay lieutenants had to be given the opportunity of a command, however small. Admirals usually preferred the older officers for such jobs as carrying despatches; they could be trusted to carry out their instructions with accuracy, not going out of the way to seek a brush with the enemy.

The largest sloops carried a fairly full complement of officers and men, not far short of that of a small frigate, which had twice the tonnage, so that quarters were close, very close. In addition to the commander, there were usually in the wardroom two lieutenants, lieutenant of Marines, sailing master, purser and surgeon; elsewhere were the standing warrant officers, the gunner, boatswain and carpenter, who remained more or less permanently with the ship whether in commission or not, having their families living on board when she was under repair or 'in ordinary'. These were appointed by Admiralty Warrant, and could not be disrated by the commander. Lesser warrant officers were the sergeant of Marines, the sailmaker, the master-at-arms, and the armourer. All of these petty officers had one or more mates, who berthed with the rest of the crew forward; then the cook and his mates, very important, the commander's steward and coxswain, and the wardroom stewards, who were usually youngsters. The Marines, usually about twenty, were berthed between the crew and the officers' quarters, in case of mutiny by night. The forward quarters were very tight indeed; it was quite impossible for the whole of the crew to sleep at the same time, but of course the exigencies of the service required that the crew be divided into two watches, four hours on and four hours off, except for the short dog watches, 4 to 6 p.m. and 6 to 8 p.m., which ensured that each watch was on a different time every day. Some captains tried a three-watch system, and even a quarter system, but these do not appear to have been successful, probably because of the difficulty of bringing in the dog watches, which were popular with everybody; hammocks were not slung, and the watch below could 'make do and mend' or get convivial on the rum ration, which was issued at noon as a rule.

Discipline in close quarters is always difficult, and depends very much on the personality of the commander. So far as his officers went, he was lacking the awful gulf which divided the post captain of a frigate from his lieutenants, as well as the superior accommodation and the certainty of flag rank on suvival. 'Fortune's favourites' had seldom any difficulty; they were usually young men of rank and education, obviously on the way up, and their 'interest' might be of the greatest in years to come. The 'plodders' found it more difficult, but experienced and good-natured officers could command their men as well as Cook. Others tried to maintain their command by severity, sometimes degenerating into sadism, and this was the reason for the few mutinies. It will be seen on Table II that two sloops were lost by the crew mutinying and taking the ship into an enemy harbour (a 10-gun cutter in 1797 and a 14-gun brig-sloop in 1800); nothing like the frightful mutiny of the frigate HERMIONE, which I have described elsewhere, but all due to the same cause – excessive and unreasonable use of the lash. It is significant that at no time during the long wars did any enemy ship come in through the mutiny of her crew. French agents spread the news through the British fleets that there was no flogging in the French Navy, which was true, and it took some time for the sailors to discover that the French equivalent for fifty lashes was seven years in the galleys, which meant hard labour, mostly on road construction, with a 24-pound shot chained to one ankle.

Flogging was always a serious matter. Only the captain could order it, although if it were recommended by a lieutenant he would have little alternative. All hands were mustered to witness punishment and it had to be noted in the ship's log, which had to be handed into Admiralty at the conclusion of the commission. Admiralty were well aware of the chief reason for mutiny and desertion, and it became known that logs were being scrutinised for punishments. During the short-lived Peace of Amiens half the Navy was put 'in ordinary' and its officers on half pay ashore; and when it came to re-commissioning, those who had acquired a reputation as floggers tended to be overlooked. Some were given command of convict hulks; some, like Bligh, were given charge of convict settlements as far away as possible; some were left on the beach. The Nelson school encouraged officers to keep up morale by example rather than by terror. Flogging was retained in all its terrors, and indeed it is difficult to imagine what sanction could have taken its place in the circumstances; but it was used with discretion, and there was no more mutiny and much less desertion. All the officers, of course, had been thoroughly birched at school, with a severity now incredible. With the spread of education all corporal punishment was discouraged, and when the Navy became a full-time well paid and pensioned career for ratings as well as officers, flogging was out: a dishonourable discharge was a much more severe penalty.

The very smallest ships, of under 100 tons and with fewer than 30 men, were not so completely officered; the lieutenant in command had another junior lieutenant, for there must always be two commissioned officers however small the vessel, but they had to do their own navigation, for a sailing master could not be spared. Boatswain, carpenter and cook were there, with their mates, leaving little more than 20 men and boys to work the ship and the guns. With a well-conditioned lieutenant in command and competent crew the atmosphere might have resembled that of a rather formal yachting party; but with a martinet in command and a tough boatswain trying to make seamen out of the sweepings of the receiving ships the little ship might be a little hell for everybody. The lieutenant commanding the smallest cutter was just as much an absolute monarch as the captain of a ship of the line, and had far fewer witnesses to restrain him.

The officers and petty officers were all volunteers who intended to make the Royal Navy a career for life. Not so with the ratings. There were a few in every ship who were volunteers, many joining through the Marine Society. This was founded in 1756 by Jonas Hanway (of umbrella fame) and had two main functions; it took in waifs and strays, many of them petty criminals, washed them, gave them some rudiments of education, and as the Navy required, passed them in with a good suit of clothes; on the other side, they took in men who were not seamen but were willing to volunteer (mostly because they were in some trouble or other), gave them some elementary maritime instruction, and passed them into the Navy as required, clean and clad. Marine Society men and boys were very welcome on board as a rule; they took a lot of training, but they were usually willing enough; they could stand the rough, tough life, for they had seldom known anything better and had seldom before been sure of their next meal; and they were unlikely to desert, for they had nowhere to go.

The majority of the men, however, were 'pressed' or picked up by the press-gang, that *very* rough and ready form of conscription. The common idea of its roughness is, however, greatly exaggerated, quite often by maritime novelists who knew better but wanted colour, 'Roderick Random' for example. The press-gang had to be commanded by a lieutenant, usually with a boatswain's mate; there were enough men with cudgels to discourage resistance, and four men with cutlasses beside the lieutenant; and all these men had to be really trustworthy, for they had every opportunity to desert. They could only press men 'using the sea', and who had used it for more than the preceding two years. They could not take any merchant service officer, boatswain or carpenter, any person (seaman or no) engaged in harvesting. Fishermen were usually exempt, although at times the needs of the Navy were allowed to outweigh the necessity of the food supply; and they could not touch a 'gentleman', a term capable of a wide interpretation. There is no doubt, however, that frequently a 'mistake' was made, and a stout young labourer or artisan was whisked away, and would be a thousand miles at sea before his relatives could get the ponderous machinery of the law in motion for his recovery.

All this was not enough to man the Navy, and in 1795 the Quota Acts were passed, whereby each town and county was required to produce a quota of 'volunteers', to the amount of roughly $\frac{1}{2}$ per cent of the population. The selection was entrusted to the justices of the peace, all estimable gentlemen, who found this a God-sent opportunity to get rid of their undesirables. The bounty was quite high – £70 – which gave offence to the volunteers of 1793, who had received £5. Apart from clearing off poachers, tramps and beggars, the debtors prisons were examined, where lay many a man for debts of less than £70. Put him in the quota, impound his bounty to pay his debts, and you are doing good all round. Except to the

Navy: these scrapings of the debtors prisons were usually quite unfit for seamen; they had usually some sort of education, had at some time been accustomed to home comforts, and hated everything about their position on the lower deck. It is not too sweeping to say that in almost every mutiny, large or small, a quota-man from a debtors prison would be found somewhere at the root of it. There was really no place for such men on a ship, and they were usually relegated to the most menial tasks, such as deck-swabbing and cleaning the 'heads', thus increasing their resentments. The quota was a drastic error: it would have been far better to have had fewer ships, all manned with 'prime seamen'.

The pay was certainly little attraction to so hard a life: an able seaman received 24s per month of four weeks at the beginning of the wars, and 33s 6d at the end, and had to find himself in clothes; but then he had lodgings of a sort, and the food was ample, although coarse and monotonous; and the drink! A gallon of beer per day was the ration, plus a rum issue of half a pint, so strong as to be almost pure alcohol. Admiral Vernon had been nicknamed 'Old Grog' because of the grogram coat he always wore; appalled at the consequences of issuing this firewater, when he was First Lord he decreed that this must be cut down with four times as much water, hence the mixture was called grog. Thus diluted, the daily ration was equal to little less than two bottles of rum at 70° proof. Admiral of the Fleet Lord Keith thought that almost every naval offence except theft arose from drunkeness; he emphasised the difference between a ship's company in the morning and in the afternoon. He felt that no more essential service could be rendered to the nation than to reduce the rum ration, but sadly concluded that it was not expedient during a war. In fact it was 1824 when the ration was cut. It is undoubtedly the case that at sea one can safely consume quantities of rum which would paralyse a city dweller, but eight pints of strong beer and nearly two bottles of rum would nowadays be considered the consumption of a hopeless alcoholic, not of a seaman who might be at any time called upon to go aloft in a storm. Still, alcohol was the only amelioration of their hard lives, and Keith was right to advise postponement. To cut the expected issue for 120,000 men in the time of war was to risk a general mutiny; with 20,000 in time of peace it was a risk which could be accepted.

The other great inducement was prize-money. The Government gave to the ship's company the full value of every prize, ship and cargo. Cases are recorded of lucky captains getting £40,000 and more in a day. Of course the seamen got nothing like that, but in such an action each man would get at least enough to set him up in a cosy little pub ashore. Such great prizes were rare, but they had existed, and as the pools competitor feels, it might be mine next time. It was sound policy of Admiralty to be so generous with prizes: the possibility of making oneself comfortable for life was much better *pour encourager les autres* than shooting Admirals. The biggest prizes fell to frigates, but a little brig, sent to harass the enemy's coastal trade, could send in as prizes dozens of well-laden coasters, as many as she could find prize crews for. Even a little 4-gun schooner had complete command over an unarmed freighter, and there were fewer to share the prize-money. There was plenty of speculation, of course, and prize agents and prize court officials became extremely rich. However, one must accept that 'where the carcase is, there will the vultures be gathered together', and it is unlikely that all the fingers in the prize-bowl, legal or otherwise, scooped out a greater percentage than, for example, an agent for a modern pop group.

Most people loathe statistics because they introduce fact where fancy loves to dwell. The popular idea is of fierce and bloody contests, in which all the casualties of the navy occurred. Fierce and bloody contests there were, but the casualties were only a small percentage of the actual losses in men: in fact negligible, so far as deaths were concerned.

Desertion was undoubtedly the largest single cause of loss of manpower. Samples taken at various periods show a fairly steady desertion rate of 500 a month, which does not appear an alarming drain on an establishment which at times amounted to 140,000 seamen and Marines; but it gives a total loss by desertion for the whole period of the two wars of more than 100,000 men – at least equal to, and probably more than, all the deaths in the service over the same period, from whatever cause. During the period of the war with the United States it was stated that 40,000 British deserters were serving in the American Navy; ten or so years later Admiralty in a more objective report estimated the number at 20,000. One figure seems too high, the other perhaps rather low; in the 'science' of statistics a good deal depends on what you are trying to prove at the time. In the first case, the point made was that the American Navy existed by tempting British sailors into that service; in the second case, the point to be made is that the loyal British tars loved the Navy so much that only 20,000 deserted to the Americans. Even taking the lower figure, it showed a pretty poor state of affairs, especially as the largest category of deserters was that of able seamen. The usual point of desertion was an American, Canadian or British port, because of the language. On account of this sailors were prohibited from going ashore at all while the ship was in commission; one can imagine the frustrations of seamen cooped up in their ship and viewing the shore, with all its attractions from green fields to brothels. No doubt many an unthinking hand got himself out of the ship just for a run ashore, and later realized that if he re-joined he would certainly receive a flogging : thus severity built up the offence it was intended to repress.

As a round figure, the total of deaths in the service during the whole period amounted 100,000. The causes of death may be given as percentages of that figure :

Disease	..	..	..	..	..	50%
Individual accident, usually when drunk				..		30%
Perils of the sea		..	..	..	..	13%
Enemy action	..	..	..	..	..	7%

Surrounded as we are by antibiotics and vaccines, we scarcely consider the possibility of death by infectious disease, but this practical invulnerability has only arrived since 1950, the long fight beginning with vaccination for smallpox and culminating with the general knowledge of advanced antibiotics. In our war period, the whole of modern medical science was quite unknown, with the exception of vaccination for smallpox, which was quite voluntary and also dangerous owing to the septic tools used. Nobody had dreamt of microbes or viruses; quinine was known and used in fevers; otherwise the usual treatment was to cut a vein and let off some blood, sometimes wiping the fleam which made the incision. Amputations could be quite dextrously performed, and every ship carried a surgeon; but there was only a physician on hospital ships and on each of the first-raters, which usually numbered six. The physicians were paid on an enormously higher rate than the surgeons, somewhere between a captain of a first-rater and a rear-Admiral, whereas the surgeons were paid less than the lieutenants, until the end of the wars – not much more than a pound a week. The consequence was that surgeons fell into two categories: young men who thought it good to have a cruise and see the world between graduating and finding a practice on shore; and those who had failed on shore, usually because of drink, and went to sea to avoid their creditors, pursue their favourable habit free of charge, and if necessary do amputations after an action. Thus, when an epidemic struck on board there was little help from the medical profession.

Scurvy was for long the chief disease in seamen, due to the vitamin deficiency in the diet; but in the wars it affected the Navy very little, as from 1796 a standard ration of lime juice was issued to all hands, and careful captains saw that, where possible, pursers kept a supply of fresh citrus fruit and potatoes, which were not on the ration but available for purchase. Smallpox, which was such a frightful killer on shore, was very seldom found at sea; partly because the air-borne germs cannot carry very far, partly because many had had smallpox and recovered, and partly because vaccination was available free to everybody, (but not compulsory until 1858). Bubonic plague, which is carried by a rat-flea, had ceased to be a menace except in the Mediterranean, where quarantine precautions were taken.

The killer diseases were all insect borne. Typhus, which is carried by a louse, marched with all the armies, who had to be billetted in all sorts of dirty quarters. Of the 25 million men whose lives were sacrified to Napoleon's ambitions, far more were killed by lice than by enemy action. In Britain it was most prevalent in gaols, hospitals and the crowded slums, and once it was conveyed on board ship it was certain that it would spread through all the jammed packs of hammocks. Almost always this disease was picked up when in a British port, and after a ship had been a fortnight at sea without any cases everybody felt better; if it began it was reasonable to assume that a third of the ship's company would die, far more than could happen in the fiercest possible engagement. The senior physicians of the Navy, observing that this fever was associated with dirty conditions (for it was rare in the upper classes), established the regulations already described, whereby every new recruit came aboard in a clean condition. By the end of the wars typhus was far less prevalent in the Navy than in similar classes of people ashore, where the presence of such vermin was regarded as normal. Thus Samuel Pepys, on a journey, 'Up, finding our beds good, but lousy, which made us merry.' 12th June 1668.

By far the greatest killers were the mosquito-borne tropical diseases, malaria and yellow fever. Malaria was not so immediately fatal, and quite frequently death could be averted or at least postponed by quinine, which was well known; but once infected the subject would be liable for the whole of his life to attacks of 'intermittent fever' and a permanent debility. Yellow fever – *vomito negro* the Spaniards expressively called it – was almost always fatal; nobody knew how it was acquired, or how it could be cured; but it was well known that to be ashore on a West Indian island was playing heads-or-tails with death.

In three years service in the West Indies, the British Army lost 40,000 dead by 'Yellow Jack'; at Waterloo, Wellington lost 1,417 British dead; Nelson lost 1,690 dead *and* wounded at Trafalgar.

Individual accident was the next most frequent killer. Sailors were called upon every day to perform feats aloft which would terrify skilled trapeze artists, and there was no safety net. A fall onto the deck was certain death, a fall into the sea probable death. No flotation gear was worn, no lifebelts were carried. The possibility existed that some quick-witted and compassionate officer might throw overboard a hen coop from the quarter-deck, but otherwise there was very little float material about the deck. A ship sailing on a good wind took a lot of stopping; to set the sails aback might carry away a topmast, turning suddenly into the wind might do the same, to wear with it meant going round in a wide circle. The usual way was to heave-to and lower a boat, which would have at least a mile to row before reaching the spot, when it would cruise around for about an hour, depending on the value of the seaman. Sometimes he was found, usually not. Very few seamen could swim, and the art was not encouraged, because it made desertion easier. In northern waters the cold killed very quickly, and in tropical seas there were sharks, although that danger, to *unwounded* men, has been exaggerated. There were many other types of personal accident. There was never full headroom between decks, and caution had to be observed at all times; but a tipsy man is *not* cautious, and there were many deaths by skull fracture from running the head against a beam 'under the influence'. The 'conveniences' for the crew were the 'heads' right forward, consisting merely of unplanked beams at the prow; many a merry sailor who went forward to relieve himself in a seaway pitched over the head, the ship sailed over him, and it might be a long time before he was missed. There were so many hard objects all around, guns and carriages, piles of shot, belaying pins and so on, that any trip or fall could be fatal, especially when drunk, when the instinct to defend the head is dulled.

Perils of the sea in our figures includes explosion, fire (which usually culminated in explosion), foundering and shipwreck. Explosion was very rare although the BOYNE, a splendid three-decker, blew up at her moorings at Spithead, 1st May 1795. The frigate AMPHION blew up alongside the jetty in Plymouth harbour, 22nd September 1796. So far as I am aware, these are all the explosion losses, which compares very favourably with modern times. In 1907 and again in 1911 the French lost a fine battleship by explosion; and during the 1914–18 war, the various combatants lost 13 large vessels by explosion in harbour. Some of the earlier versions of nitroglycerine explosives were found to be very unstable under certain conditions, whereas gunpowder was not affected by the climate.

Accidental fire was was as rare. I am only aware of three cases: the QUEEN CHARLOTTE, 100 guns, off Leghorn, 17th March 1800; the AJAX, 74, off the Dardanelles, 11th February 1807; and the RESISTANCE, 44, in the Banka Straits, 24th July 1798. None of the small warships was lost by such accident, either explosion or fire. It is an error to suppose that a wooden ship is more liable to fire than a steel one; a metal hull can contain plenty of wood and burn out just as completely. In a small ship there were very few places out of observation of anybody, and the first requirement in case of fire is to deal with it immediately.

Foundering was a more serious cause of loss, because the small ships were often out in heavy weather. There was very little foundering among the larger ships (frigates and above) and always it was an old ship which should have been taken out of commission long before; but many of the foundered small ships were quite recent and in good condition. Table III gives a list of all the small ships that foundered, or were supposed to have foundered, during the wars, and the fate of the crew. Studying this, a pattern seems to emerge: there are certain areas of sea which produce more founderings than others.

The table, indeed, lists the areas in which the fiercest storms are expected to be encountered. The very large losses in the West Indies may occasion some surprise nowadays, when the

West Indies are considered a yachtman's paradise, because of course one must always believe the advertisments. But during the hurricane season the West Indian yachtsman puts his vessel into dry dock if he can. At that time there was only a vague idea of a season for hurricanes. Nowadays every hurricane is noted and watched from its birth in the doldrums; the course and speed of the eye of the storm is accurately prognosticated, as well as the force of the winds which swirl round it. At that time there was no idea whatever that a hurricane obeyed any laws at all and could be avoided by prudent navigation; it was the Wrath of God, not an explicable natural phenomenon. It was not until 1830 that Lieutenant Reid of the Royal Engineers read a paper on 'The Law of Storms' to the Royal Society. Near the dead-calm eye of the hurricane, winds up to 200 miles an hour may be encountered, and no small sailing vessel can stand up to them : it must be overwhelmed or capsize, and in such a sea no boat, no man, can live for a minute. The North Atlantic losses were mostly ships sailing to or from Halifax, and it is quite possible that some of them put down as foundered may in fact have run upon icebergs. It was very seldom that there were any survivors to make a report. The North Sea and the English Channel are well known as stormy waters, and many a hurricane which originated in the tropics expends its dying fury round the Island. At Unst in Shetland an anemometer reading of 177 m.p.h. was obtained on 15th February 1962. No brig could ride out that. Losses in Eastern waters were very few, because there were very few sloops operating in that area. It was too far for a sloop, until the Cape of Good Hope was taken and made a naval base, and most of the Eastern sloops were Bombay-built.

It is interesting to notice that the number of losses of captured sloops was very little short of losses of British-built ones, although they were not more than a quarter of the sloops in commission; so that the losses of captured sloops was three times the average for British-built sloops. There is no reason to suppose that the foreign-built ships were in any way inferior in design or construction; on the contrary, a ship built in Toulon of Adriatic oak was universally acknowledged to be superior to any British vessel. The possibility exists that if a ship endured a heavy cannonade before surrendering, her timbers would be shaken in a way that might be overlooked in the repair yard, and only show itself in the stress of the storm.

It will be noticed that of the 66 ships lost 48 were lost with all hands, or in 4 cases almost all. This is inevitable in the circumstances: in the midst of the ocean, if the ship itself is overwhelmed by the tempest, what possible hope is there for any man? In shipwreck there is some sort of land somewhere near, and it was quite usual for all or most of the crew to be saved; in action with an enemy there would be casualties, usually light; but foundering was the ultimate catastrophe.

It would be tedious, for me especially, to produce a similar analysis of the 147 wrecks, but we might look at the year of the heaviest losses, 1809. In that year 6 sloops foundered with all hands, three saved in 2 cases. Fifteen were wrecked. One, on the Manacle, lost all hands except a boy; from another, off Martinique, only 19 were saved; in all the other 13 all the crew were saved, except eight in one case and two in another. This may be taken as a typical average, throughout the wars, of the fearsome difference between foundering and shipwreck.

With all those ways of perishing miserably, is it surprising that the sailor looked forward avidly to action with the enemy? Glance again at the little table on page 41; the sailor did not have this in front of him, but he knew the odds well enough. If he were fated to die, even odds he would die in a crowded foetid hospital in the Caribbean, vomiting his guts out in hopeless agony; only three to one against falling off the rigging; eight to one against drowning after a long desperate battle against the elements at their fiercest; and fourteen to one against death in battle. Knowing this, the seaman went merrily into battle, with his mind on prize-money, his eye on the enemy, and his hand on the gun.

3

First Blood

The French government declared war on Britain on 1st February 1793, and immediately ordered the whole navy to be put on a war footing. They impounded all the British merchant shipping in French harbours, more than 70 ships against 8 French merchantmen in British ports. They also urged all the merchants of the sea ports to fit out their fastest ships as privateers and sail forthwith against the returning British ships, which could not yet have heard of the war. The largest of the French privateers were fitted out by the merchants of Bordeaux, but the most nimble were the smaller ones manned by the Bretons, seamen born. A privateer was simply a licensed pirate, who would be treated as a prisoner of war if captured. There was always more of the pirate than the warship about them, discipline was usually lax, and as well as bringing their prizes into French ports they showed great dexterity in robbing their captives of personal possessions.

The brig-sloop SCOURGE was rated as 16 guns, but in time of peace carried only eight 6-pounders, and had not yet mounted her war armament nor complement, for she had only 70 out of her full crew of 90. Under Commander George Brissac she was cruising to the west of the Scilly Islands when she fell in with the French privateer *Sans-Culotte,* with a crew of 81 men, armed with eight long 8-pounders and four 12-pounder carronades, giving her 12 guns and 56 pounds weight of broadside, against the eight guns and 24-pound broadside of the brig. The early privateers were merely the swiftest and strongest of the available merchant ships, with ports cut for their guns, but lacking the stout bulwarks built into the vessel, and the stern discipline built into the crew, of a warship, however small. The the half-armed SCOURGE drew up and engaged; for three hours the fight continued while the ships circled round in the choppy seas, each trying to get a weather advantage of the other. Eventually, after a loss of 9 killed and 20 wounded, the *Sans-Culotte* hauled down her colours and surrendered to a vessel of less than half her gun-power.

This was a most creditable affair for the SCOURGE, whose loss was only 1 man killed and 1 wounded – the very first British blood shed at sea in the wars which were to end more than 22 years later, for this action took place on the 13th March 1793. Nevertheless, there was little notice taken of the engagement, because it was with a privateer, not a French government vessel. Had the *Sans-Culotte* been a regular French naval ship, commanded by a commissioned officer, no doubt there would have been promotions to post rank for the commander and to commander for the lieutenant; but as it was there was nothing but the prize-money, which, as there was no rich cargo, amounted to little. All through the wars this attitude continued, even when the merchants of Bordeaux were sending out privateers as powerful as frigates and commanded by such naval heroes as Captain Bergeret. Given the choice between taking without conflict a few well-laden French merchantmen, yielding lots of prize-money, and engaging a well-armed privateer, with plenty of danger and neither profit or glory to be won, it was only a disciple of Nelson who would go for the privateer. This was an error on the part of Admiralty, which should have treated an engagement with a privateer in exactly the same way as an action with a government ship. Every privateer captured reduced the task of protecting the merchantmen and discouraged *les autres.*

α

It would appear that *Sans-Culotte* was quite a favourite epithet in the first fervour of the Revolution, although I am unaware of any French officer appearing on the quarter-deck in this uniform. One of the very finest ships in the Royalist Navy, the *Dauphin-Royal,* 120 guns, far bigger than anything in the Royal Navy, was re-named *Sans-Culotte* after the Revolution; but Bonaparte, before embarking at Toulon on his expedition to Egypt, renamed her the *Orient*; under which more vice-consular name she blew up at the Battle of the Nile.

The first British Naval officer to lose his life in the wars was Lieutenant John Western. King George III had sent an expedition under the Duke of York to assist the Dutch, who happened to be on the British side at the time. During the amphibious operations which ensued, Lieutenant Western was in command of a shallow-draught gun-boat, and while he was personally aiming a 12-pounder gun he was shot through the head. Casualties were yet few; the Duke of York attended the funeral in Dordrecht Church, and ordered a monument to be erected to his memory. It is to be hoped that the stone-cutters got paid for their labours. However, as the wars increased ceremony lessened, and a warrior did well enough if he were inhumed below wolf level.

A packet-boat, always referred to as a packet, was a small ship, usually cutter or schooner rigged, designed for carrying the mail to any part of the world as well as such passengers as might gain favour with the packet superintendent at a port of call. They were very lightly armed, merely to deal with any fast privateer, and relied on their speed to avoid any more powerful opponent. They were invariably commanded by a steady, elderly, 'plodder' lieutenant, who would carry out his orders without deviation in search of adventure, but was officer enough to fight to the death if necessary in defence of his mails.

HM packet ANTELOPE, Lieutenant Curtis, left Port Royal, Jamaica on 28th November 1793, with mail for England; and three days out, off Cuba, met two French privateers, schooners, apparently well armed and manned. Immediately the ANTELOPE bore up to return to Jamaica, with the two privateers in hot pusuit; one she completely outsailed, but the other kept up all day and all night and all the following day until four o'clock in the afternoon, when the wind fell away to a dead calm. The privateer, which was now made out to be called the *Atalante,* now got out her great sweeps and commenced rowing up to the ANTELOPE, at the same time hoisting the red flag at the main, to inform the attacked that no quarter whatever would be given; always a foolish action, since there is no point in killing an adversary who has ceased to resist, whereas he will fight like a wildcat if surrender also means death.

While the *Atalante* was slowly sweeping herself forward, Lieutenant Curtis had time to consider. He had left Jamaica with a crew of 27, of whom 4 had died of fever, including the second mate; 2 were down with fever, unable to leave their hammocks; so that he had a total of 21 men, far too few to man sweeps, even if he had them. The *Atalante* on the other hand carried 65 men, more than three times his number. For guns, he had six 3-pounders, the smallest gun in the Royal Navy, with a bore of about $2\frac{1}{2}$ inches; whereas the *Atalante* had eight of the same calibre. For responsibility, he had the Royal Mail and also his passengers, some of whom were French Royalists, who might expect short shrift from the Republicans. One of them a former midshipman of the French Royal Navy, volunteered his services, and the other gentlemen assured him that while they were not seamen they could use their swords. Fight it would be, then.

The *Atalante* came alongside at about eight in the afternoon, and the two ships exchanged somewhat scattered broadsides, whereupon the *Atalante,* finding she had to do with an armed ship and a resolute crew, sheered off for the night; but at five the next morning, before first light, she came on again, threw grappling-hooks into the ANTELOPE, fired a broadside, and under cover of the smoke attempted to board. The broadside had the most devastating effect : Lieutenant Curtis was killed, as were also a French passenger and the steward; the first mate was shot through the body and had to leave the deck, although he lived to tell the tale; and the command now devolved on the boatswain, Mr Pasco, supported by the French midshipman aforementioned, M. Nodin, who conducted himself like a hero. He took the helm and worked the ship, and moreover, having a musket and a pike, he defended the stern and quarters against all boarders, shooting them down with his musket, or, if unloaded, leaving the helm to run forward and poke them overboard with his pike. Meanwhile, amidships, Mr Pasco with his minute crew and the passengers repulsed all attempts to board, until the privateer cut the grapples and would have made off; but the bold boatswain ran aloft and lashed the foresquare-sail yard of the schooner to the shrouds of the ANTELOPE. Now a well-directed fire was poured into the deck of the *Atalante*, whose crew now called for quarter, after an action, right alongside, of two hours. Quarter was granted, in spite of the privateer having gone into action with the red (no quarter) flag flying, and next day the ANTELOPE brought her prize into Annotta Bay, Jamaica.

As might be expected in so close and desperate an affray, the casualties were extreme in proportion to the numbers originally engaged. The ANTELOPE out of 21 lost 3 killed, including her commanding officer, and 4 wounded, including her first mate. The *Atalante*'s first and second captains were killed, and 30 men (some accounts say 20, with fair probability) and 17 wounded, out of a total of 65 altogether. Thus one ship lost a third and the other two-thirds of the total complements, as big a casualty list between the two as was ever to be endured again in the whole of the wars. This was an engagement creditable to both parties, but especially to the much smaller British packet-ship, with all the incidents: the French M. Nodin, taking the helm in hand and at the same time guarding the quarter-deck; the French gentlemen repelling boarders with their small-swords; and above all the heroic Boatswain Pasco, taking a command he could never have expected and conducting it with the coolness and initiative of a long-commissioned officer.

There was never a better-fought action during the whole of the 22 years of warfare; but it was merely between a packet and a privateer, and there were neither honours nor rewards for the heroic victors, except of course a bit of prize-money from their capture. It was assumed as a matter of course that any British ship whatsoever could deal with any French privateer, an assumption which was to be very rudely shaken some time later. But however it has been ignored and forgotten, it was a splendid action, bringing out the highest qualities of fighting seamen just as much as at Trafalgar, and *here* at least it will not be forgotten.

4

The Young Viking

Thomas, Lord Cochrane, was one of 'fortune's favourites'. Not only was he son and heir of the ninth Earl of Dundonald, his uncle, Sir Archibald Cochrane, was a distinguished naval officer. His father had served in the Navy, but would rather his son had joined the Army; however, the young man's mind was quite determined on the Navy, and eventually he joined as a midshipman under his uncle, setting foot for the first time on the deck of a warship in June 1793, at the advanced age (for a midshipman) of seventeen years. However, the care of his uncle had put him 'on the books' five years earlier, thus defeating the careful regulations of Samuel Pepys, and enabling him to be appointed acting lieutenant before he was twenty, years before he ever saw a shot fired in anger. Thirsting for service and command, he could never forget that at twenty Nelson was a post captain.

Cochrane was in many ways typical of the Lowland Scottish aristocracy, of Norse origin. Very tall, and even as a young man of a commanding presence, he was well aware of 'the deference due to a man of pedigree'. Where that deference was paid, he was the most affable and charming man imaginable; but he was fiercely resentful of anything resembling a stretch of authority by his seniors in the service. Before action he would gravely consider all the factors; when action was decided on, he was as fierce and headlong as any of his Berserker ancestors, yet always cool and watchful for any circumstance of which he might make use. A 'mariner of infinite resource and sagacity', an ideal commander, but a prickly subordinate.

After service in various ships he found himself, at the end of 1798, a lieutenant on board the BARFLEUR, the flag-ship of Lord Keith (also a Scotsman), Commander-in-Chief of the Mediterranean Fleet. This was the usual position from which 'fortune's favourites' could expect fairly early promotion to commander. Discipline on a flag-ship was always strict, with much formality on the quarter-deck, and First Lieutenant Philip Beaver was the very man to enforce it. He took occasion to reprimand Cochrane in the wardroom, and Cochrane gave offence, not so much by his words but by his disdainful demanour. Beaver immediately demanded a court-martial on Cochrane, which could not be refused. The details are too tedious to recount, and indeed the Admiral found the same. Cochrane was acquitted of whatever he was accused of and advised to respect the position of a first lieutenant, but Beaver was rebuked for his methods; the whole fleet had been delayed a day, when the wind had come fair and they might have been a hundred miles on their way, and this for the most trivial complaint. Beaver, however, was soon promoted post captain, and served with some distinction, dying at the Cape of Good Hope in 1814. Early in 1800 Keith made Cochrane commander in the gun-brig-sloop SPEEDY, and no doubt felt easier for having cleared his quarter-deck of both a martinet and a firebrand.

The SPEEDY was quite small for her class, being 158 tons, with a crew of 6 officers and 84 men; only 2 of the officers were commissioned, Cochrane and his lieutenant, Richard William Parker, the officers otherwise being of warrant rank. The quarters must have been uncommonly tight, for the tonnage only comes to $1\frac{3}{4}$ tons per man, the least I am aware of; a frigate had about 4 tons per man. She could only carry 10 tons of water, about 25 gallons per man, so that she had to re-water every few weeks. The commander's cabin was not big enough for a chair, being entirely occupied by a table surrounded by lockers, forming both storage and seating. The headroom was only five feet, making it difficult for a man of Cochrane's height to get in at all; and when it came to shaving, he had to lift off the skylight, stand up through the opening and set out his tackle on the quarter-deck. Her armament was minute – fourteen long 4-pounders, throwing a shot about the size of a cricket ball. On one occasion Cochrane walked the quarter-deck with a whole broadside – seven shot – of his ship in his coat pockets. Cochrane asked for, and was allowed, two 12-pounder long guns as fore and stern chasers; but there was not room enough to work them, and the timbers would not stand the recoil. Later he asked for 6-pounders instead of his 4s, but the ports were not big enough. The only 'improvement' he was able to make was in his rig: the mainyard requiring to be replaced, a spar was supplied longer than the original; it was ordered to be cut down to size, but instead of doing so Cochrane had the end planed so as to make it appear that it had been cut, and got away with it, so that he could spread in his main course and main-topsail more canvas than the ship was designed for. This may or may not be an improvement. It would appear that Cochrane was under the vulgar delusion that the more sail you hoist the faster you can go. In fact length on the waterline is the limiting factor, and once the optimum sail area for length has been reached, more canvas will by no means increase the speed, but rather decrease it by depressing the bow. The design of sailing ships, indeed of any ship, is a very complicated business, and it is best to accept the ship as it comes from the yard; but then Cochrane always felt that he could do a little better, and history shows that in matters he fully understood this was true.

Cochrane was very proud of his first command. He had not much to survey, but he was monarch as far as it went. This precisely suited him, and he soon endeared himself to his men by his steady but kindly discipline, his care for their comfort, or rather to alleviate their discomforts, and the occasional treat such as fresh vegetables when in port, not only pleasing the men but keeping them healthy and alert. He exercised them at the guns far beyond the Admiralty allowance of powder and shot for practice, and trained them in boarding tactics. Very soon he had a keen and compact company, trained to his hand, eager to do anything he set them at.

The first order was a small convoy job, which was neatly executed, beating off some gun-boats and capturing a French privateer in 1800, bringing the convoy of 14 ships safely into Leghorn. He then rejoined Lord Keith off Genoa, where the French under Massena were occupying the town. Soon, by capitulation, Massena gave up the town and retreated to Nice, and Keith gave Cochrane the orders which exactly suited him – to cruise on the coast of Spain and attack anything in sight. SPEEDY had a wonderful time all June and July, sending seven or eight prizes into Leghorn, where the SPEEDY anchored on Agust 3rd. Lord Keith was highly pleased with the enthusiasm and success of his compatriot, and invited him to share all the festivities which happened to be going on ashore. In a fortnight SPEEDY was at sea again, with orders to harass the coast of Spain but not to risk his vessel against heavy stuff. However, after capturing a small privateer, they fell in with the MUTINE, under a post captain who had a number of French prisoners on board; he ordered Cochrane to take these on board and ship them to Leghorn, which he did rather sulkily, and remained at Leghorn until 14th September, refitting. On the 22nd he captured a large Neapolitan vessel with a French prize crew on board, and brought her into Port Mahon on 5th October. Here he was informed that the depredations of the SPEEDY had attracted the attention of the Spanish authorities, who were fitting out a frigate especially to 'abate the nuisance'. Now the 'infinite resource and sagacity' began to show. There was in the Mediterranean a Danish brig, the *Clomer,* not unlike the SPEEDY: Cochrane painted the SPEEDY in the *Clomer*'s colours, found a Dane somehow and appointed him quartermaster, and found him a Danish naval officer's uniform. The SPEEDY sailed from Port Mahon into the worst winter weather in living memory, and found very little reward. On 21st December a vessel was sighted, which appeared a large and deep-laden merchantman; but as they neared she hoisted Spanish colours and opened her ports to show a formidable battery. SPEEDY hoisted Danish colours, but the Spaniard signalled her to heave-to, and lowered a boat. SPEEDY complied, and also ran up the quarantine flag. When the boat came alongside, the Danish quartermaster explained that this was the *Clomer*, two days out from Algiers, where the plague was known to be raging; but the officer could come on board and see for himself. The invitation was declined, and the ships parted company. The Spaniard was the *Gamo, a* xebec-rigged frigate. Xebec denotes any ship with square sails forward and lateen aft; usually they are quite small coasters, but the *Gamo* was a small frigate of over 600 tons, with two masts square-rigged and a lateen on the mizzen. Her force has been sometimes exaggerated, but in fact she was very much the equivalent of a British sixth-rate 28-gun frigate, mounting twenty-two long 12-pounders on the main deck and eight long 8-pounders and 2 carronades, 24-pounders, on quarter-deck and forecastle, but with a much larger crew than the British equivalent, 319 against 194. Obviously, with a six-to-one superiority, she could eat up the SPEEDY at one mouthful; yet some of the officers of the brig thought they would have liked to have a go at her. Cochrane promised he would think about it, and if it were at all feasible there might be another meeting.

SPEEDY kept on cruising between Cartagena and Barcelona, with great success, coming into Port Mahon on the 24th January with a convoy of prizes. Thence she made for Malta, where Cochrane got himself involved in a silly duel with a French officer of the Royalists, who were there on the Allied side. Fortunately neither was killed, for there were present all the elements of an 'Allied' split. No doubt a Royalist French officer had laid hands upon Cochrane at a fancy dress ball, when he was disguised as a British tar; and to lay hands on a Scottish gentleman is death, naturally : but there were provocations. On the whole, the incident tended to strengthen the establishment view that Cochrane, although a bonny fighter, was a danger to authority, known to be of a Whig family and probably a Radical. This was in fact true, and he remained so all his life; but of course events overtook him and the Radical of 1800 became the staunch establishment of 1860.

Another profitable cruise on the coast of Spain left the SPEEDY with a crew of only 54, due to the prize crews sent with the captured ships to Port Mahon. Off Barcelona a large ship was sighted sailing close under the land, and she was eventually made out to be the *Gamo*. Cochrane piped all hands, told them what was before them, and gave his orders. As the ships approached the *Gamo* fired a gun and hoisted her Spanish colours, the usual way of demanding that a strange ship should identify herself. The SPEEDY hoisted American colours and continued to approach. In the odd sort of sea-etiquette of the period it was perfectly all right to show false colours so long as one hoisted the true colours before opening fire; to fire under false colours laid the whole crew open to the penalties of piracy. The Spaniard hesitated long enough for the SPEEDY to go about on the other tack, when she ran up the British ensign, and the *Gamo* fired a broadside without hitting anything. A second time she fired, also without effect; while the SPEEDY came on in perfect silence, until she ran alongside and locked her yards in the Spaniard's rigging.

This manoeuvre was not bravado : during the previous encounter Cochrane had taken a long look at the *Gamo*, and had noted that not only was her main battery mounted fairly high, her ports did not allow for the guns being depressed. The low-velocity cannon of the period needed a high trajectory to carry any distance; it was a matter of tossing the shot rather than shooting it with velocity. If the port were made large enough to allow of depressing the gun as well as elevating it there would be very little bulwark left to give an impression of protection to the gun-crew. Locked alongside, the SPEEDY was so small and so low in the water that the shot of the *Gamo* roared through her rigging, with damage to the cordage and sails but very little to her men; whereas the little guns of the SPEEDY, being elevated and double-shotted, sent their light shot smashing up through the sides and deck with such effect that the first broadside killed the captain and boatswain. The Spanish next-in-command saw his disadvantage, and gave the order for boarding, which was heard just as clearly on the SPEEDY. When the Spaniards were assembled for boarding, the SPEEDY sheered off, and put a broadside and a volley of musketry into the close ranks. Again and a third time was this manoeuvre repeated, until the Spaniards gave up the idea of boarding and stood to their guns, however little effective.

This, however, could not continue; the SPEEDY was in exactly the position of the lady who went for a ride on a tiger; as long as she remained close enough she could get along well enough, but she could not get away. Cochrane determined to board the *Gamo* with all hands. The surgeon, Mr Guthrie (descended, I believe, from a locally famous Covenanter family), volunteered to take the tiller, and with two or possibly three boys formed the whole ship's complement. With admirable skill he laid the SPEEDY right alongside the *Gamo*, and the boarders leapt up her side, one party at the head and the other at the waist, which was as far as the SPEEDY extended. The boarders at the head had been ordered to blacken their faces and generally make themselves look like pirates, and when they emerged through the gun smoke, yelling like fiends, the Spaniards wavered for a moment; and in that moment they were assailed in flank and rear by the main party. Seeing an opportunity, Cochrane sent a hand to haul down the Spanish colours; the Spaniards supposed that their officers had surrendered the ship, and laid down their arms. It was a legend in the Navy that the surrender was expedited by Cochrane calling to the SPEEDY 'Send another fifty men!' to which the surgeon replied 'Fifty men – aye aye Sir!'

All troubles were not over, for the unwounded prisoners

numbered about 270, almost seven times the unwounded of the SPEEDY. The officers were transferred to the sloop, and the men battened down under hatches; but there must have been very little sleep for Cochrane and his men during the next few days, until they brought their big prize into Port Mahon.

This was perhaps the most astounding single-ship encounter in all recorded history. There have been cases where the weaker ship has defended herself courageously, and sometimes successfully; but never before or since has a ship actually attacked another of an altogether superior class, and conquered. The bare statistics show the amazing disparity of force :

	SPEEDY	*Gamo*
Tonnage	158	Over 600
Main-deck guns	14, 4-pounders	22, 12-pounders
Quarter-deck guns	None	8, 8-pounders,
		2 carronades, 24s
Weight of broadside	28 pounds	190 pounds
Total crew	54	319

Of these crews, the SPEEDY lost three killed and nine wounded,* including Lieutenant Parker; the *Gamo* 14 killed, including her captain, and 41 wounded, total 55 casualties, one more than the whole crew with which the SPEEDY went into action.

The news of this astonishing action was rapturously received in England, but Authority was quite cool about it. There was no haste to promote Cochrane post captain, which had rewarded many lesser victors. It may be that Authority felt that the risk was too great and should not have been taken, disregarding the months of thought that had gone into the problem. There may have been jealousy of Cochrane's success, both in glory and in prize-money : in the year's cruise the humblest seaman in the SPEEDY had earned more in prize-money than the regular pay of almost any officer. At any rate, Cochrane's next job

* In his *Autobiography of a Seaman* Cochrane gives the wounded as 18, but he was over 80 years of age at the time, writing 60 years after the event. All other accounts give 9, from the official record, which is also a more usual proportion to the killed.

was to go peaceably to Algiers to expostulate with the Dey about the seizure of a merchant ship, surely a task more suitable for a civilian diplomat, and unsuccessful.

Once more Cochrane was sent to cruise off the coast of Spain, and almost at once captured a Spanish privateer of 8 guns. This he fitted out as a tender to the SPEEDY, and gave the command to his young brother Midshipman the Hon. Archibald Cochrane, who had been with him throughout his service in the ship; a decidedly high-handed proceeding which was unlikely to endear him to Authority. Later they fell in with the KANGAROO, Captain Pulling, and under his orders engaged in a fierce and protracted battle with ships and forts at Oropesa, until they had expended almost all their shot after nine hours' firing, for the SPEEDY could only load 1,400 shot. They now ran in as if to board the ships and attack the fort by land, at which the defenders of the fort 'retired in confusion' and the ships ran themselves ashore; three of them, however, were brought off.

When Cochrane returned with his usual clutch of prizes to Port Mahon he found, to his intense chagrin, that the *Gamo* had not been bought into the service but had been sold very cheaply to the Dey of Algiers. He had confidently hoped that it would have been bought in and that after repair he would command it as a post captain, and again he suspected official jealousy. This may have been an element, but more probably the xebec did not fit at all into the rigging system. Apart from the lateen-rigged mizzen, the sail arrangements on the two square-rigged masts were quite different from anything in British sail lofts. Cochrane's view was that this was all to the good; the lateen rig had proved itself for a thousand years to be the handiest for coasting in the Mediterranean, and the totally un-British appearance was a far better camouflage than a Danish quartermaster.

The next assignment was less rewarding: to convoy a very slow-sailing packet ship with mails to Gibraltar. However, he relieved the tedium by examining all the anchorages along the coast, and came upon a few merchant ships near Alicante. They ran themselves ashore: it would take too long to bring them off, so Cochrane fired them. One of them was laden with oil, and produced a tremendous blaze which, on a very dark night, was visible over a wide area. This attracted the attention of a squadron of three French ships of the line making for the Atlantic, and at five o'clock on the morning of 3rd July 1801 they fell in with the SPEEDY. For four hours they coursed her like greyhounds with a hare, while Cochrane tried every dodge his inventive brain could devise. He had all his guns thrown overboard, and indeed it would have been unwise to have fired them, since the view of the day on the laws of warfare was that it was quite wrong, even criminal, to shoot when there was no possible hope of success. Away went the anchors and the boats, while the SPEEDY tacked and wore and dodged without success; the big French ships were faster and almost as handy, and at length she came under the broadside of the *Desaix*, and the cruise of the SPEEDY was over.

Cochrane never commanded a brig again, because after he was exchanged he eventually got his post rank. His subsequent career as a frigate captain I have related in *The Frigates*, and his later services are part of South American history; but we may have a glimpse of him at the end of his career, when he was the tenth Earl of Dundonald, Admiral and Commander-in-Chief, North American station. From the local newspaper in Bermuda, 21st May 1850:

On Thursday last the noble Earl, the Commander-in-Chief of the Navy, gave a ball, in His Lordship's usual magnificent style, to above 350 persons – comprising the elite of these Islands. . . . The ball was a full dress one; and His Lordship, in full uniform – covered with orders, won in many a desperate encounter – stood to welcome a crowd of guests. Many beheld for the first time this distinguished hero – His Lordship appeared in excellent health and spirits, delighting all with his good humour and urbanity.

5

Heroes Before Agamemnon

There were heroes before Agamemnon, and before Cochrane there were commanders of the little SPEEDY – equally courageous, equally capable, not so brilliant perhaps – and, unlike the predecessors of the King of Men, their names 'stand remembered in the known account of time.'

The SPEEDY has already been described (Chapter 4): a little brig of 158 tons, fourteen 4-pounder guns and about 80 men. In 1798 she was commanded by Hugh Downman and her job was to make a pest of herself on all the coasts of Spain, which was very vulnerable to this kind of attack. The rocky Sierras made a canal system impossible, and as the roads were in rather worse condition than the Romans had left them, practically all traffic had to go by sea.

On 2nd February 1798 the SPEEDY captured a coasting brig, and put into her a prize crew consisting of the sailing master and twelve seamen. The next day, at dawn, about fifty miles west of Vigo, in winds light and variable with a great swell of sea, there appeared a large brig bearing down under all sail on the SPEEDY. This was the *Papillon,* French privateer of 360 tons, four long 12-pounders and ten long 8s with 160 men, making her in tonnage, fire-power and numbers rather more than twice the force of the SPEEDY, which cleared for action. Owing to the lightness of the wind it was 3 p.m. before the

Papillon opened fire at a range of half a mile, while the SPEEDY endeavoured to shorten the range. The cannonade had the usual effect of causing the wind to drop almost to a calm*, and the two ships drifted for more than four hours, firing away in a desultory fashion without much damage to either party, owing to the uncertain heading of the ships and the great swell. At 7.30 p.m. a light evening breeze came up and the *Papillon,* which sailed much better than the SPEEDY, made off out of gunshot, although the SPEEDY got out her sweeps and tried rowing.

At midnight the privateer came upon the brig which the SPEEDY had captured the day before, and fired on her. Mr Marshall, the sailing master, seeing that resistance was out of the question, battened under hatches the twelve Spaniards who were on board, and with his twelve men took to their boat and escaped in the darkness. They had a long twelve-mile pull before they regained the SPEEDY with the bad news. The privateer, instead of handing the brig back to their Spanish allies, put on board a French prize crew of ten men.

At dawn on the 4th the dawn wind enabled the SPEEDY to come up within gunshot of the *Papillon,* which made away until noon, when she put about and made towards the British brig to attack. At 12.30 p.m. a hot and close engagement began, which continued for an hour and a half, when the fire from the *Papillon* perceptibly slackened and the SPEEDY closed in with thoughts of boarding; but the privateer went about and made off right before the wind under all sail. The SPEEDY followed as best she might, but she was the slower ship in any case and was badly cut about in the rigging. As neither ship had a chase-gun they exchanged musket shots for some minutes until the range became too long. Darkness set in, and by 7 p.m. the *Papillon* was completely out of sight.

The SPEEDY now gave up the chase and went right about, beating up slowly against the wind in the hope of falling in with

* See Appendix 1.

her prize again. It may have been luck or it may have been seamanship, but at dawn the prize was sighted to windward, and by 10 a.m. the SPEEDY was alongside and re-took her.

The ten French now prisoners had been put on board the prize during the night before the heavy action, and could therefore give no information about the casualties on the *Papillon,* but they were surmised to be heavy, to cause her to run away from a ship of half her force. The SPEEDY lost a lieutenant, boatswain and three seamen killed and four severely wounded, and was so much knocked about, especially in masts and rigging, that she had to put into Lisbon for a complete repair. Her action against a ship so much more powerful was indeed a notable victory, but as the enemy was a privateer and was only beaten off, not captured, little notice was taken of the affair.

When the SPEEDY was recommissioned after repair she was commanded by Jahleel Brenton, based at Gibraltar. On 9th August 1799 she was casually in company with a privateer, the DEFENDER, of Gibraltar, when she sighted and chased three small Spanish warships, having a total of twenty 6-pounders among them. These ran for shelter into a small sandy bay and moored parallel to the shore and very near it, showing an excellent defensive line of broadsides. The shore was so steep-to that no soundings could be found within 200 yards of the Spaniards, so the SPEEDY and the privateer sailed up and down for about two hours, firing away in a desultory sort of way without much effect, Commander Brenton finding out the hard way that it is much easier to hit a moving target than to hit from a moving platform. The privateer, seeing little chance of profit, having only twenty-two of her men on board, and not being under Admiralty orders, made out to sea, informing the SPEEDY that she was going to pick up more men.

The SPEEDY now ran right in, and found anchorage within thirty yards of the middle vessel, opening at once a fierce cannonade. The Spaniards returned it with more good will than skill, until after three-quarters of an hour they lost heart and took to their boats, first cutting the cables of their ships. Two drifted on shore, but the one opposite the SPEEDY was boarded immediately, only two dead men being found on board. The boats were now put out to bring off the two ships which were ashore; quite a hazardous operation, for the Spaniards remained in the thick scrub on the steep shore, keeping up an irregular fire of musketry while the guns of the SPEEDY sprayed the bushes with grape-shot. On such a steep-to shore the ships could not go hard aground; both were got off, and the SPEEDY brought into Gibraltar all three ships, with a total gun-power more than twice her own, and with the loss of no more than two men wounded.

On 3rd October the SPEEDY was passing Gibraltar in heavy weather, wind east, when she saw ten small ships coming out of Algeciras. As a British convoy was in sight Commander Brenton concluded that they were Spanish gun-boats coming out to attack it, and stood towards them. It turned out, however, that they were not gun-boats but eight merchant coasters with two armed vessels, a cutter and a schooner, hoping to slip along the coast unobserved in the dirty weather. When the SPEEDY approached the little convoy scattered, two anchoring under the guns of a fort, while four ran west before the wind pursued by the SPEEDY, and anchored in a bay on the east side of Cape Trafalgar, covered by a fort and an old castle. The SPEEDY was now in the position dreaded by all mariners: embayed with a strong wind driving her onto a lee shore. Commander Brenton anchored half a mile off shore, to give sea-room to work outwards, and opened fire first on the fort and the castle, without any apparent return. With the low-velocity guns of the period the wind made quite a difference, and while the 4-pounders of the SPEEDY could quite well range a mile down wind, the guns of the forts would probably find half a mile too far.

The SPEEDY now turned her guns on the anchored merchant-men, whereupon the crews took to their boats and made ashore, having cut the anchor cables to set the ships adrift.

Commander Brenton now ordered Lieutenant Richard William Parker to take the boats of the brig and either bring off or destroy the ships; a fairly tall order, but the commander knew his lieutenant. The boats were launched and came to the ships, but owing to the heavy surf it was equally impossible to bring them off or to set fire to them. However, they boarded both and brought away all the small arms 'to witness if I lie'; and having satisfied themselves that the ships were complete wrecks, settled down to the long and hazardous pull back to the brig.

Three days later, on 6th November 1799, the SPEEDY was lying-to off Europa Point in a stiff breeze from the west, to escort two ships past the danger area: a brig bound for Trieste and a ship, the UNITY, of great importance, being laden with wine and spirits for the Fleet. Twelve vessels came out from Algeciras, and this time they were all gun-boats carrying 24-pounders: two schooners with two apiece and ten feluccas with one apiece. They could thus bring to bear 336 pounds weight of shot against the 28 pounds of the SPEEDY's broadside. Naturally she made for the gun-boats, opening fire at 3.30 p.m. as they converged on the merchant brig which, under cover of this fire, got clear away and sped through the Straits on the wind. The gun-boats then turned their attention on the UNITY and at 5 p.m. commenced firing on her; but the SPEEDY drove right through the gun-boat flotilla from astern, so close as to carry away quite a number of oars, at the same time cannonading with both broadsides while keeping up a fire of musketry from every man not needed at the guns. What with the rowers sent sprawling as the brig cut through the oars and the rapid fire, the Spaniards fell into confusion and allowed the UNITY to escape; but the SPEEDY kept up the combat, until at 6.30 p.m. the gun-boats desisted and ran for shelter under the guns of Fort Barbary.

The SPEEDY had only two men killed and one wounded, but she was very much damaged in the rigging, and had so many heavy shot below the waterline that she could not make Gibraltar in the strong wind, which would have heeled her enough to let too much water in through the shot-holes, so she ran before the wind for Tetuan Bay, where she did not arrive until 2 a.m. the next morning. Here she anchored to plug her shot-holes, and having made herself more or less seaworthy she stood out and soon came safely into Gibraltar. The Spanish gun-boats remained three days under the guns of the fort and then, instead of returning to Algeciras past the SPEEDY, they went to Malaga where they lay unharmed and harmless for two months.

This desperately unequal combat was fought right under the Rock of Gibraltar, bristling with guns, not one of which was fired in support of the SPEEDY. In explanation the Governor, General O'Hara, informed Commander Brenton, 'I have made arrangements with the Governor of Algeciras, to prevent this town being kept in a constant alarm and annoyance by the Spanish gun-boats, which are in consequence never to be fired on from the Rock.' By all the laws of odds, the SPEEDY should have been either captured or sunk by the gun-boat flotilla, and the governor was quite content to see this happen under the guns of the most powerful fortress in the world, to ensure that nothing should disturb his quiet otiosity!

6

Shipwreck

In 1806–7 Balkan politics were as confused as usual. Since the French occupation of Egypt, Turkey had been in alliance with Britain, and also with Russia, quite extraordinarily; there was a Russian fleet in the Mediterranean. However Turkish diplomatic relations had been resumed with France, and there was a powerful French army assembling on the east coast of the Adriatic. The French Ambassador to Constantinople, General Sebastiani, was using the usual wiles of threats, promises and bribery to persuade the Turkish government to close the Straits to the Russians and at least to cool off towards Britain. In those circumstances the British government had to take account of possibilities, and Admiralty sent orders to Vice-Admiral Lord Collingwood, C-in-C Mediterranean, then cruising off Cadiz, to send a small squadron to reconnoitre the Dardanelles and the fortifications, in a friendly sort of way, just in case it might be necessary to be unfriendly later. Lord Collingwood detailed Rear-Admiral Sir Thomas Louis, in the CANOPUS, 80, with two 74s, a frigate and a sloop. Leaving the Fleet on 2nd November 1806, the squadron arrived at Malta on 8th December, and on the 21st anchored off the famous island of Tenedos, about twelve miles south of the entrance to the Dardanelles.

Here they lay for a week, waiting for a favourable wind; for as there is a constant current running out of the Strait, which is very narrow, there was no possibility of beating up against a wind off the east. Also they had to collect pilots, who had to be Greeks, for the Turks were not in the least anxious to impart their navigational secrets. Greece was still a province of the vast Turkish empire, but a very restive one : the Greeks looked upon the Turks as their hated oppressors, and on the British as friends whose intervention would some time or other secure their independence; which did indeed happen in 1827.

Having obtained pilots and a good wind, the squadron entered the Strait, and about ten miles inside anchored in a small bay, just short of the heavily fortified narrows. From here, on the 27th December, the CANOPUS proceeded alone to Constantinople, while the other ships made unobtrusive observations from their anchorage. Having transacted his business, with which we have nothing to do here, the Rear-Admiral returned, joining his squadron on 30th January 1807 and immediately sending off the sloop with despatches for Vice-Admiral Lord Collingwood and for England.

The sloop was the NAUTILUS, 18-gun quarter-decked ship-sloop, about 380 tons, with a complement of 122 men. Commander Edward Palmer was an elderly 'plodder' type of commander, perfectly competent in his profession, well liked by his officers and men, unlikely to engage in a brilliant action. Having outlived ambitions of the captains' ladder and flag rank, he looked forward to a quiet retirement on the modest half pay of a retired commander.

The Isles of Greece are much more romantic to enthusiasts like Byron or a travel agent than to those who have to navigate among them in winter. It is difficult enough nowadays, when the waters are charted and buoyed and lighted like Piccadilly Circus, but then it was really hazardous. The islanders, nominally fishermen, were usually more profitably employed as wreckers, smugglers or pirates; charts were not to be completely relied upon; and in winter, in those shallow waters, the fierce squalls kick up a short steep sea almost instantly. The ancient Greeks restricted their voyaging to the summer months, and even then they went ashore every night. However, a sloop of war is not a pleasure yacht, and the NAUTILUS was on duty.

The night came down dark and squally, and the Greek pilot suggested to the commander that they should heave-to and wait for daylight. This was done, and when the pilot could discern his day marks they proceeded through the Archipelago: tricky work; but after the ship had passed between Falconera and Antimilos the pilot turned over to the Commander and went below. Palmer, also feeling tired, pricked out on the chart the proper course for the vessel and also turned into his bunk. It is not precisely known who was left in charge on deck, but presumably the lieutenant and the sailing master. Now the night fell very dark, lightened by almost constant lightning, with an increasing gale from the NE; the NAUTILUS scudded along under double-reefed topsails only at about nine knots. At 2.30 a.m. land was seen abeam; this was taken to be the island of Cerigotto (Andikithera*) and therefore there was nothing but clear sea ahead. The wind and sea increased, far worse than the night before when the ship had hove-to; but the commander was in his bunk and his orders were clear: push on regardless of weather, and anyhow they had passed Cerigotto and all was clear. At 4.30 a.m. the lookout hailed 'Breakers ahead!', and almost immediately the NAUTILUS crashed at full speed upon an uncharted reef.

According to a contemporary account all the men below were thrown out of their hammocks by the shock, but this is impossible: no shock on the hull can throw a man out of a hammock. No doubt they were all startled, leapt up and made a rush for the ladder to the deck, which broke under the strain, leaving most of the men milling about without orders and without object except to get out. There was a period of panic, which the commander and his lieutenant did their best to quell; discipline was to an extent restored, and the officers were able to evaluate the damage. It was clear that the ship must very

* The names given are those in use at the time: the name in parentheses is the modern one.

shortly become a total loss, and the commander and the lieutenant, going below to the commander's cabin, were able to set fire to the despatches and the code of signals. Legalistically, this terminated their responsibilities for their orders, and it would appear that they felt that all other responsibilities had also terminated; there is no further evidence of any kind of chain of command.

Everybody had now more or less got on deck, where the sea was breaking so heavily that they all got into the rigging, in the hope that the ship would hold together and the breaking seas pass beneath. A rock above water was now seen to leeward, and the possibility existed that if the mainmast came down it would fall upon this rock. This did in fact happen about first light, but there was such an undisciplined rush to get over to fairly dry land that several were pushed off into the sea and drowned, one had an arm broken and there were many injuries. Meantime about half-a-dozen sailors took to the whaler and made away without orders. Commander Palmer very properly remained on board until he was sure that every man had left, when he too crossed the shaking spar to the rock.

As daylight advanced the prospect became plainer and grimmer. The reef on which they stood was awash, and while the wreck of the NAUTILUS afforded some protection, it was quickly breaking up and they would shortly be exposed to the full force of the seas. A little distance away was a somewhat higher rock and it was found possible to wade to it, in peril from the many heavy pieces of wreckage which were tossing about all around, some having men clinging to them and hopelessly calling for help where help there was none. The island they finally reached was about 400 by 300 yards and more or less awash except in the centre; here, in the lee of a trifling eminence, they were able to make a fire with a flint, gunpowder and driftwood. It was frightfully cold, the very seawater freezing in the puddles, but the fire, the most primaeval of all comforts, put some heart into the men and they went about collecting driftwood until they had a really satisfying blaze. With odd planks and pieces of sailcloth they put up a bit of a shelter, opposed to the wind and open to the fire, and even got down to taking off their soaked clothing and drying out in front of the luxurious warmth.

At dawn they were cheered by the sight of a small boat approaching the rock; this turned out to be their own whaler, which had been to the uninhabited island of Pera (Pori) where there was no water; so they had made for the light of the fire. There was too much sea for the boat to land, but one of the men invited the commander to make his way through the surf to the boat; this Commander Palmer refused. His place was taken by the Greek pilot, who said there were some fishermen on the nearby island of Cerigotto (Andikithera) who might be induced to help. The boat left, but hope of success was lessened by the renewal of the storm, which drove the waves higher and higher until they extinguished the fire, their comfort and their hope; and drove the men to the highest part of the rock, where they passed a rope round the pinnacle and hung on all night, being constantly dashed against the rocks by the relentless waves until they were all agonisingly cut and bruised, and some, totally exhausted, lost hold of the rope and were swept down into the sea.

Morning broke grey and threatening, although the wind had abated a little; nothing was to be seen except some bodies tossing in the water between the reefs, or thrown upon the rocks. When suddenly, 'Sail ho !' A small ship was seen making directly for the rock. Everybody was signalling frantically with anything they could get. The ship came near, hove-to and lowered a boat : they were saved! The boat approached within fifty yards and was seen to be crewed by men in the dress of European sailors, when suddenly the coxswain waved his hat and the boat at once put about and returned to the ship : Two more boats were lowered and the three parties employed themselves for most of the day collecting the more valuable wreckage from the NAUTILUS, paying no attention whatsoever to the frantic cries and gestures of the famished castaways. As evening approached they all returned to the ship and sailed away with their loot.

It is difficult for us who have been bred under the noble traditions of the Life-Boat Institution and the Humane Society to realise how completely callous people who make a trade of wrecks become. This area had been notorious for thousands of years, ever since Nauplius lit false fires on Point Caphareus to decoy to destruction the Grecian fleet returning from the sack of Troy. But all over the world people who profit from wrecks are noted for their ruthless disregard of the human wreckage – indeed, are just as likely to murder as to save them, so that there may be no witness or claimant. Sir Walter Scott noted a Shetland superstition that if you saved a man from the sea he would be sure to do you a serious injury sooner or later, and has told how on a remote island the natives cut a rope by which eight shipwrecked sailors could have saved themselves, and let them all drown. When Admiral Sir Cloudesley Shovel was wrecked on the Scillies in October 1707 he was washed ashore still alive; an island woman took his emerald ring from his finger and left him to die. Even in 1838, when the steamship KILLARNEY went ashore east of Cork and the survivors made their way to a rock in a little bay, the local peasants paid no attention to them, only to looting; and when the Coastguards eventually rigged a long rope right across the inlet, the peasants came at night, cut the rope and took it away.

The short winter day was succeeded by another long night of suffering, but about midnight they were roused by a hail from the whaler, which returned from Certigotto; amazingly, without a scrap of food, only some water in earthenware jars which could not be got through the surf. The whaler kept off, definitely in fear lest the castaways might seize the boat; but they gave an assurance that the next day they would all be taken off by the fishing boats of Cerigotto, whither the whaler now went. The rest of the night was made even more hideous (it was possible) by the ravings of some of the survivors who had become insane, it was thought from drinking seawater.

On the fourth morning came the sun, the first they had seen since the shipwreck, but it brought little comfort. In all the wide sea it brightened there was no sign of life, no sail, no hope. The day dragged on, and still no hope. They were in the last pangs of starvation, and there on the rocks lay the bodies of their comrades. Was it not better that they should feed on their shipmates rather than the lobsters?

We of this country have supped full of horrors, and the idea of cannibalism does not now arouse the loathing it did a hundred years ago. Its prevalence in certain areas has been attributed to dietary deficiency rather than savage wickedness, and the assertion of the biochemists that all forms of life are essentially identical has had its effect on the moral issue: a steer is as much a fellow creature as a stockbroker. If it is ethical to cut out a dead man's heart in an attempt to prolong another's life, it is certainly ethical to eat it for the same purpose. But regular cannibals had at least their fires and their ovens; here was the uttermost of human misery: the unfortunates huddled separately over the rock, each gnawing fiercely at a lump of raw flesh that had yesterday been a comrade.

That evening the commander and the first lieutenant died, along with a few of the seamen.

Next day there was still nothing to be seen, but some of the men bestirred themselves to make a raft of the wreckage. It was so poorly constructed that when it was pushed out on the sea it came to pieces. Five men now gathered what they could of the remnants and made a very small raft, on which they embarked and were quite swiftly carried away by the current; but they were never seen again.

In the afternoon the whaler again approached, and the men explained the great difficulty they had had in persuading the fishermen of Cerigotto to come out in such unsettled weather, but they had promised to come immediately the weather made a rescue possible. About a dozen of the men attempted to swim out to the whaler: two were taken aboard, which was quite as many as safety permitted, one was drowned, and the rest had to struggle back to the rock as best they could.

The day wore on. One survivor has described his sensations as he watched the sun setting, quite sure that he would never see it again. His sight was failing, unable to focus; he was incapable of connected thought of any kind; his strength was entirely gone, and he lay there quite inert, unable to move a limb, only aware dimly of the sun going down, down for ever. Suddenly there was a shout: the boats had arrived! With a perceptible shock all his lassitude left him: he could see, could think, and arose and made his way through the water to the nearest boat.

At Cerigotto the inhabitants entertained the castaways as well as their very limited means allowed for a fortnight, and then transported them the 25 miles to Cerigo (Kithera), the classic Cythera, where the sea-born Aphrodite came ashore. More important at the moment, there was a British vice-consul. He settled matters with the rescuers and arranged for lodging and medical attention for the rescued, and eventually arranged their passage in a Russian ship to Corfu, then under joint Russo-Turkish occupation, where they arrived on the 2nd March 1807, two months after the shipwreck.

Out of a total complement of 122 men, 58 had been lost. Eighteen were drowned at the time of the wreck, 5 disappeared on the raft, and the other 35 died of starvation on the rock. A sad tale, but it has to be told: life at sea was by no means all one gay adventure.

It would appear that the commander fell short of the qualities expected in a naval officer: amiable, it seems, but weak and easy. In dirty weather and dangerous seas he ought not to have allowed the pilot to leave the deck, but having done so, he should certainly not have turned in himself; there is only one place for the commander in times of danger. After the ship-wreck, instead of hoping that the mast would fall right, it could and should have been *made* to fall right; and after it was down, there ought not to have been the panic rush along it to the rock, whereby many were pushed off and drowned. The whaler should not have been allowed to go off on its own. The hull lay most of the night before it broke up, but no attempt was made to organise salvage of food and water. After the commander was dead, *somebody* had enough initiative to make a raft: how much easier the first day while the men were fresh and strong! Hard situations need hard men: Captain Bligh was not an amiable character, but he brought eighteen starving men in a 23-foot open boat for 3,618 miles, without a casualty.

7

Jane's Brother

In March 1800 two British vessels were cruising in the Gulf of Lyons: the 32-gun frigate MERMAID, Captain Robert Dudley Oliver, and the 16-gun brig-sloop PETEREL, Commander Francis William Austen. Captain Oliver ordered Commander Austen to cruise along as close inshore as possible, while he himself would keep company just out of sight of the shore. The PETEREL was to snap up any small prizes available, and if heavier stuff came out was to lure it offshore into seduction reach of the MERMAID: live bait, in short.

On the morning 21st March the PETEREL sighted a convoy of fifty vessels making for Marseille and Toulon, escorted by three armed vessels: a ship, a brig and a xebec. Closing in, the PETEREL cut off and captured two of the merchantmen laden with wheat, put prize crews into them and sent them off. Later in the day the armed vessels came up and brought the PETEREL to action off Cape Couronne. The commodore of this squadron was Captain Raccord, in the xebec *Lejoille*, with six long brass 6-pounders and 50 men; the ship was the *Cerf*, with fourteen long brass 6-pounders and 90 men; and the brig was the *Liguri-enne*, with fourteen long brass 6-pounders and two 36-pounder brass carronades, and 104 men. The PETEREL was therefore out-numbered and out-gunned by more than two to one, but engaged the enemy hotly. The MERMAID now came in sight, although at a great distance to leeward, so that it would take hours before she could beat up to take part in the fight; nevertheless the two first-named vessels ran themselves on shore to avoid the action, leaving the brig alone to continue the battle. This she was well able to do, having rather more gun-power and man-power than the PETEREL, plus the aid of a shore battery of four heavy guns. A running fight of an hour and a half ensued until, within six miles of Marseille, the commander of the *Ligurienne,* Lieutenant Pelabond, was killed, and his successor surrendered.

A surprising feature of this duel was the casualty list, after a fight of ninety minutes: the *Ligurienne* had, beside her commander, one other killed and two wounded; while the PETEREL had no casualties whatever, and only trifling damage. Of the ships which ran ashore the *Cerf* became a total loss, but the *Lejoille* was got off and taken in to safety. The *Ligurienne* was a very fine little brig, nearly new and well found in every respect. But her construction was unusual, being fastened with screw-bolts so that she could be taken to pieces and set up as required. The prisoners said that she had been specially constructed in this manner for service with the Egyptian expedition, and there may have been some idea of transporting her over the Isthmus to the Red Sea before it was discovered that the Bombay station had the Red Sea well under control. However that may be, the construction side of Admiralty felt that screw-bolts were likely to work in a seaway, and she was not taken into the Royal Navy.

In August of the same year the PETEREL was in the Eastern Mediterranean in the squadron commanded by Sir Sidney Smith, who was under the orders of Admiral Lord Keith, Commander-in-Chief, Mediterranean. At this time Napoleon, or rather General Bonaparte, had left his army in Egypt and returned to France; his successor, the admired General Kleber, had been assassinated; and *his* successor, General Menou, was by no means admirable. The British strategy was to maintain a strict watch on all the coasts of Egypt; to prevent reinforcements or supplies reaching the French army there; and to prepare for landing a powerful British army to annihilate French authority in Egypt. Egypt was nominally under Turkish suzerainity, and Turkey was in a somewhat wary alliance with Britain, and even with Russia.

The PETEREL, detached on reconnaissance work, was coasting near Alexandria when on 13th August 1800 she sighted a large hull, dismasted and lying on the shoals of Aboukir Bay not far from where the CULLODEN, Captain Troubridge, had stranded while pressing in to join the Battle of the Nile. As the PETEREL approached to investigate, a number of small dhows were seen to leave the ship and make for the shore. At noon the PETEREL anchored in four fathoms and sent a boat aboard the apparently deserted vessel. Very shortly it returned with thirteen Greeks on board, who told the story.

The ship was a Turkish 80-gun line-of-battle ship, which had stranded by night under so much sail that she was dismasted by the shock. In the morning the captain, Indjay Bey, had surrendered to the local French forces, under threat of bombardment from the shore. A considerable part of the crew had escaped in the boats, but the captain and the rest of the crew were taken ashore by the French, except for the Greeks, who had hidden themselves effectively. They did not want to be prisoners of the French, nor did they want to escape to resume their servitude to the Turks; all they wanted was an opportunity to desert. The French intention, the Greeks knew, was to take off all the guns and especially the stores, which they needed badly, and then float off the empty hull if possible.

Commander Austen now sent off his pinnace with the sailing master Mr John Thompson and nine men, with orders to set the ship thoroughly on fire, which was done so effectively that when they left her at 2.30 p.m. the wreck was on fire from stem to stern. The PETEREL waited at anchor until 5 p.m. when, satisfied that the ship was a total loss, she weighed and resumed her patrol.

It was not quite certain how the Turks would regard the

burning of a Turkish ship, but Hassan Bey, the commanding officer of the Turkish naval forces co-operating with Sir Sidney Smith, took the correct view that by surrendering it had become a French ship, and signified his approval by presenting Commander Austen with a Damascus sabre and a sable pelisse. Not long after he was made post captain, and thus promoted out of sloop commands. We glimpse him later in command of the CANOPUS, reckoned the finest two-decker afloat (French-built, of course); later still in command of an obsolescent 64-gun ship, the ST ALBANS; not that it mattered as far as promotion went, for that was by seniority only (Chapter 2); all he had to do was to keep on living, and this he did very well, dying at 91. He went up through all the ranks of the Service, was Commander-in-Chief, West Indies, and was awarded the Grand Cross of the Bath. Without doubt, His Excellency Admiral of the Fleet Sir Francis Austen G.C.B. would have been surprised to have been foretold that the only reason for including him in a naval saga was solely because of his half-forgotten sister Jane, who had not married, did a bit of writing, and died at Winchester more than forty years before him.

8

The Viper Has Fangs

A favourite command for a young lieutenant was a cutter – one of those swift little ships which were the errand boys of the Navy. Nowadays Admiralty can communicate instantly with any ship in any part of the world and has been known to take over an operation from the SNC on the spot, with disastrous result; but then the only means was by written orders carried by a ship. Usually this was a cutter : a light single-masted ship of about 100 tons, built for speed and windward qualities, with a crew of about 50; well armed, usually with fourteen 4-pounders in the earlier years, later with ten. With the cutter rig ships could sail closer to the wind than any square-rigged vessel, and were supposed to be able to escape from any larger ship, which did not always happen. The gun-power was enough for a fight, although the crew was rather too small to work the ship and fight her too, which was one of the reasons for reducing the fire-power to ten guns. They were remarkable sea-boats, and could sail anywhere in the world.

On 13th March 1797 the 14-gun cutter VIPER, Lieutenant John Pengelly, having done an errand to Algiers was returning to Gibraltar. Passing north of the little island of Alboran she sighted a sail and went NW in chase. This sighting was a Spanish privateer brig, much the same force as the VIPER, having six 4-pounders, four 6-pounders and eight swivels, with 42 men.

The cutter overtook the brig in half an hour and commenced firing, gradually closing the range until the Spaniard tried to stave her off by throwing on her deck flasks filled with gunpowder and sulphur, which the crew got rid of overboard without much trouble. When the privateer saw that the VIPER was preparing to board, she hauled down her colours and surrendered. She had a fair amount of damage, with two killed and six wounded. The VIPER had about 40 shot in her hull and one through her mast, but had no casualties whatever, so that there was nothing to dim the pride with which she brought her prize into Gibraltar.

On the 26th December 1799 the VIPER, still commanded by Lieutenant Pengelly, was off the coast of his native Cornwall not far from Falmouth when she sighted a suspicious sail and went to investigate. Soon there was seen the unmistakable rig of a French *chasse-marée,* which was in fact the privateer *Furet,* Captain Bouvet, armed exactly as the VIPER with fourteen 4-pounders. She had actually picked up a prize that very morning and sent her to France with a prize crew, leaving the *Furet* with 57 men. These privateers were a continual plague in the Channel: fast and seaworthy, manned by the intrepid and expert mariners of Britanny, they could nip out of port in almost any weather, pick up a prize or two, and be back among their rocks and races before any warship even heard of them. Even if they did meet an armed ship, speed and skill would generally bring them clear away. On this occasion the *Furet* saw nothing about the cutter to cause alarm, and waited to engage; but after a cannonade of about three-quarters of an hour decided that this was not a good idea and made off. The VIPER was just as handy and as well manned and engaged her in a running fight for an hour and a half, until damage to the *Furet*'s rigging allowed the VIPER to come alongside, when two broadsides were decisive and the privateer surrendered. She was extensively damaged and had lost four killed and eight wounded, including her captain and second captain. The VIPER had only two slightly wounded (one, Lieutenant Pengelly) and had to have a new mast after she brought her prize into Plymouth; with some triumph, for these odd-looking luggers were hard to catch and hard to beat.

December in the Channel, July in the West Indies – never a dull moment for a cutter. Now she was attached to a squadron under the command of Sir Edward Pellew, lying off Fort de France, Martinique and commanded by Acting Lieutenant Jeremiah Coghlan. Jeremiah was a rarity among 'fortune's favourites'. A poor boy, he had entered the merchant service as a ship's boy in 1793; three years later he distinguished himself for courage and resource in the rescue of the crew of a wrecked East Indiaman. The account came to the notice of Sir Edward Pellew, then in command of the INDEFATIGABLE, and he forthwith wrote to the young hero, offering him his patronage if he cared to join the Royal Navy. Imagine the feelings of a poor ship's boy on receiving such a letter from so distinguished a captain! He accepted, joined the INDEFATIGABLE and was immediately rated midshipman, quite correctly, for he had the requisite sea experience. Pellew never regretted his offer, and when he moved to the IMPETEUX, 74, in command of a squadron, he took Jeremiah with him. Now, with most of his required five years as a midshipman behind him and in command of a fine cutter as acting lieutenant, Jeremiah burned to justify Sir Edward's patronage.

Fort de France was the principal French naval base in the West Indies, and was appropriately guarded. A line-of-battle ship and two frigates were in the harbour; the narrow entrance was covered by three batteries of heavy guns and gun-brigs and smaller gun-boats on constant watch and patrol. Altogether the coast defences mounted more than 250 guns. It was impossible to contemplate a serious attack on such a fortress, and indeed it was not taken until 1809, and then by a fleet of 28 warships of all sizes and an army of 10,000 men. Still, Coghlan felt that the VIPER should have a bite somehow, and exercised his brains on all sorts of unlikely schemes.

The outermost of the gun-brigs was the *Cerbère,* and

Jeremiah studied her with the loving care of a hunter. She was moored broadside on to the channel, close under the batteries, and mounted three long 24-pounders and four 6-pounders, with 87 men. At length Coghlan thought of something and went to Sir Edward, who gave him permission to try. He asked from the flag-ship the 10-oared cutter and twelve volunteers, in which he was to go himself along with Midshipman Paddon from the VIPER and six of her men; there was also another boat from the VIPER and a third from the frigate AMETHYST. On the very dark night of 26th July 1800 the little flotilla set out.

The general idea in a cutting-out-by-boats action was to have a number of boats boarding the attacked vessel at different points, to confuse the defenders who could not tell when yet another boatload might come aboard. In this case such tactics did not work, for the two smaller boats could not keep up with the 10-oared cutter and lost all touch in the darkness, so that the cutter was alone when she reached the *Cerbère,* which was fully alerted to the attack. Undaunted, Coghlan attacked on the quarter, leapt over the bulwark and fell into the meshes of a trawl-net which had been hung up to dry. Thus entangled, he was wounded in the thigh by a thrust from a boarding pike, and he and his handful of men were all bundled overboard. They now pulled forward and boarded again on the forecastle, were able to establish themselves and commenced a fierce fight with the defenders; but once again they were defeated and forced overboard. Undiscouraged, they returned to the attack with renewed ferocity, and this time, after a desperate struggle, they actually carried the ship. The other two boats arrived in time to help tow the brig out, which they did under a heavy fire from the batteries, which scored no hits.

Out of 87 defenders, there were 6 killed and 20 wounded; the 22 who conquered them had 1 man killed and 8 wounded, including Coghlan in two places and Paddon in six.

This was a splendid affair: it is difficult to get men to charge a second time after a repulse; to charge and win on a third attempt is very rare indeed and tells better than words the quality of the score of volunteers and their young leaders. The action was fully appreciated by those who were best able to judge. The prize-money for the *Cerbère* belonged to the whole squadron, but the officers and men unanimously decided that it should all go to the boat's crew which had done the job. In his report to the First Lord, Earl St Vincent, Pellew refers to 'my admiration of that courage which, hand to hand, gave victory to a handful of brave fellows over four times their number, and of that skill which formed, conducted and effected so daring an enterprise.' St Vincent went out of his way to encourage so promising an officer: he sent him a fine sword, and even strained the rules – very rare for him – to confirm his commission as lieutenant six months before he had served the necessary five years as midshipman.

This was a very fair start, and by 1805 Jeremiah Coghlan was commander of the 18-gun ship-sloop RENARD, cruising in the West Indies. On 20th March 1805 off the north coast of Dominica a sail was sighted and chased, on which the stranger, nothing loath, shortened sail to engage. This was a 20-gun privateer sloop, which had had a rather chequered career. Originally a Bermuda trader, she was bought into the Royal Navy in 1795, armed, and renamed the LILY. In 1804 she was captured by a French privateer, taken into Guadeloupe and fitted out as a privateer under the name of *General-Ernouf*, after the governor of the island. Like the RENARD, she had two long 6-pounders, but while she had two more carronades, hers were all old pattern British 12-pounders, very short and of little power, while the RENARD's were 18-pounders of an improved type; and although the French ship had a larger crew, Coghlan had trained his men into a fine team, keen and taut, as might be expected of him.

The *General-Ernouf* began the action, firing irregularly at a range far too long to be effective. The RENARD waited until she was alongside her opponent, at about 40 yards, when she gave her a simultaneous broadside of devastating effect, every shot crashing into her hull, followed by a rapid succession of broadsides equally well controlled and equally accurate, such as the privateersmen had never dreamt of. After half an hour the *General-Ernouf* was seen to be on fire, and ten minutes later she blew up in a great explosion. The RENARD had only one boat left undamaged by shot; this was immediately launched, and the RENARD sailed slowly around towing pieces of timber through the water. By these means 55 men were rescued, the remaining 105 of the French crew being lost. The RENARD had no casualties whatever, showing how effective a defence is a rapid and accurate fire on the enemy.

Although it was common practice to set fire to a captured vessel which was not worth bringing away, it was very seldom indeed that one took fire and blew up during an engagement. The case of the *Orient* at Aboukir springs immediately to the mind, but the sensation which this caused shows how rare it was at the period – strangely enough, considering the amount of gunpowder, slow-match and other combustibles always about during battle.

Jeremiah Coghlan must have reflected, as he was writing in his cabin that afternoon, that just ten years before he had been a merchant ship's boy, the lowest form of marine life, everybody's kickabout; and here he was in command of a fine warship, writing his official letter to the Commander-in-Chief to report a very complete victory with no losses on his ship. He had further to go, because it was not long before he became a post captain, although he never achieved flag rank. It was too late in the war, and there were nearly 700 on the captains' ladder in front of him; still, it was the highest rank to which one could be *promoted*. Jeremiah Coghlan is a standing proof that whatever has been said, and truly said, about influence and connections, it was still possible for a youth in the humblest civilian rank, without money or influence of any kind, to reach high Naval command by sheer merit. How would he fare today?

9

The Hirelings

In addition to the potential of the Royal and private dockyards, there was another source of ships for the Royal Navy — merchant ships already in service, which could be either bought or hired. The larger ships such as the East Indiamen were usually bought, for the alterations they required and the service they might have to undertake would make it difficult to return them; but very often the smaller ships were hired. Quite frequently there was a need for small ships with a special rig which did not come within Admiralty specifications but suited a particular area at the time, and there was a perennial shortage of small swift vessels for carrying despatches and important passengers. The usual practice was that Admiralty hired a vessel complete with her crew, paying the owners so much per month, sometimes for a definite period and sometimes indefinitely, and put a commissioned officer in command, the former skipper generally remaining as sailing master. Out of the hire the owners paid the skipper and crew, and kept the ship seaworthy; but war damage fell on Admiralty. This suited all round: Admiralty had immediate use of a ship and crew; the men were fed and paid as they usually were plus having a chance of prize-money, although they were outside the Navy scheme for pensions for wounds; and for the owners, while it was not so potentially profitable as fitting out a privateer, at least there was a sure income and no financial risk.

On 28th September 1795 the hired cutter ROSE, Lieutenant William Walker, was on a passage from the fleet at Leghorn to Bastia in Corsica. She was armed with eight 4-pounders, but carried a crew of only thirteen men and one boy, conforming to merchant rather than Navy standards, which would have given her forty or fifty; even a 4-pounder gun weighs almost half a ton, and was in the Navy handled by four men, and there must be enough others to work the ship and replace casualties. Of course, only one broadside was manned as a usual thing, although the possibility always existed of a ship being engaged on both sides. The little cutter, with her miniscule crew, had on board a King's Messenger, doubtless with important despatches, two ladies, and £10,000 in coin.

At 4.30 in the morning the only man on deck, the steersman at the tiller, saw three suspicious ships to leeward and called the lieutenant. The ships were recognised as French privateer feluccas, which were known to be well armed and to carry crews of from forty to sixty men; they were also very fast and handy. Lieutenant Walker decided that he could best defend his weighty responsibilities by attacking, called his men, cleared for action and made for the nearest felucca. Intending close action or boarding, he had each gun loaded with three shot, which one could do safely enough with 4-pounders, tough little pop-guns.

Lieutenant Walker intended to run his opponent on board amidships and attack with the cutlass. With this in view he took the tiller himself, but as they neared he went forward to lead the boarders. The steersman did not quite carry out his orders, but with the bowsprit carried away the felucca's mizzen mast and swung under her stern; really a far better manoeuvre, for she was now able to give a most effective raking broadside. Coming round on the lee side, she was almost becalmed by the huge lateen sails of the felucca, but was able to fire her other broadside, on which the privateer hauled down her colours and her captain called for quarter. Lieutenant Walker had not a man to spare to put on board, so he ordered the captain to brail up his sails and lie-to, threatening to sink her with all hands if she attempted to escape, while he made after the next privateer. Coming close alongside, a single broadside of his treble-shotted 4-pounders, aimed low, actually sank her. Leaving the crew to sink or swim as they preferred, Walker went after the third, which, however, made off to windward. No British-built ship could outsail a felucca on that tack, so abandoning the pursuit he returned to his first capture, which still had twice as many men alive as his whole crew. It was impossible to spare a prize crew, so Walker battened the whole crew down under hatches, put on one sentry and a steersman, and took the ship in tow, bringing her in triumph into Bastia.

The first privateer had originally a crew of 42 men, of whom 13 were killed and an unstated number wounded; they reported the other two feluccas as manned with 56 (all lost) and 48 (all escaped), so that the little ROSE had taken on, in men, ten times her number. The captured felucca was armed rather as a pirate, well fitted for taking merchantmen : she had one long brass 6-pounder and four 1-pound swivels forward, while on her gunwales she mounted twelve wall-musketoons. The ROSE had only one man wounded, and that by the accident of a gun-carriage running over his foot on the recoil, crushing it badly; a painful and crippling wound, but William Brown declined to leave the deck, saying he could use a musket sitting as well as anybody. The ship, however, was extensively damaged.

This splendid little action was quickly known around the Mediterranean, and Walker received the congratulations both of Sir Gilbert Elliot, Governor of Corsica, and of Admiral Hotham, C-in-C at Leghorn; but as the ROSE was not a King's Ship, and the action was with privateers, it was not reported in the *Gazette* and Walker had no promotion nor recognition of any kind.

The hired cutter COURIER, twelve 4-pounders and 40 men, Lieutenant Thomas Searle, was on her way from Yarmouth to the Texel, where an amphibious operation was mounting. On 12th May 1799 she came across an enemy brig just in the act of capturing a British merchant sloop. The brig was a privateer of 16 guns, probably 6-pounders, and the action continued for almost two hours, when the brig made off; the COURIER chased her until midnight but lost her in the mists. Next morning a two-masted ship was descried, but on closer approach it turned out to be a small schooner, the French privateer *Ribotteur,* with four 3-pounder guns and 26 men, which surrendered without resistance; she had been a consort of the brig chased the day before. The loss of the COURIER in the two little engagements was five men wounded.

On 11th August 1799 the COURIER was part of a light squadron mudlarking in the shallow narrow passes between the Dutch islands. One objective was to retake the brig *Crash*, which had been captured by the Dutch and now lay moored in a narrow strait off Groningen. She was armed with twelve heavy carronades, 18, 24, and 32-pounders, and was well situated and difficult of access, the wind blowing dead against the attackers in a very narrow and shallow passage. The main force was two sloops, which had great difficulty in tacking among so much mud and so little water. The COURIER with her cutter rig could sail much nearer the wind, so Lieutenant Searle was sent ahead to engage the *Crash* and prevent her escaping before the sloops could come up. This he did with effect, although within very close range of the big carronades of the brig. To engage 32-pounders with 4-pounders seems a tall order, but the COURIER in fact sustained no casualties, although naturally some damage. Eventually the sloops came up and the brig surrendered.

The CRASH was repaired overnight and along with the COURIER sent inshore to cover a boat operation against a battery on shore. In the shallows and rushing tides both grounded and were got off with difficulty, having taken no part in the action which, however, was completely successful, the boating party carrying the battery, spiking the heavy guns and taking away two brass light 4-pounders as souvenirs.

On the evening of the 22nd November 1799, while the COURIER was cruising off Flushing, a cutter was observed to bring-to a bark, and the COURIER went to investigate, upon which the cutter made off. The bark was a British merchantman, and informed the COURIER that she had been held up by a French privateer. Lieutenant Searle at once chased northwards all night, and at 9 a.m. overtook about thirty miles east of Lowestoft. The privateer was well armed with fourteen 4-pounders and 44 men, Captain Lallemand, and the action lasted an hour, when the French ship surrendered. She lost four killed and six wounded, while the COURIER had one killed (her sailing master) and two wounded.

All this small stuff was good service, and satisfied Admiralty that Lieutenant Searle was of captain quality; he was promoted commander and eventually captain, a considerable encouragement to other lieutenants in command of hired vessels, which was generally considered the lowest form of commissioned-officer life.

Another fortunate lieutenant was William Wooldridge, in command of the hired brig PASLEY, with fourteen old-type 12-pounder carronades and two long 6s, and 54 men and boys. On 21st July 1801 she was about thirty miles south of Majorca in light irregular winds when she came up with a large Spanish xebec of 22 guns, which demanded her surrender. The natural reply was a broadside, and the action continued for more than an hour. The wind died away completely because of the cannonade (see Appendix 1), and the xebec, having had enough of this rough stuff, got out her sweeps and rowed away. The PASLEY also swept after her, but having a much smaller crew could not keep up, and the xebec got safely to Ibiza and took shelter under the shore batteries. Her name and losses are not known to me; the PASLEY had one killed and two wounded.

On the 28th October 1801, about seventy miles SE of Cartagena, the PASLEY fell in with a three-masted Spanish privateer polacre, the *Virgen-del-Rosario*, with eight long 12-pounders and two long 24s, and 94 men. Coming up from windward, she chased the PASLEY, came alongside, and there commenced a furious cannonade which lasted for an hour. The PASLEY's weak old carronades (pages 16, 87) were no match for the heavy long guns of the Spaniard, so moving ahead she crossed the bows of her opponent, caught her bowsprit, lashed it to her capstan, and instantly boarded. There ensued a most desperate hand-to-hand battle on the deck, but after fifteen furious minutes the *Virgen-del-Rosario* was completely conquered. As usual in a boarding action, the losses were very heavy – kill or be killed.

The PASLEY had three killed, including the gunner, her sailing master mortally wounded, and seven wounded, including Lieutenant Wooldridge and the mate. The privateer had 21 killed, including almost all her officers, and 13 wounded.

It is difficult to praise in words the cold courage of Lieutenant Wooldridge: finding himself quite out-gunned by his powerful opponent, he boarded a ship which had almost twice his man-power, and carried her with the cutlass. Admiralty approved, and made him commander and then captain; in command of the frigate MEDIATOR on 11th April 1809 he led in the fireships for the attack on the French fleet in Aix Roads (*The Frigates*, pages 112–3).

Lieutenant Thomas Henry Wilson commanded the hired cutter LARK, with twelve old-type 12-pounder carronades and two long 4-pounders, and a crew of 50 men and boys. Cruising off the Texel, he fell in with, and engaged, a French privateer, which ran herself ashore. In the tides and shoals the LARK was unable to get close enough for effective action, and had to give over; on the night tide the privateer was able to get off and away.

A few days later, on the 25th April 1800, the LARK came up with a well-known French cutter privateer which had been having a fine time capturing British merchantmen in the narrow seas: the *Imprenable*, with twelve long 3-pounders and two long 8s, 60 men. After a sharp engagement with the LARK she too ran herself on shore, from which unsinkable position she fought for another hour, when her men began to escape to the land to join a party of soldiers numbering perhaps a hundred. Here they took up a position among the dunes, to oppose with musketry any attempt to bring off their ship. Lieutenant Wilson, however, was getting a little peeved with this running-ashore tactic. He had only two boats. He ordered the sailing master to take the larger with as many men as she would hold, and land a little distance away, to take in the flank the musketeers among the dunes, while he himself in the small boat boarded the cutter. Everything happened according to plan (O Rarity!) and Lieutenant Wilson brought his prize into Yarmouth Roads without a single casualty.

Success is gratifying, but there are occasions where doing one's duty to the last is the only gratification. On 3rd April 1804 the hired cutter SWIFT, 77 tons, eight 4-pounders, 23 men and boys, Lieutenant Leake, bearing despatches to Vice-Admiral Lord Nelson off Toulon, was overtaken by a French xebec privateer of double her size, gun-power and crew. Seeing the probable outcome of the impending battle, the despatches were weighted and hove overboard, and in the furious engagement which ensued the lieutenant and many of his men were killed and the cutter captured. As has been said, these small errand-ships depended on their speed to keep out of trouble, and it was bad luck to fall in with a xebec, which is even faster under Mediterranean conditions; but Lieutenant Leake did his duty to the last.

In 1808, by one of those changes of political wind which we need not here examine, Britain was in alliance with Sweden in opposition to Denmark and Russia. Vice-Admiral Sir James Saumarez, wearing his flag in the VICTORY, commanded a strong fleet in the Sound, and had detached Rear-Admiral Sir Samuel Hood with the 74s CENTAUR and IMPLACABLE to cooperate with the Swedish fleet. Having occasion to communicate with the Rear-Admiral, Saumarez sent his despatches by the hired cutter SWAN, Lieutenant Mark Lucas, with ten 12-pounder carronades and 40 men.

On 24th May 1808, off the island of Bornholm, a strange cutter was seen making out from the land towards the SWAN; this seemed to be much the same sort of ship, perhaps larger, and well manned. After the usual manoeuvring for the wind, false colours, and so on, the two ships engaged at about 4 p.m. about a mile from a battery on Bornholm, which opened fire without any effect at that range. The enemy had apparently a fairly large long gun mounted in her stern, and in endeavouring to bring this to bear she hung in stays. While she was thus immobile the SWAN was able to get in several broadsides, and shortly she blew up with a massive explosion. The cannonade and explosion had practically killed what wind there was; the battery on Bornholm was firing with more rapidity, and boats were pulling out from the shore. Lieutenant Lucas did not wait to seek for possible survivors, and therefore the Danish cutter was not identified. In his official letter Vice-Admiral Saumarez gave high praise to Lieutenant Lucas for his spirited action, although another Commander-in-Chief might have felt that it was more important to deliver his despatches than to trail the coat; but Saumarez was the last man in the world to discourage a fighter.

10

The Mails Must Get Through

Packet-ships have already been described (Chapter 3), as well as the splendid action of the ANTELOPE with the French privateer *Atalante*. In fact, when a packet *was* engaged it was usually with a privateer, because these were the only enemy ships fast enough to catch up with packets, which were generally fast cutters able to sail very close to the wind and designed to evade any enemy ship of war. Privateers had also to be fast, to overtake merchantmen and get away from warships; moreover they carried very large crews for their size, for boarding, providing prize crews, and manning the long sweeps they used extensively in calms.

In the Royal Navy then as now it has been usual to give some idea of the ship by its name; thus one could be fairly sure that the ROYAL SOVEREIGN would be a ship of the line, the AMAZON a frigate, and the CURLEW a brig. Not so with the mail packets, which were frequently given very high-sounding names, seemingly fitter for three-deckers than for tiny cutters. Thus the PRINCESS ROYAL was in fact a cutter of 6 guns, four 4-pounders and two 6s, and a crew of 32 men and boys, commanded by Lieutenant John Skinner as a nice light job for a semi-cripple, for he had lost his right arm in a frigate engagement in the War of the American Revolution. On 12th June 1798 the PRINCESS ROYAL left Falmouth for New

283

York, carrying the mails and seventeen passengers, including the commander's sister and her maid.

On the 21st June, at dawn, there appeared a large brig, which made all sail in pursuit. This was the Bordeaux privateer *Aventurier,* of 16 guns, fourteen long 4-pounders and two carronades, 12-pounders, with a crew of 85 men and boys, nearly three times the force of the packet, which very properly set all sail to escape. The privateer now got out her sweeps, as there was practically no wind and the sea very smooth, and after fourteen hours' rowing came within shot of the PRINCESS ROYAL, when both ships fired to try the range. Apparently satisfied that she could take the packet without trouble, and being disinclined to risk a night engagement, the *Aventurier* took in her sweeps and lay astern of the PRINCESS ROYAL.

Dawn comes early at midsummer, and at 3.30 a.m. the *Aventurier* appeared alongside within pistol-shot, and opened fire. All the passengers had volunteered their services, making a very useful addition to the minute crew of the PRINCESS ROYAL. The most valuable was a Navy lieutenant who was on his way out to join his ship, the ST ALBANS, 64; he took charge of the after 6-pounder and showed himself to be a highly skilled gun-layer. The other fourteen gentlemen were issued with a musket apiece, and were as cool as ever they were over spaniels, while Miss Skinner and her maid were employed below, sewing and filling bag-cartridges for the 4-pounders. The guns were hove about so that five of the six could bear on the broadside, and they were served as steadily as if there were no such things as musket-bullets and cannon balls whistling and crashing around. They fired broadsides only, taking their time from the ST ALBANS lieutenant, and while they were reloading the sporting musketeers made the enemy keep their heads down.

For two hours this cannonade of sixteen guns continued against six, when the *Aventurier* decided to call it a day, got out her sweeps and rowed off eastward. Immediately the lieutenant's 6-pounder was hove around to bear as a stern-chaser, and before the privateer was out of range he got off two shots, both of which crashed through the stern of the *Aventurier* to the cheers of the crew of the PRINCESS ROYAL, who then went to breakfast before seeing to the repairs. These were not too difficult : several shot in the hull, all above water; the boats and spare spars knocked about, and the sails and rigging cut; but the masts and spars undamaged and, strangest of all, not a single casualty.

The *Aventurier,* on the other hand, had two killed and four wounded, all her masts shot through and nineteen shot in her hull; so badly knocked about, in fact, that she had to give up the adventure and go back to Bordeaux to be completely re-fitted. There she landed thirty civilian prisoners, British and American, taken from former prizes during that cruise, and from these all the details of the *Aventurier*'s losses were ascertained.

As always when the battle was against a privateer, however well equipped, there was no particular recognition of this splendid little action. There was no prize to show, only the story of a privateer beaten off; but a story fully authenticated, proving that an elderly and one-armed packet commander was still a King's Officer, completely capable of a heroic and successful action against enormous odds.

The WINDSOR CASTLE was not a three-decker flag-ship but the Leeward Islands packet, Acting Commander William Rogers, six long 4-pounders and two 9-pounder carronades, with a crew of 28 men and boys. The carronades were unusally small, the smallest normal carronade being a 12-pounder, but 9s were probably as heavy as the WINDSOR CASTLE could mount. On 1st October 1807 she was making for Barbados with no passengers but very heavy mails when she sighted a large top-sail schooner approaching under a press of sail. This was the privateer *Jeune-Richard,* having six long 6-pounders and a single long 18-pounder on a traversing carriage, so as to be worked on either side; her complement was 92 men. Not wishing to speak her, the packet cracked on all sail to get away; but the schooner was much the faster ship and came up hand over fist, hoisting French colours and opening fire, which was returned.

Coming within hail, the privateer demanded the surrender of the packet, which was refused. The schooner now came close alongside, threw in grappling-hooks and tried to board; but Commander Rogers had issued pikes to his crew, which they used so effectively as to repulse the boarders with considerable loss. The French now cut the ropes of the grappling-hooks with the intention of giving up the attempt, but the yard of the topsail was so entangled in the packet's rigging that the ships remained locked together. Both sides now prepared for a second hand-to-hand combat. Preparing for the worst, Commander Rogers had all the mailbags hung out overside on the disengaged side, and stationed two boys with hatchets to cut the ropes and let the mail go if the enemy should appear to get the upper hand.

The privateer's men now gathered together on deck with the intention of making a concerted rush; but Commander Rogers had prepared one of his 9-pounder carronades, loaded to the muzzle with grape-shot and musket-balls, and this was now fired with fearsome effect into the crowd on the opposite deck. Without giving the enemy a second to recover from the blow, Commander Rogers leapt upon her deck, followed by five of his men, all that could be spared of the survivors. This tiny body of determined men fell upon their confused and frightened opponents, and in spite of apparently overwhelming numbers drove them all below with heavy loss and fastened the hatches on them : then down came the French colours.

The casualties in this desperate engagement were extremely heavy, as almost always in a boarding action, when it is kill or be killed. Out of a total of 28, the WINDSOR CASTLE lost 3 killed and 10 wounded. Out of 92, the *Jeune-Richard* lost 21 killed and 33 wounded, much more than half her crew; this left, however, 38 unwounded men to be kept prisoners by the 15 remaining of the packet's complement. Fortunately, the privateer had been well provided with handcuffs and shackles for her expected prisoners; almost all the men of the WINDSOR CASTLE were posted round the hatchway of the *Jeune-Richard*; and the prisoners were called up one by one and each put in irons as he appeared.

The action had lasted almost the whole day, but there was little hope of rest. Commander Rogers divided his remaining fifteen men between his two ships and brought them both triumphantly into Barbados.

This was the most fiercely contested naval engagement of the whole of the wars. In no other case is the total of casualties more than half of the total of combatants.* One reason may be that privateers, especially in the West Indies, were reckoned to be no better than pirates in their treatment of prisoners, particularly if wounded; there was therefore more cause to fight desperately rather than surrender. But above everything stands out the character of Acting Commander William Rogers, who showed all the virtues of the greatest captains. Not only did he inspire his men to resist apparently hopeless odds; he arranged for the destruction of his mails in case of failure, at the same time he was planning the heroic coup which won the fight. Such conduct cannot be excelled. As usual when the enemy was a privateer, there were no promotions nor honours for the victor. Proabaly Rogers was not particularly disappointed; not in every naval officer burns the fiery ambition of a Nelson or a Cochrane, and there are many – many I have met! – who are satisfied to do their duty, and do it well.

* But see ANTELOPE and ATLANTE, page 52, chapter 3.

11

The Wolverine

During the early period when every novelty was welcomed, a Captain Schank came up with an invention to allow all the guns of a small ship to fire on the same side. Until then there had been one gun at each port, and consequently only half of the guns carried could be used at the same time, except on those very rare occasions when a ship was engaged on both sides at the same time; and then there were usually not enough men to work both sides simultaneously. It was worth while to try Captain Schank's idea, naturally as cheaply as possible.

A bark-rigged merchant ship, the RATTLER, 286 tons, was purchased, renamed the WOLVERINE, and rated as a 14-gun brig-sloop. As armed by Captain Schank she carried four 12-pounder carronades on her quarter-deck and one on her forecastle, quite ordinary; but her main deck carried two long 18-pounders and six 24-pounder carronades, each mounted on its gun-carriage on a heavy pivot. Eight ports were cut on each side, and grooves were cut in the deck to fit the wheels of the gun-carriages, so that all eight guns could be quite readily run across from one side to the other. Conservative persons shook their heads over the idea of running 15 tons from one side of a ship to the other, and pointed out that she could only fight from the lee side of an enemy, so that the weight of the wind on the sails would counteract the weight of her whole battery on one side; and thus voluntarily to give up the weather gauge was against Naval tradition. However, the idea of a small sloop bringing a couple of long 18s into action was very attractive. With a crew of 70 men under Commander Lewis Mortlock she was attached to the Channel Fleet.

Cruising off Boulogne on the 4th January 1799 in thick weather, the WOLVERINE discovered two large luggers close in to windward. In those waters luggers could scarcely be any other than French privateers, which in fact they were, the *Furet* and the *Rusé,* of fourteen and eight 4-pounders respectively, and each with 70 or 80 men. To encourage them to come closer, Commander Mortlock showed Danish colours, and the *Furet* came so close that her bowsprit projected over the WOLVERINE's quarter-deck. Immediately Commander Mortlock ordered British colours to be hoisted, lashed the bowsprit to his mizzen-chains with his own hands, and ordered to open fire.

Unable to bring her broadside to bear, the *Furet* had nothing for it but to try boarding, and her men came pouring onto the WOLVERINE's quarter-deck with great vigour, but were with difficulty repulsed. Meanwhile the *Rusé* came up on the other side, and boarded by the forecastle, so furiously that practically the whole crew had to leave the guns to repel this new invasion. While they were so occupied, some of the men of the *Furet* boarded again, and one man leapt up on the roof of the round-house encouraging his comrades. Commander Mortlock came rushing from forwards, the Frenchman put a pistol to his face and pressed the trigger, the pistol missed fire, and Mortlock pushed the Frenchman overboard with a thrust of his pike.

The *Furet* now set the WOLVERINE on fire by throwing bags of combustibles in through the cabin windows, and while the ship's company were engaged with this new assault both luggers made away. As they left, the *Furet* fired a parting shot which mortally wounded the Commander. Losses on the WOLVERINE were 10 casualties, of the luggers between 30 and 40.

The indecisive nature of this combat was due to the error of judgment on the part of the British commander in lashing the

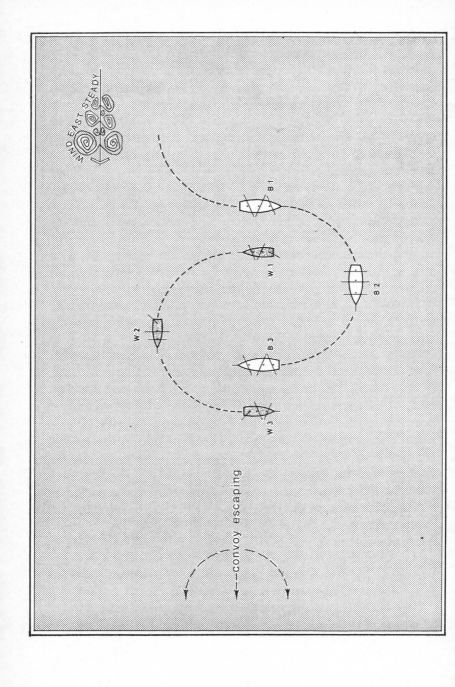

WIND EAST STEADY

B.1

W.1

B.2

W.2

B.3

W.3

convoy escaping

Furet to his rigging and thus making a boarding action inevitable against an enemy with more than twice his numbers. Had he stood off and engaged with gunfire, his two long 18s alone could have sunk both luggers if they did not surrender, and his six 24-pound carronades had at least equal range with the little 4-pounders of the enemy, with a really devastating effect. It would appear that Commander Mortlock had not been given a course in the tactical use of the unusual little ship he was to command.

The next action in which the WOLVERINE was engaged was in consort with the ARROW, as described in Chapter 14. In this action the ARROW was commanded by Nathaniel Portlock, and the WOLVERINE by William Bolton, who better understood the capacity of his vessel. Anchoring 70 yards from his Dutch opponent, with a spring on his cable, he could have brought his six big carronades into action as well as his long 18s if the *Gier* had not surrendered at the first shot.

On 24th March 1804 the WOLVERINE, under Commander Henry Gordon, was well out in the Atlantic escorting a convoy of eight merchantmen to Newfoundland. The wind was fair from the east, and in this direction were descried two large sail, bearing down on the convoy. By 2.30 p.m. it was clear that they were enemies, and the WOLVERINE, signalling the convoy to get away as best they could, turned to meet the strangers. One of them took no part in the encounter and has not been identified; the other was the *Blonde*, formerly a 24-gun ship-corvette of the French Navy, now a privateer, of about 600 tons and 240 men, with 30 guns, the main battery being twenty-four long 8-pounders on the main deck.

. W 1 WOLVERINE lies-to, while the convoy makes its escape. B 1 *Blonde* comes up and engages WOLVERINE, but finds cannonade hotter than expected. She therefore sets sail and crosses the stern of the WOLVER-INE, to engage her from the other side (B 2). W 2 This the WOLVERINE can by no means accept, and crosses the bow of the *Blonde*, in order to engage her from the only side which her peculiar armament admits (W 3 and B 3), which position is maintained until the end of the engagement.

At 4 p.m. the *Blonde* was well within range and the WOLVERINE hove-to on the starboard tack to give the *Blonde* a broadside; the *Blonde* hauled to the wind heading south, fired her broadside, and then wore again to pass the stern of the WOLVERINE, intending to rake her and come up on her lee side. This the WOLVERINE could not permit, for apart from a possibly disastrous raking fire in the stern, owing to her peculiar armament she could only engage from leeward; she therefore had to wear also, when the *Blonde* hove-to on the larboard beam of the WOLVERINE, to windward, and opened a heavy fire with musketry as well as the great guns, at less than pistol-shot distance. The WOLVERINE had now her desired position to leeward, but before she could fire, all her main guns had to be trundled across to the larboard side, and in doing so one of her two 18-pounders jumped the grooves and became hopelessly jammed, not only useless but a hindrance to the working of the other guns. When the other guns were in position a spirited fire was opened in spite of all handicaps, not the least of which was the fact that being heeled away from her antagonist she exposed a good deal of the underwater section of her hull.

The WOLVERINE was now incapable of further manoeuvre, could not in duty abandon her convoy and therefore could not try to escape by sailing away, even if that were possible; there was nothing for it but to hammer away at the hopelessly unequal battle, merely to give the convoy the longest possible time in which to escape. For nearly an hour the WOLVERINE kept up her resistance, until a fifth of her crew were casualties, her sails and rigging cut to pieces, many shot taken between wind and water, and her hold full of water, when she surrendered. No sooner had the *Blonde* taken off all the crew as prisoners than the WOLVERINE heeled and sank, thus proving, if proof was needed, that she had been fought to the last.

The loss of the WOLVERINE was taken rather badly by the great British public, who could not imagine that a privateer could be more than twice as powerful as a King's Ship; indeed, the *Annual Register* referred to the *Blonde* as 'a paltry privateer'. However, she was captured in the same area in August of that year by the 38-gun frigate LOIRE, Captain Frederick Maitland, with some trouble, and her actual force was ascertained. Admiralty had no doubts as to the merit of the action; although a prisoner of war, Commander Gordon was promoted post captain, and the name WOLVERINE was continued in the Royal Navy.*

The WOLVERINE was the last attempt to pull a magical quart out of a pint pot. Compared with the French, the ships were still over-gunned and under-manned; but the Navy had done with trick ships.

* In the same waters during the Second Great War, the destroyer HMS WOLVERINE, Captain James Rowland, D.S.O. and bar, in command of a small flotilla, performed notable service escorting the Halifax convoy.

12

Mutiny

As is generally known, there were two Fleet mutinies in 1797, one at Spithead and the other at the Nore. The former was settled within a month, among demonstrations of fervent loyalty by the mutineers. They had received all their demands about rations, pay and so on; there had been dismissed an admiral, four captains, and 54 other officers, commissioned and warrant; and a general amnesty was decreed and scrupulously observed. The mutiny at the Nore was a more serious business. A president, Richard Parker, had come to the fore, and had taken upon himself the pomp and circumstance of an admiral; there was suspicion of communication with the enemy, and definite threats to take the Fleet over to France, Ireland or America. When the mutiny was quelled Parker was courtmartialed and hanged within six weeks of the outbreak, and 412 of his supporters were courtmartialed later, of whom 29 were hanged, 9 flogged, 29 imprisoned and the rest pardoned.

Amongst those who got off scot-free was one Jackson, who had acted throughout the mutiny as secretary to Parker. He was obviously a literate person and was also a competent seaman, as were indeed most of the 'delegates' of the mutineers. Early in 1800 he was captain of the foretop in the DANAÉ, 20 guns, 9-pounders, Captain Lord Proby.

Early in 1800 the DANAÉ was one of the 'close inshore' squadron of the fleet engaged in the blockade of Brest; the squadron consisting of the 38-gun frigate LOIRE, Captain Newman, and four smaller ships. On 6th February they captured the fine French frigate *Pallas,* 38 guns, which was trying to make the port, and later a few merchantmen, so that all the ships of the squadron had a number of French prisoners on board, and a number of the most reliable seamen had been detached as prize crews.

On 14th March 1800 the DANAÉ chased the 16-gun brig-corvette *Colombe,* which, however, escaped and anchored in Camaret Bay under the guns of Fort Conquête, while the DANAÉ cruised hungrily around the entrance to the bay. This was the moment for which Jackson had been waiting. He had been preaching the seditious doctrines of the Nore mutineers to his shipmates, and being, like most mutiny leaders, much better educated than the usual foremast hand, he had found a considerable following. After dark on the 15th March, at 9.30 p.m., aided by his partisans he released the French prisoners and rushed the quarter-deck, where the only officer was the sailing master. They struck him down, with a serious cutlass wound in the head, threw him down the main hatch-way, and battened down the grating, placing two boats weighted with shot on top of the grating. Thus if by any means the grating could have been cut through from below, the boats with their loads of shot would have fallen on the heads underneath.

All the officers were in their cots except Lord Proby and the officer of Marines. They attempted to make their way to the deck by the after hatchway, but found it heavily guarded; Lord Proby was wounded in the head by a cutlass and forced down, while the hatchway was secured. They now took stock of the situation. Besides the officers, 40 of the crew remained loyal, but all the arms they could muster amounted to ten cutlasses, four muskets, and a few pistols; in any case, they were so securely battened down that there was no possibility of any attempt to re-take the ship. However they were in control of all the stores, and they could hope that if the weather held the ship would have to hold off to sea, and when the ready provisions were exhausted the mutineers would have to make some move. Unfortunately the wind changed, and next morning, the 16th March, the DANAÉ ran in Camaret Bay and anchored alongside the *Colombe.*

Jackson now sent the jolly-boat to apprise the captain of the *Colombe* of the situation, and shortly the first lieutenant, with an armed party, came on board the DANAÉ and asked Lord Proby if he surrendered; the reply was 'To the French nation but not to mutineers.' Both ships now made for Brest. For some hours they were followed by two powerful British frigates, the ANSON, 44, Captain Durham, and the BOADICEA, 38, Captain Keats; but Jackson made the correct answering signals, and the captains concluded that this was a British ship chasing a French brig, with which she was obviously well able to cope; so they stood away. Lord Proby, however, took advantage of this distraction of attention to weight the box containing the private signals and heave it out of a cabin window.

On the 17th the two ships arrived at Brest, where Jackson and his confederates were horrified to find that they were treated like any other prisoner ratings and all marched off to Dinan prison, while the officers whom they had handed over were treated with the utmost consideration. In October 1798 a squadron from Brest had been engaged with a British squadron off Lough Swilly in Ireland and several of the French ships were captured, including the frigate *Bellone,* Captain Louis-Leon Jacob. He had been very properly treated by his captors, duly exchanged, and was now waiting at Brest for another command. He was very happy to repay hospitality, and in particular enabled them to pay their way by very handsomely exchanging their Bank of England paper for French gold. On his suggestion Admiral Bruix allowed most of the officers to return to England, on parole not to serve until regularly exchanged. Later Lord

Proby stood court-martial for the loss of his ship and was honourably acquitted.

Far different was the case of the mutineers. The brief Peace of Amiens two years later brought release to all prisoners of war, but they had nowhere to go. Mutiny, even in the sense of refusing to obey an order, was a hanging matter; but mercy might be sought. There was no possibility of mercy for mutineers who had wounded two officers and handed their ship over to the enemy. Nothing remained for their lifetime but a miserable Ishmaelite kind of existence. Some might take French service; some might make their way to Bordeaux and sign on some of the many American merchantmen which used that port; but always there was the possibility of a British warship closing in and a smart lieutenant coming aboard with his armed boat's crew to look for deserters. One thing was certain : they had alienated themselves for life from their friends, their families and their native land.

13

Commander Maurice
and His Unsinkable Sloop

Martinique was the principal French colony in the West Indies,
a sizeable island of some 400 square miles, bigger than any of
the British West Indian islands. At Fort de France, the capital,
it had a magnificent harbour, fit to accommodate the largest
fleet; on the west coast near the southern end, it was sheltered
from the prevailing easterly winds and yet accessible in all
weathers except hurricanes. The harbour was so heavily fortified as to be impregnable from seaward, and every possible
landing beach on the island was covered by cannon, nearly
300 heavy guns being allocated to the island's defence; there was
also an infantry force of about 2,500 regulars, and about the
same number of local militia. Such a harbour was invaluable.
Here merchant men could assemble in safety until the Atlantic
was more or less clear, or could run for shelter if chased. Every
kind of warship could take on stores, refresh its crew, and wait
to pounce on any possible prey, with a safe refuge if
unsuccessful.

The extreme SW corner of Martinique is Diamond Point,
about five miles south of the entrance to Fort de France
harbour; and a mile offshore lies, or rather stands, the Diamond
Rock, a shaft of volcanic origin standing right up out of the
sea from out of fair depths. It is very similar to the Bass Rock
at the entrance of the Firth of Forth, although somewhat

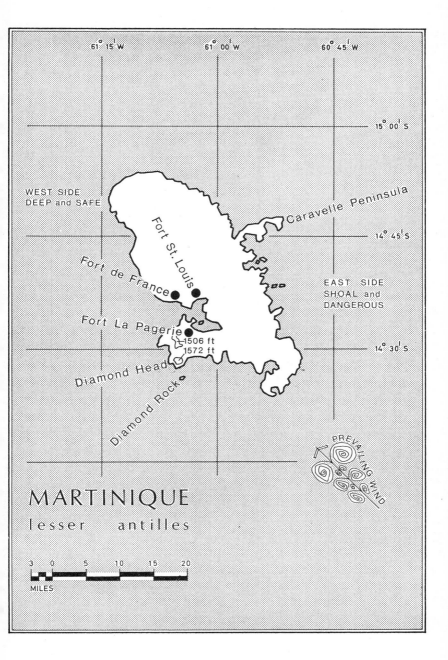

MARTINIQUE
lesser antilles

West side: 61° 15' W, 61° 00' W, 60° 45' W
15° 00' S
14° 45' S
14° 30' S

WEST SIDE
DEEP and SAFE

Fort St. Louis

Caravelle Peninsula

Fort de France

Fort La Pagerie

EAST SIDE
SHOAL and
DANGEROUS

1506 ft
1572 ft

Diamond Head

Diamond Rock

PREVAILING WIND

3 0   5   10   15   20
MILES

H

higher, about 600 feet; as on the Bass, the cliffs rise perpendicularly out of the sea, and the rock is quite inaccessible on all sides except at a place on the west where a landing is practicable in suitable weather. The route slopes obliquely upwards through broken and dangerous ground to the NW side, whence a steep wooded ascent leads to the summit. Unlike the Bass, the Diamond Rock has no spring of water, and was uninhabited.

At the end of 1803 the British line-of-battle ship CENTAUR, 74, Captain Murray Maxwell, having on board Commodore Samuel Hood, was cruising off Fort de France to intercept all passage whether in or out. It was found that those of the French who knew the area used to dodge around the Diamond Rock and often escape thereby into Fort de France. To prevent this, and make the rock a danger instead of a refuge to the French, Commodore Hood decided to take possession and fortify it, thus denying to the French the strait between the rock and the point.

There was no opposition from the enemy, to whom such an idea had never occurred; there was only the silent resistence of the rock and of gravitation. A 24-pounder gun weighs 2½ tons, and to manhandle such a dead weight up a 600-foot cliff was a task to be attempted only by such accomplished officers as Samuel Hood and Murray Maxwell* and the men they had trained. The ship moored at a convenient distance off the rock, and an anchor cable was rigged from the deck to the top of the rock. Running on the cable was a large pulley, from which the gun was suspended, so that the cable took part of the weight and kept the gun clear of any obstruction; the actual hauling was done by two hawsers attached to the gun, with a hundred men on each. In this way not only the guns but the gun-carriages, ammunition and all stores were safely landed. The principle is now of course well known and commonly applied, but it was new in 1803.

* *The Frigates*, page 168.

Five heavy guns were landed, three 24-pounders and two 18s. One of the 24s covered the landing-place and a wide area as well, one was on the NE side commanding the strait between the rock and the point, and one was more than half way up the rock looking towards the entrance of Fort de France harbour. Although far out of range of the harbour any ship entering or leaving from east or south had to give it a wide berth. The two 18s were mounted on the summit of the rock, with an all-round field of fire; the view over the sea from this point was extremely wide, and there was a little disappointment that the range of the guns was not similarly enhanced. A good supply of powder and shot was landed, with small arms and ammunition for 120 men, and provisions and water for four months. An armed launch was provided for such allies as might offer. Lieutenant James Wilkes Maurice of the CENTAUR was promoted commander of this stout vessel, which was duly registered in the Navy List as HM Sloop of War DIAMOND ROCK, as from January 1804.

The crew of the new sloop had a wonderful time: they were freed from the perils of the sea, and also of the enemy, for the French had nothing bigger than a frigate in the West Indies, and even a frigate dared not venture within range of the plunging fire from the Rock's heavy guns; a single shot from such a height would plunge through all the decks and the bottom of a ship, either sinking her at once or putting her out for a lengthy repair. No ship could use the channel inside the Rock, while the launch could pounce out by night on any un-suspecting merchantman bound for the complete safety of Fort de France. Moreover, as well as an extraordinary field of view the British had an equal field of vision for their signals. They reported every ship and every movement they saw, whether or not there was any ship in the vicinity to receive the signal; and the French on shore could never tell. The occupation of Diamond Rock might be only a preliminary to a large-scale invasion of Martinique itself.

The 13th of May 1805 brought a busy day not only for the

lookouts but for the gunners. A great fleet passed HMS DIAMOND ROCK and anchored in Fort de France harbour, consisting of eleven French and five Spanish line-of-battle ships, seven frigates, and six lesser vessels, to all of which the British paid iron tribute as they passed. During the night another French 74 came in, and on the 16th a big Spanish 80-gun ship. For her the DIAMOND ROCK hoisted French colours, so that she came close alongside, when the colours were quickly changed and the Spaniard received an unexpected salvo to hasten her on her way into Fort de France harbour.

This was Admiral Villeneuve with the French Toulon Fleet, who had successfully lured Nelson and the Mediterranean Fleet to the West Indies, and was now to return to Europe, pick up the fleets from Ferrol and Brest, proceed with overwhelming numbers into the Channel and give Napoleon command of the 'damned ditch' for the three days he needed to make himself master of the world. For reasons never fully explained, Villeneuve remained for the rest of the month of May in Fort de France harbour. He may have been waiting for information about Nelson's movements, or it may be that the bombardment from the Rock had necessitated repairs; at any rate the Admiral decided not to take his fleet out until the threat from the DIAMOND ROCK had been eliminated.

For this service he detailed a formidable squadron, consisting of two 74-gun ships of the line, a frigate, a corvette and a schooner, with eleven gunboats, and nearly 400 regular infantry. This force sailed from Fort de France harbour on the 29th May 1805, but owing to the prevailing winds it was the 31st before it got to windward of the sloop and was in a position to attack.

Seeing the force which was approaching, Commander Maurice decided that he could not hold the landing-place nor the lower guns; so he scuttled the launch, spiked the two lower guns, and prepared to defend the higher part of the Rock. For three days the ships bombarded the works with more than 200 guns, while the infantry forced ashore at the landing-place, losing three gun-boats and two rowing boats full of soldiers.

Meanwhile the powder on the DIAMOND ROCK was running low, and the provisions and water for four months, which had been put on board in January of the previous year, had been replenished from time to time, but a fresh supply was overdue and no supply ship could approach. Commander Maurice thought it best to talk terms while he could at least make a show of renewed resistance, and put out a flag of truce. The French were quick to respond, and the schooner came in with a similar flag and a senior officer. Very honourable terms were soon arranged, officers to retain their swords, men to march out under their officers' orders, the company to be taken to Fort de France and thence by the first available cartel to the most convenient British ship or base, without further conditions. It would appear that Admiral Villeneuve was extremely anxious to have this outpost abandoned.

Out of 107 remaining men on the Rock, the losses in this last engagement were only two killed and one wounded in the sloop's company; the French loss was certainly very heavy, but has never been stated from their side, so that there are only estimates: none from the French naval commander, a 'hasty calculation' by the commander of the landing troops of about 50 casualties among his men, the estimate of Commander Maurice of about 70 casualties in the landed force, plus the five large boats sunk by gunfire and whatever casualties were suffered among the bombarding warships.

The following day, 4th June 1805, Admiral Villeneuve with all his fleet sailed unchallenged past the Diamond Rock, bound for Basse-Terre and Europe.

Commander Maurice stood his court-martial for the loss of his sloop DIAMOND ROCK, and was not only honourably acquitted but highly commended for his firm and judicious conduct, which was, indeed, not forgotten six years later, when a somewhat similar command was vacant, but Maurice was by then a post captain, so *that* story must be told elsewhere.

14

The Arrow and the Dart

There was no lack of experimental building in the early part of the wars, especially when Jeremy Bentham was Inspector-General of all naval works, for he rather fancied himself as a naval architect and saw no reason to look to French models for all improvements when he could do better himself. He had no difficulty in having his designs carried out so long as he restricted himself to sloops and below; my Lords Commissioners were strangely conservative when it came to frigates and ships of the line.

In 1796 two sloops to Bentham's designs were ordered, and put in commission at the end of the same year. They were 386 tons each, and much more resembled a rich yachtsman's ship of 1870 than a warship of 1796. They had considerable overhangs both forward and aft, their breadth was much less than usual for their length, and instead of the usual tumblehome of all gun-carrying vessels of the period, their breadth increased from the waterline to the deck. The idea was that as they heeled more and more flotation would be presented at the waterline, which was in fact true, but it was the bulk below the waterline that mattered more, the metacentric shelf was too high. This was met by setting the guns very low and adding to the deadwood of the keel, so that eventually they turned out to be very stiff and fast. Their armament was enormous, all

32-pounder carronades, 24 on the main deck and two on each of forecastle and quarter-deck; later the DART added another two on the quarter-deck. This gave a weight of shot, at carronade range, equal to the main battery of the VICTORY and far greater than the most powerful frigate; but sloops they were and sloops they remained, to be commanded not by a post captain but by a commander.

The idea behind the ARROW and the DART was to produce a very fast ship with a very powerful short-range armament, which could easily escape from a more powerful or longer-ranged ship, or else bring to close action any ship she could tackle. Unfortunately, owing to the 'exigencies of the Service' – euphemism for the stupidity of superiors – neither had much opportunity to demonstrate their particular capabilities.

The great victory off Camperdown in 1797 had assured Britain the command of the North Sea, and it was very seldom thereafter that the Dutch came out in any strength, remaining among the shoals and dangerous channels of the Texel. On the 9th September 1799 Vice-Admiral Mitchell, cruising offshore with a strong squadron, had information of a ship and a brig in the outer channels, and detached in search of them the ARROW and the small WOLVERINE, also an experimental ship, Commanders Portlock and Bolton (Chapter 11). The ARROW was not the ideal ship for this mudlarking, having a fairly deep draught, 12 feet 8 inches, for her tonnage, but by careful seamanship and the aid of some Dutch pilots they were able to nose their way in, slithering over the flats on the flood tide and finding some channel on the ebb. At length, on the 12th, they found the vessels they sought, moored in an advantageous position in a narrow channel near Harlingen. The brig was nearer, and Commander Portlock ordered the WOLVERINE to engage her, while he passed on to meet the much larger ship beyond.

The WOLVERINE came boldly up, anchored very neatly, and fired one preliminary shot; whereupon the Dutchman fired three guns to leeward and hauled down her colours. She turned out to be the *Gier*, with fourteen long 12-pounders and 80 men. Commander Bolton took her pilot and sent him aboard the ARROW, whose Dutch pilots had refused to take her any further. The ship the ARROW was now to engage was said to be the *Draak*, Lieutenant Van Esch, oddly but heavily armed with six brass howitzers, 50-pounders, two long 32s and sixteen long 18-pounders. As the ARROW worked her way with difficulty against wind and tide in the narrow channel she came under heavy fire from the long guns of the *Draak*, which her crew had to endure as best they might for twenty minutes before they got within carronade range. At last they came abreast, and the ARROW opened fire with her mighty broadside of 32-pound shot, while the *Draak* fired her howitzers, which appeared to be loaded with langridge; the enemy did not attempt to reload them, but kept on firing with one 32 and eight 18s against the ARROW's broadside of fourteen 32s, which could be fired at almost twice the rate of the long guns. This could not go on for long: after a quarter of an hour the WOLVERINE was seen approaching and the *Draak* surrendered. Casualties were light, one killed and nine wounded in the ARROW, and apparently only two killed and three wounded in the *Draak*; but it subsequently transpired that many of her casualties had been sent in by boat to Harlingen, under cover of the gun-smoke. She was fired by her captors, being an old ship in poor order; but the *Gier*, a new brig of 324 tons, was taken into the Royal Navy.

While advancing, both the ARROW and the WOLVERINE flew, as well as the British ensign, the orange flag of Nassau, which was hauled down before action commenced. It transpired that the ready surrender of the *Gier* was due to a reluctance of the crew to fire on the orange flag. This had already been exemplified a fortnight earlier, when a whole Dutch battle fleet had surrendered to a British fleet flying the orange flag with the British and having a proclamation from the Prince of Orange; the officers were willing to fight it out for their honour, but the crews mutinied and refused to fight. They were just as brave as the men who had fought at Camperdown, but they didn't like the way that Holland was becoming a satellite of the French Republic. The Dutch, of all nations, like to know what they are fighting about; the reason why.

At the commencement of 1805 the ARROW was in the Mediterranean, based at Malta, her commander now Richard Budd Vincent. In January she was detailed, along with the bomb-ketch ACHERON, Commander Arthur Farquhar, to escort a convoy of 35 merchantmen to England. It would have been difficult to have found two less suitable ships for convoy duties. The ARROW relied upon her speed to run out of trouble, or to bring her formidable carronades within range; but what use was her speed when she was tethered to the lumbering convoy? As for the bomb-ketch, she was built for one purpose only : to toss big explosive shells into stationary targets such as towns or anchored fleets. Her mortars were useless against a moving target, and her other guns gave her less fire-power than the smallest brig. A proper escort would have been two frigates or an old line-of-battle ship, but nothing such could be spared; Nelson had only two frigates with the Mediterranean Fleet, and as for ships of the line! Everybody knew that the crunch was coming, that 1805 must see the decisive action which would determine whether Napoleon was to dictate his terms from St James's or be repulsed for ever from the shores of the Island.

On the 17th January 1805 the French fleet in Toulon put to sea, with eleven of the line and seven frigates, with orders to pass through the Straits of Gibraltar, pick up as many Spanish allies as might be ready for sea, and proceed to the West Indies. However, two days out a violent storm scattered and damaged the fleet, which returned to Toulon with two battleships disabled and two frigates missing, the *Hortense* and the *Incorruptible*; these had weathered the storm very well, and were cruising about east of Gibraltar waiting for the fleet or further orders. These were new frigates of the most powerful types, the *Hortense* rated as 40 guns but actually mounting 48, the

Incorruptible rated as 38 but mounting 42; both had crews of 340 to 350, plus 300 soldiers on each.

At dawn on the 3rd February 1805 Commander Vincent sighted Cape Caxine on the African coast about thirty miles to the south, and kept on his course for the Straits, W by N, with a light breeze from the NE. The ARROW was leading the convoy, now 34 ships, one having been lost in a storm, and the ACHERON was covering the rear when she descried two large sails to the eastward, sailing on much the same course as the convoy. This was reported to the ARROW, which acknowledged the signal. At 10.30 a.m. Commander Vincent ordered the ACHERON to investigate the strangers, and at 11.15 a.m. Commander Farquhar signalled that the ships looked suspicious and were large frigates. Commander Vincent now left the head of the convoy and ordered it to be led by the DUCHESS OF RUTLAND, the most like a warship of all the motley fleet; they had been sailing in two lines fairly well apart and were now ordered to close up. At 12.30 p.m. the ACHERON showed her colours and fired a gun; as the frigates made no reply there could be no further doubt that they were enemies. On this Commander Vincent ordered the convoy to make all sail for Gibraltar, and signalled the ACHERON to join him, which she was not able to do until 4.30 p.m. owing to the very light and uncertain wind. At 5 p.m. it fell dead calm. The two commanders now had a conference and decided to remain between the convoy and the French frigates, both the convoy and the enemy being about five miles from the escort.

Up to this time there had been uncertainty on the French side as to what precisely they had met. It might even have been Nelson himself with the Mediterranean Fleet! The apparent detachment of two small vessels to reconoitre them did nothing to contradict this possibility; but when they saw the main body crowding on all sail to get away, and observed the clumsy disarray of the ships, no doubt was left; it was a large convoy with a very weak escort, a gift from heaven. The calm was a pity, but it affected all ships alike, and only delayed the capture for a few hours. One thing was dubious, whether to take the prizes into Cartagena or risk it for Toulon.

The frigates, with their fine lines and great sail power, were able to ghost a little during the night, and when a very light air came up from the SW at 11 p.m. they were only three miles from the escort and less than seven from the convoy. The ARROW and the ACHERON were in close line ahead, but the frigates were fairly widely separated. Shortly after 4 a.m. on the 4th February the *Hortense* passed to leeward of the ARROW without firing, but on coming abreast of the ACHERON opened fire on her rigging, causing considerable damage but no casualties; the French wanted their prize as intact as possible. The ACHERON fired her pitiful little starboard broadside of four guns, then went about and fired the larboard ones, without any observed effect. At 5.30 a.m. the *Incorruptible* came up and passed both British ships without firing, although the ACHERON fired two guns at fairly long range.

Dawn came at 6 a.m., with a very light wind from the NW. The two frigates were seen between the escort and the convoy, in line ahead going south, the *Hortense* flying a broad pendant to denote the commodore. The ARROW now signalled the DUCHESS OF RUTLAND to engage the enemy, which signal was neither acknowledged nor obeyed. The DUCHESS looked rather like an old 44 or 50-gun two-decker, and had some guns, so that at least a show of entering the combat might have made the frigates hesitate; but she kept on westward with the convoy leaving the escort to its fate.

What that fate was could not be a matter of doubt, only of time. By skilfully drawing the British fire during the brief night encounter the French had satisfied themselves that both were armed only with carronades; the sloop could not have more than 28 of these, and the bomb-ketch 8. The complement of a sloop was 125 men and boys, and of a ketch 67; a total of 36 carronades and 192 men and boys, plus passengers in the ARROW, seven male invalids, two females and an infant. The British very well knew the classes and force of the frigates;

the *Hortense* with 48 guns, the *Incorruptible* with 42, mostly long 18-pounders, only 8 out of the 90 being carronades; and a total complement including soldiers of about 1,300 men. To engage such an overwhelming force was mere suicide; but if the convoy was to escape, suicide appeared to be necessary.

The French ships lay between the convoy and the escort, headed south in the waft from the NW, while the convoy beat up to windward. The ARROW now made sail on the starboard tack, the ACHERON followed her closely, and they sailed westward to the attack. The frigates now sailed eastward to meet them, to engage to leeward. At 7.30 a.m. the action commenced, the *Incorruptible,* leading, passing the ARROW and giving her a broadside *en passant*; to which the ARROW replied, thus necessarily giving the range of her carronades while the *Incorruptible* sailed ahead to engage the ACHERON. The *Hortense* now engaged the ARROW, keeping almost out of the effective range of her carronades while smashing her through and through with long 18-pounders.

The ships slowly passed each other in the light air, and when out of shot the French went about and returned to the attack, the *Hortense* now leading. The ARROW turned into the wind, intending to present her broadside to the approaching prows, hoping to get in at least one raking broadside for each of them; but what with the very light wind and her crippled rigging, she did not answer the helm, and received the whole broadside of the *Hortense* in her starboard quarter, without being able to make any effective reply. The *Hortense* now pushed on after the ACHERON, leaving the ARROW to be finished off by the *Incorruptible*. This, however, was neither quick nor easy. Without hope and without fear, Commander Vincent and his men carried on the fight for nearly an hour, when, with a third of his men killed or wounded, all the rigging shot to pieces, the steering disabled, four guns dismounted, and many shot below the waterline, Commander Vincent ordered the colours to be struck.

The ACHERON resisted for twenty minutes longer, for those

bomb vessels were so strongly built to carry their mortars that they could take a tremendous hammering. For more than an hour she carried on this extraordinary fight of 8 guns and 67 men against 48 guns and 650 men until she was nearly shot to pieces, when Commander Farquhar ordered the ensign to be hauled down.

Both the British ships had all their boats shot to flinders, so that the French had to get out their boats to bring off all the prisoners. No sooner had all the people been taken off the ARROW than she turned on her side and sank. The ACHERON did not sink, but she was such a wreck as to be useless as a prize, and the French set her on fire.

The delay was vital for the convoy; of the 34 ships only 3 were captured by the French, including the DUCHESS OF RUTLAND, which had forfeited honour without gaining safety. It was the old story, so often repeated in the annals of the Navy : the warships must sacrifice themselves so that the convoy may get through. The action was properly appreciated by Admiralty, and both commanders were promoted post captains while they were still prisoners of war. Never was the discipline of the Royal Navy better vindicated than in this action; no hare-brained rushing on unconsidered odds, but a cold acceptance of certain defeat and probable death, pursuant to orders. In all the long account of the Price of Admiralty there is no more glorious defeat than the ARROW and ACHERON.

15

The Dart

Dunkirk has long been famous in British history. From Tudor times it was noted as a nest of pirates and privateers, with ships of surprising speed and handiness which could swoop out from their strategic position, gather up a scoop of prizes in the Straits, and be safely back within their sands and shoals before any effective action could be taken against them. Cromwell had taken it from the Spaniards, as an ally of the French; Charles II had sold it to Louis XIV. Although it could not serve for ships of the line, as could the Scheldt and the Texel, it was a perpetual nuisance to all the small British ships passing the Dover Straits to or from London River and the harbours of the east coast.

In 1800 there lay in Dunkirk four French frigates, much larger vessels than commonly used the port, but as they had got in they could come out, and such a strong squadron could not be tolerated on the very doorpost of Britain's gateway. Accordingly, in June 1800 there was assembled a motley squadron of two small frigates and fifteen smaller vessels, under the command of Captain Henry Inman, to winkle them out. Difficulties arose; no pilots could be found who would undertake to bring the frigates into Dunkirk, although the French ships already there were much larger and deeper in draught. Even for sloops it was impossible to find local pilots, the fact being that everybody who knew the sands was engaged in the smuggling traffic, and dared not give mortal offence to the Dunkirkers. At length it was decided to smoke them out with fireships, and a squadron was made up thus: the DART, Commander Patrick Campbell; gun-brigs BOXER and BITER, Lieutenants Norman and Gilbert; hired cutters KENT and ANN, Lieutenants Cooban and Young; and four fireships. The master of the ANN volunteered to pilot the DART, the others to follow closely; and the night of the 7th July 1800 was chosen for this extraordinary venture, in which a light detachment from the outside squadron was to enter the port and drive out from their moorings four powerful frigates, which were more than a match for the whole of the squadron.

About midnight the DART sighted the French frigates moored in line ahead. As she approached, she was hailed in turn by the first two frigates, and replying in French was allowed to pass unmolested; the third, however, the *Incorruptible,* opened fire on the DART, which replied with double-shotted carronades. The close range suited the DART ideally, but without staying to fight it out she ranged on, laying out a stern anchor, and ran aboard of the last frigate, the *Désirée*, the DART's bowsprit passing between the forestay and the foremast. Instantly the first lieutenant, James McDermitt, leapt on the frigate's forecastle, followed by a division of seamen and Marines, and after a fierce encounter cleared the decks. He was wounded, however, and expecting the enemy to counterattack he asked for another officer and reinforcements. Meantime the cable of the stern anchor had been cut, allowing the DART to swing close alongside, so that the second lieutenant, William Pearce, with the second division was able to board by the quarter-deck and drive all the French below with heavy losses. Immediately Lieutenant Pearce cut the mooring cables, made sail on the *Désirée* and took her off over the sands on the top of the tide.

Meanwhile the fireships, well handled, had been set alight and steered for the frigates, which were also fired upon at short range by the DART, BOXER and BITER; but cutting their cables and setting sail the French made off downwind through the channels to safety. One went ashore on the Braak sand, but was got off next tide and the three frigates eventually returned safely to their original anchorage.

The difference in the losses was most remarkable. In this fierce boarding action the DART had only one man killed and eleven wounded, while the *Désirée*, with nearly three times the number of crew, had over a hundred killed and wounded, including nearly every officer; exemplifying once again that in the confined area of a deck total numbers do not matter nearly so much as the fighting qualities of the front rank. Speed and ferocity are the essentials; the slow and half-hearted are better elsewhere.

The *Désirée*, a fine new frigate of 1,015 tons, was taken into the Royal Navy as a 36-gun frigate, and the command was given to Captain Inman, who had commanded the whole squadron. Commander Patrick Campbell was promoted to post captain and given command of the ARIADNE, a 20-gun post-ship of about half the force of the sloop he had to relinquish as below the dignity of a post captain. First Lieutenant McDermitt was promoted commander. Earlier in the war there would probably have been a frigate and a knighthood for the commander of such an action, but the public was growing a little blasé and saw nothing all that much out of the way in a sloop of 386 tons boarding a frigate of 1,015 tons and carrying her with the cutlass.

In the ARROW versus the *Incorruptible,* and the DART versus the *Désirée*, we have sister ships encountering sister ships with very different results, for reasons which are clearly due to whether or not a ship was employed for the duties for which she was designed. Had the ARROW encountered the *Incorruptible* casually on the high seas, she could no doubt have sailed away into safety; but she was tethered to her convoy, so that the frigate could lie out of accurate carronade range and batter the ARROW to pieces with her long guns. In the other case, the narrow channels between the sands enabled the DART to come close up, when her 32-pounder carronades were devastatingly effective and the moored *Désirée* was a set target for boarding. However the lesson was read, after the loss of the ARROW there were no more of her type constructed, although the DART had a long and honourable war service before being relegated to the Coastguard.

16

The Hard Way to a Commission

In the early days of the wars Admiralty was always open for experiment, thus creating new classes of very few ships. It was after experience was gained that the idea became fixed of as few classes as possible each with as many ships as possible; seldom attained, because of the inherent dislike for scrapping any obsolete ship so long as she floated.

In 1796 Admiralty purchased from the Honourable East India Company nine large ships, all built at Bombay of teak, from 1,170 to 1,430 tons; two-deckers, flush-built, without either quarter-deck or forecastle, making them very weatherly in high winds. The larger carried 56 guns, the smaller 54; 18-pounder long guns on the lower deck, 32-pounder carronades on the upper. They were rated as fourth-rate, but not for the line of battle. They were intended for a specific purpose : to act as flag-ships on the various stations in the West Indies. The teak would last better than oak in tropical waters and the armament was more than enough to meet any French frigate, while if ships of the line approached the flag-ship could draw under the guns of the shore forts. None of them saw much action, although the CALCUTTA, Captain Woodriff, during a homeward voyage in 1805 fell in with a French squadron off the Scillies and was captured; in 1809 the *Calcutta* was destroyed by the IMPERIEUSE, Captain Lord

Cochrane, during the action in the Basque Roads (*The Frigates*, Chapter 10.) The rest of the 54s and 56s were gradually phased out of service by that time.*

In all ships the great enemy is boredom. In a warship at sea, under a good captain, this foe may be met by strict attention to duty, constant vigilance and the changing conditions of weather and rig; but in harbour boredom got the upper hand, especially in flag-ships. Thus in 1796 one of the newly-purchased 54s, the ABERGAVENNY, Captain Henry Vansittart, was sent out as flag-ship to Port Royal, Jamaica. During the whole of 1797 and most of 1798 she swung at her moorings, without the least incident to relieve the tedium. The commodore and his staff were kept busy enough with the frigates, sloops, brigs and schooners under his command, which were constantly employed in collecting information, convoying merchant ships and capturing enemy ones, and continually fighting the enemy privateers and pirates which swarmed in those waters; but the officers of the flag-ship could only watch the little ships busily plying their office while they hung about on the moored flag-ship. Owing to the risk of infection on that fever-haunted island the ship had to lie well out, and for the same reason shore leave was almost impossible; they were thrown on their own resources, and after the first year these began to wear thin.

The usual grumble in the wardroom was that while the officers of the cruising ships were picking up prize-money, and the captain on the station had his share, the officers of the flag-ship had neither a part in others' pickings nor the opportunity to get any for themselves. At last the idea grew up – why should the flag-ship officers not get a little ship of their own, to be rated as tender to the flag-ship, and to cruise for prizes? The captain was approached and was quite agreeable – no doubt delighted that an occupation had been found for some of the company and an interest for all. He could not allow any of the

* The earnest student will observe that in 1814 56-gun flush-decked ships reappear in the Navy List. These were, however, quite different ships.

ship's boats to be used, but he would allow anybody to volunteer and would provide arms and ammunition. In a place like Port Royal, where prizes were being sold almost daily, almost any kind of small vessel was to be had, at a price. What the wardroom's funds could run to was a large frigate's launch, with a 1-pounder swivel gun mounted in the bows and fit to carry up to 30 men with provisions for a month.

The question now arose, who was to command her? A certain lack of enthusiasm was observed, as the officers pondered on exchanging their comfortable cots, well-served wardroom table and deck promenade for the cramped bare boards and hard fare of an open boat, perhaps for a month on end, and for what? Any prize-money won by the tender would be divided among the captain, officers and crew of the whole ship. Obviously the first lieutenant could not go, nor the signals lieutenant; there was an excuse for everybody, but a volunteer was found, Acting-Lieutenant Michael Fitton.

Fitton was no enthusiastic youngster but a most experienced seaman, who knew exactly what he was letting himself in for. He had nearly twenty years of service behind him, having come aft through the hawse-hole,* and was most competent in navigation as well as all the other duties of a naval officer. In spite of his 'age for rank' he was not at all the typical plodder but an active and ambitious man who chafed in the rather invidious rank of acting lieutenant. He wore the uniform, performed the duties and enjoyed the privileges of lieutenant's rank, but only during the captain's pleasure. His substantive rank was master's mate, and the only way to get his commission was by the recommendation of his captain after some meritorious service. Here was his chance.

Some financial arrangements had to be made : the wardroom agreed that out of any prize-money accruing, only half would be divided among the officers and the other half would go towards providing a bigger and better ship; the lower deck

* The term for promotion from the lower deck.

agreed that the volunteers for the launch would have half of the prize-money, and the non-combatants the other half among them. The captain issued powder and shot for the swivel, a few muskets, and a cutlass per man; the acting-lieutenant had his sword and pistols. Thus manned and armed the ABERGAVENNY's tender set forth to seek the enemy, surely the lightest and weakest warship ever sent out; about half the size and man-power of the Viking longships of eight hundred years earlier.

Fighting power, however, is always relative; a 1-pound gun could overawe a merchantman with no guns at all, and in a boarding action the discipline and dash of the man-o-war's men could always drive below the irresolute and ill-disciplined crew of a Spanish privateer. Prizes were brought in, prize-money accumulated, and at length Mr Fitton found himself commanding a real seagoing ship, decked all over, the schooner FERRET, with six 3-pounder popguns and a crew of 45. Treading the deck of the ship under his command, Fitton felt that he could go anywhere and tackle everything.

The opportunity came. On 5th October 1799, while cruising off the NE of Jamaica, the FERRET sighted a larger schooner under British colours, having eight ports on each side. She didn't seem right, somehow. No 16-gun schooner was known in the Royal Navy, and both her ensign and pendant seemed to be far too big for the ship. The FERRET tacked to speak her, but keeping the weather gauge just in case; sure enough, as they drew close the stranger hoisted Spanish colours and opened fire. Mr Fitton knew quite well that this was a ship of much greater force than his; in fact, it was afterwards ascertained to be a Spanish privateer with fourteen long 6-pounders and a crew of at least 100; he had not the least idea, however, of doing anything other than engaging. The cannonade lasted for half an hour, when the Spaniard broke off and made sail to the NW, closely followed by the FERRET; so closely, in fact, that observers on shore, seeing the respective sizes of the schooners, concluded that the FERRET had been captured by the Spaniard and sent word overland to Captain Vansittart that he had lost his tender.

Far different was the fact. When the wind dropped after sunset Mr Fitton got out his sweeps, and at 11 p.m. came alongside the privateer and the contest was renewed. After half an hour a breeze came up, and the Spaniard made sail and put into the fortified harbour of Santiago de Cuba, having had 11 killed and 20 wounded. The FERRET had no casualties at all, but was badly cut about in the sails and rigging and had to return to Port Royal, not at all depressed, having engaged a ship of twice her manpower and nearly five times her gunpower, completely defeated her and chased her into harbour with heavy casualties.

During 1800 the accumulating prize-money allowed the purchase of an 8-gun schooner, named the ACTIVE, which then cruised far and wide throughout the Caribbean, sending in many prizes and destroying even more small but dangerous craft not worth the trouble of bringing into port. In December she returned to Port Royal and was scheduled for an extensive overhaul. To pass the time Acting-Lieutenant Fitton applied for and received permission to transfer himself and his well-tried crew to one of the prizes he had sent in, a Spanish felucca of 50 tons, not really big enough for her sonorous title of *Nostra Senora dos los Dolores,* easily enough shortened to 'Dolly'. She was an odd sort of vessel, flush-decked without any bulwarks and armed with a single 12-pounder, which was too heavy to carry in a firing position while under way. It sat on a traversing carriage on a screw-jack, by which it could be lowered into the hold or raised when it came into action. With her felucca rig and big disappearing gun she was the ideal pirate; nothing less British could be imagined. She was able to penetrate all the pirate's nests and be taken for one of themselves.

In January 1801 they set out for a cruise along the Caribbean coast of South America – the only area which can correctly be called the Spanish Main. They picked up and destroyed a number of small pirates and privateers, not worth sending in; but a few days of rough weather showed them that the felucca was not as staunch as they had supposed. Mr Fitton anchored off a small desert island, where he rigged a tent, landed his crew and stores, and hauled the ship ashore for examination. It was not encouraging; the deck leaked at every seam, keeping the men continuously wet and cold, for which they were so little prepared that nearly half of them were sick; the big beam on which the gun rested was badly sprung, and it was obvious that it would stand very little more gun-raising; the sails were torn and the rigging in poor condition, but there were no spare sails or rope. Without pitch or oakum there was nothing to be done about the deck, and the sprung beam could not be repaired, but Mr Fitton cut down the rig from felucca to lugger, using the off-cuts for patches sewn in position with twine obtained by ravelling down the remnants of canvas. Scarcely had they got the ship re-rigged and everything embarked than so fierce a squall blew up that both cables parted, leaving the little ship with no means of anchoring.

Undismayed, Mr Fitton made for Cartagena, intending to cruise from there along the coast as far as Portobello in the expectation of capturing some sort of vessel which might take them to Jamaica. When nearing Cartagena a Spanish coast-guard schooner approached, the *Santa-Maria*, armed with six long 6-pounders and ten swivels, with a complement of 60 men. The ships were quite close when Mr Fitton screwed up his one gun and began an engagement which lasted half an hour, the lugger making up for the disparity in guns by its greater weight of shot and the celerity with which the gun was served. They fired round-shot and grape alternately, the Spaniard apparently incurring many casualties, until she broke off and made for the island of Varus. The lugger tried to grapple her without success, and both ran ashore at the same time, within ten yards of each other. Without hesitation Mr Fitton sprang overboard, and with his sword in his teeth swam to the Spaniard, followed by all of his men who were fit; they swarmed up the side and after a short fierce encounter carried the schooner.

Once again Mr Fitton had captured a vessel of three times his gun-power and twice his manpower, for almost half of his 45 men were sick. His casualties were two killed and five wounded, the Spanish five killed and nine wounded, including the unfortunate commander, Don Josef Coréi, who had both hands shot off together. A most creditable little victory, and Mr Fitton found himself in command of two ships; but unfortunately both were fast ashore, while the local Spaniards were gathering and commencing musket fire. It soon became clear that it would be impossible to get the Spanish schooner off, so they took the anchors and cables out of her to haul off the lugger; but before this could be done they had to throw overboard their one gun – indeed its supporting beam was so strained that it could never fire again. Once afloat they took all the stores from the schooner, set all the prisoners ashore dead or alive, set fire to the ship and made off, as anxious to avoid an enemy as they had been to encounter one. In four days they reached their base, with no food or water left, no prizes, and only a splendid little victory to their credit.

The captain and the commander-in-chief did justice, and at long last the coveted commission came through, and it was Lieutenant Fitton who commanded the flag-ship's tender. By January 1805 this was the schooner GIPSY, with ten 4-pounders and 45 men. She was sent by the commander-in-chief to deliver despatches to the PRINCESS CHARLOTTE, 36-gun frigate, Captain Gardner, the rendezvous being off Cape Antonio. While hanging about there the GIPSY was chased by five privateers, two schooners and three feluccas, and at once made out to sea in the hope that they would separate in the chase and give a chance of capture. This did happen; the larger of the schooners outsailed all her consorts such a distance that the GIPSY was able to tack towards her and engage her in a running fight; so much to the disadvantage of the Spaniard in attempting to escape she ran on the Colorados reef and became a total loss. Misliking what they saw, the rest made off under all sail and were not seen again. The GIPSY remained on her station for three days until the PRINCESS CHARLOTTE came up, and Lieutenant Fitton was able to hand his despatches to Captain Gardner.

The exploits of Fitton and his 45 men, as they fought their way up from an open boat to a 10-gun schooner, may seem a chronicle of very small beer; but the merit of an action depends in no way on the numbers engaged. The story demonstrates once again how a compact body of daring and resolute men, well commanded, can triumph again and again against apparently impossible odds.

17

The Pelican

The PELICAN was one of the first 18-gun brig-sloops to be fitted out with sixteen 32-pounder carronades and two long 6s, giving her quite a broadside at close range. She was commanded by John Clarke Searle, an excellent officer, with a usual complement of 121 men and boys, whom Searle had worked up into a very good crew indeed. In 1796 she was cruising in the West Indies and took some prizes, which had to be given prize-crews to take them to Jamaica, so that by 23rd September she had only 97 of her crew on board when she sighted a large sail to windward. This was soon made out to be a French frigate of the 36-gun class, in fact the *Médée*, mounting 40 guns altogether, and with a crew of about 300 men – about three times the PELICAN in tonnage, gun-power and crew. Commander Searle judged it prudent to take evasive action, but the *Médée* was much the faster ship, and overhauled rapidly; flight was therefore impossible, and it was either fight or surrender. Thinking he perceived a certain wavering among the men, Commander Searle called them aft and assured them that if they carried out his orders exactly as they had always done, they would at least beat off the frigate if not take her. The men gave him a cheer, cleared for action and shortened sail to fighting rig.

As the frigate approached, she opened fire; but the brig did not return this until the two ships were close enough for carronades, when her first broadside killed the man at the wheel, wounded three others, and disabled a gun. The cannonade went on furiously for nearly two hours, during which the PELICAN was damaged about the spars and rigging but had only one man slightly wounded. At length the *Médée* turned away, exposing her stern for a moment, when the PELICAN was able to put in a raking broadside, causing further damage and casualties, which now amounted to 33 killed and wounded. The *Médée* now fairly made off for Guadeloupe, and the PELICAN was in no condition to follow; well content with having beaten off her big opponent, she set to repairing the damage.

This was at 9 a.m. At 10 a large sail was reported, and by 11 the PELICAN was able to make sail in chase, overtaking at 3 p.m. This was the ALCYON, a British store-ship, which had been captured by the *Médée* a few days before and was now re-taken by the PELICAN. She was taken in tow, but the wind fell away to a dead calm while there was still a heavy swell on the sea, so she was cast off and the two ships drifted about on the swell all night.

Dawn found them fairly near the coast of Guadeloupe, near the French naval harbour of Anse-le-Barque, the ALCYON much closer inshore than the PELICAN; there was also descried the *Médée* at anchor within gun-shot of the ALCYON. She now got out her boats and soon re-took the store-ship, while the PELICAN, helplessly becalmed, could only look on. The morning breeze off the land now came up, and another frigate came out of Anse-le-Barque to stand by the *Médée*, so Commander Searle judged it prudent to use the same breeze to go off to the nearby Iles des Saintes, then in British occupation.

The French captain was so impressed by the 32-pound shot from the PELICAN that he reported that he had been engaged with a frigate which had had her mizzen mast removed; sufficiently improbable that the Governor of Guadeloupe actually sent an ADC to the Saintes under a flag of truce, to enquire about the vessel. This was a fine vindication of the policy of arming these small ships with heavy carronades, proving to the whole Royal Navy that a brig so armed could actually take on a frigate, given the right officers and men. There was no prize to show, however, and no special recognition was made by Admiralty, although Searle was made post quite shortly after.

In 1797 the PELICAN was still in the West Indies, with the same well-trained crew, but now under Commander John Gascoyne; he, however, fell ill and had to be put ashore, the command devolving on Lieutenant Thomas White. Cruising off San Domingo, a strange brig was sighted approaching from northward, the wind being east. The PELICAN went to meet her, hoisting British colours, on which the approaching brig hoisted French. She was the privateer *Trompeur,* with twelve long 6-pounders and 78 men, not really a match for the PELICAN; but she had a consort at a little distance, a schooner with 60 men. As they passed each other both opened fire; the PELICAN swung neatly round the stern of the *Trompeur,* giving her a raking broadside, continued round and came up close alongside within most effective carronade range. It would have been better tactics for the Frenchman to have stood off to try the long-range effect of his long 6-pounders, but the ships kept up a close and furious action for more than half an hour, the French captain plainly seen on the quarter-deck encouraging his men, who stood to their guns like heroes.

Now the schooner came up, and her large crew could be seen assembling on deck with the evident intention of boarding the PELICAN on her disengaged side. To be boarded on both sides is a very awkward situation: Lieutenant White gave up hope of capturing the French brig, and determined to get her out of the way. Approaching even closer, he ordered the muzzles of the carronades to be depressed, so that the 32-pound shot went through her side and bottom. At the third broadside she went down by the head and sank in five minutes. The schooner now put about and went off to windward; instead of chasing her, which would probably have been unsuccessful, Lieutenant

White got out his boats and was able to save 60 Frenchmen, including the gallant captain, so that only 18 were lost. The PELICAN had one killed and five wounded.

Without the intervention of the schooner, the result of the meeting would not have been in doubt. Lieutenant White showed great judgment and resolution in destroying the brig before he could be assailed by superior numbers, and once again he demonstrated the mighty fire-power of 32-pounder carronades, properly handled.

A well-built wooden ship lasts a long time. Ships which fought the Armada were still in the line of battle under Blake, so it was not surprising that the PELICAN was still in service in 1813, after twenty years of warfare. She was now commanded by John Fordyce Maples, cruising in home waters. On the 12th August 1813 she came into Cork for stores and re-fitting, but within an hour she was out again, beating against a half-gale. The American brig *Argus* was actually in St George's Channel, capturing and burning all the shipping she met. Next day at evening a fire was seen, and a brig standing away to the SE. The PELICAN went in chase, but lost sight after nightfall. Early next morning the same brig was seen, having just set another ship on fire, and now making for a group of merchant ships. There was no doubt that this was the *Argus*, and the PELICAN made after her with all sail; nor was there any attempt to escape, for her Captain William Henry Allen was anxious to try his ship against a British brig. The two were a fair match, the *Argus* having eighteen carronades, 24-pounders, and two long 12s, with a remaining crew of 125 men.

At six that morning, St David's Head in sight about fifteen miles to the east, the ships drew alongside, hoisted their colours and opened fire. With her veteran crew, the fire from the British brig was for once superior to the American. In less than five minutes Captain Allen was mortally wounded, and the command fell to Lieutenant William Henry Watson, who handled her with great skill despite the serious damage to her spars and rigging. The PELICAN now sought to cross the stern of the *Argus,* but was prevented by adroit manoeuvring. After the carronade had continued for twenty minutes the *Argus* was so much damaged as to be practically disabled; the PELICAN was now able to cross her stern, raking her from stern to stem with her heavy 32-pound shot, and then came round on her starboard quarter. Passing up her broadside, the PELICAN grappled at the bow and immediately boarded. There was very little resistance, and the American colours came down after a fight of three-quarters of an hour.

The PELICAN had two killed and five wounded, and was so slightly damaged that she was perfectly fit to fight the battle all over again. The *Argus* had 14 killed or mortally wounded, and another 14 wounded. Although seriously damaged, she was temporarily repaired and sent into Plymouth under command of Lieutenant Thomas Welsh of the PELICAN, with all the wounded and a half of the prisoners, while with the other half Commander Maples proceeded to Cork to make his report to Admiral Thornborough. Captain Allen of the *Argus* died at Plymouth and was buried with all honours.

This engagement was received with great approval in Britain. The succession of American frigate victories had been broken in March by the victory of the SHANNON, but the presence of American sloops in home waters had caused considerable alarm, particularly among overseas traders and their insurers, who were greatly comforted by the decisive defeat and capture of the *Argus.* It was observed that at least some of the defeats could be put down to recently constructed ships and raw crews, whereas when a veteran crew which had long served together under the same command, as in the SHANNON and now the PELICAN, met a ship of equal force it was victorious. The shaken belief in the British invincibility on the seas, the faith of all men's childhood, was restored.

18

The Hornet

Shortly after the declaration of war in 1812, the government of the United States decided to send a squadron into the Pacific, consisting of two frigates and a sloop, which was almost a quarter of the whole available American Navy. The story of the two frigates has already been told (*The Frigates,* Chapters 13 and 15), but the sloop also had a varied and adventurous career.

The BONNE CITOYENNE, 20-gun post-ship, Captain Pitt Barnaby Greene, was on a voyage from the River Plate with coined silver to the value of £500,000; grounding on a shoal off the east coast of Brazil in mid-November, she put into the port of Salvador (Bahia) for repairs. Early in December the 44-gun big American frigate *Constitution* and the 18-gun sloop *Hornet* arrived off the port, waiting to pick up their consort the *Essex*, frigate, for their projected cruise. While time hung heavy, the *Hornet* sent in a challenge to the BONNE CITOYENNE to come out and fight, the *Constitution* promising not to interfere. This Captain Greene very properly declined: if he were victorious, it was very unlikely that the great *Constitution* would really see her consort taken clear away as a prize without happening to fall in with them a day or two later; and Captain Greene's duty was to get his much-needed coin to England, whatever scrap was offered. The two sloops were very nearly a match, the American being a trifle heavier in gun-power and number of crew.

The *Essex* did not arrive; the *Constitution* went off and sank the JAVA, and then had to go home for repairs; which left Captain James Lawrence in the *Hornet* to wait for the BONNE CITOYENNE to come out, or whatever might turn up. What did turn up was the MONTAGUE, 74, Captain Manley Hall Dixon, and the *Hornet* had to carry out some very neat evading action to save herself from this line-of-battle ship. Having got clear away she made for the Caribbean, while the MONTAGUE escorted the BONNE CITOYENNE on the next stage of her important voyage, leaving Salvador on the 26th January 1813 and arriving at Portsmouth in good time for her cargo to help to pay the armies which were closing in on France.

The *Hornet* picked up some prizes on the Caribbean coast, and on the 24th February sighted a British brig at anchor among the shoals at the mouth of the Demerara River, making repairs to her rigging. This was the ESPIEGLE, 18-gun brig, Commander John Taylor. She was temporarily incapable of movement, but to get at her the *Hornet* had to make a wide sweep round the sandbanks; and while doing so came across yet another British brig, the PEACOCK, Commander William Peake, sixteen carronades, 24-pounders, and two long 6s. Both ships were seen from the ESPEIGLE until about 1 p.m., when they were manoeuvring for the windward gauge, and went out of sight to the SE. The ESPIEGLE, in no great haste to get her rigging completed, made no attempt to come to the aid of her consort, and next day went into the port of Demerara, for which Commander Taylor was afterwards court-martialled. He was lucky to be acquitted on the capital charges, being merely reprimanded for not having exercised his men sufficiently at the guns; so it was perhaps well for him that he did not engage the expert gunners of the *Hornet*.

The PEACOCK was the smartest sloop in the Royal Navy. Her paintwork was perfection, her spars shone with varnish, her deck was holystoned snow-white, every piece of brass sparkled, every carronade was black-leaded and oiled, even their breech-ropes were encased in pipe-clayed canvas. The only thing odd about her guns was that they were never fired – a smoky messy business at the best.

After the usual manoeuvring for the wind, the two sloops passed each other on opposite tacks, exchanging a broadside as they passed. Unfortunately the first broadside left the PEACOCK almost unarmed on the larboard side: some of the carronades overturned; some drew the fastenings from the ship's side; some of the breeching-ropes broke, rotten under their pipe-clayed sleeves. The PEACOCK wore around to come up again with her starboard side to the enemy, possibly with some hope that this side might be better; the *Hornet* ran in close on the PEACOCK's starboard quarter and in a quarter of an hour reduced her to flinders. Her commander and four others were killed and 33 were wounded; her mainmast was down, and she had six feet of water in the hold; not only were her colours down, but she hoisted an ensign upside down on the foremast as a signal of distress. The *Hornet* had one killed and two wounded, plus two seriously injured by an accidental explosion.

No time was lost in getting out boats, nor was any effort spared to save the ship and crew they had so skilfully defeated; but she was going too fast, and even while they were throwing overboard the beautifully polished guns, she sank straight down in 33 feet of water, so that her foremast stood up like a beacon. Three Americans and four of the PEACOCK's men saved themselves by clinging to the foretop until they were rescued; the American lieutenant and his men were able to jump into their boats just in time; four of the PEACOCK's men took a small boat and made off in the confusion, ultimately making their way into Demerara; probably about five were drowned. Had it not been for the promptitude and efficiency of the *Hornet*'s men in coming to the rescue, very few of the PEACOCK's crew could have been rescued.

The *Hornet* had a slight advantage in weight of broadside and number of crew, but as usual the difference was qualitative:

K

it was a battle between expert gunners and skilled valets, between a strongly built well-practised ship of war and a light vessel fit for any review. Had the PEACOCK had the commander and crew of the REINDEER, of exactly the same force, she would indeed have put up a fight, but probably not with success. Apart from the splendid fighting efficiency of the ship, great courage was shown by the *Hornet* in engaging a sloop apparently her equal while there was another a few miles away which might be expected to come into action with all speed; but even if the ESPIEGLE had come in, with her equally unpractised crew, it is unlikely that the two together could have met the devastating fire of the *Hornet*. It was perhaps as well for British *amour propre* that the ESPIEGLE had a pressing engagement in Demerara.

Perhaps the greatest single difference between the times we are speaking of and today is in communications. Nowadays any event of any importance is known throughout the world within minutes of its occurrence; Napoleon had the same means of communication as Alexander of Ashurnasirpal – horse and sail.

Land communications could be improved by road-making and organisation, but over the oceans wind, weather and accident ruled supreme. The news of Nelson's decisive victory at Aboukir was of the most urgent importance, but it was not received in London until exactly two months later. Thus conferences rolled on for months after the events of war had negated their terms of reference, and war continued uselessly after peace had been declared. Having said all this, it is still difficult to justify the American government in despatching a squadron to the Pacific on 20th January 1815. Peace had already been signed at Ghent on the 24th December 1814, and while it is probable that the government did not know this, they certainly knew that negotiations were well advanced and that a peace was absolutely essential : America's overseas trade had been annihilated,* cutting off her sole source of revenue, the Customs, and

* See Appendix 2.

the states of Massachusetts and Connecticut were preparing to secede from the Union and make a separate peace. In such circumstances, to despatch a squadron to the Pacific, whence it could not be recalled for many months, was the action of reckless desperadoes rather than a responsible government.

The squadron consisted of the *Peacock* (of which more later), the *Tom Bowline*, brig store-ship, and the *Hornet*, now commanded by James Biddle who, as a lieutenant, had hauled down the colours of the FROLIC when she was captured by the *Wasp* (1). The first rendezvous in case of separation was Ascension Island, then uninhabited,* and as the store-ship sailed rather slowly the *Hornet* pushed on ahead to reconnoitre the situation at Ascension, a frequent sighting-point for vessels from India to Britain. It is said that on the 20th March Commander Biddle was informed by 'a neutral' that peace had been signed three months before; this is very possible, but actual evidence is lacking.

The PENGUIN was an 18-gun brig, very much the same as those already described, with sixteen 32-pounder carronades and two long 6s; hastily constructed under contract the previous year and manned by excellent officers, but with a crew which could only be described as the sweepings of the receiving ships. The commander, James Dickinson, had been first lieutenant of the frigate CERBERUS in the glorious action off Lissa, told elsewhere (*The Frigates*, Chapter 12), and had been promoted commander thereafter. He had an excellent lieutenant, MacDonald, and good warrant and petty officers, but his crew were very mixed: some young 'quota men', some very old repressed men (some over 70 years of age) and 17 young boys. With this lot Commander Dickinson was sent out to the Cape; while there, the local C-in-C, Vice-Admiral Tyler, had information of the American privateer *Wasp* (page 179) as having been seen on the India trade route, and sent Dickinson out in search; drafting him, however, twelve Marines out of his

* Ascension was first garrisoned by Britain in 1815, as part of the elaborate arrangements for Napoleon, on St Helena.

flag-ship, showing exactly what he thought of the manning of the PENGUIN.

Patrolling on the line Cape of Good Hope–St Helena–Ascension, the PENGUIN came across the *Hornet* off the north end of Ascension, the limit of her beat; the British vessel had had no news of peace and, coming up, hoisted her colours and fired a gun as a demand to the stranger to show hers. This she did, passing on the opposite tack and firing a broadside, to which the PENGUIN replied, with the same wretched result as on her former consorts, that many of the carronades upset or tore away from the bulwarks. Any apprentice artificer nowadays knows that the same bolt-mounting which is rock-firm in oak will tear right through pine, but the same fittings had been accepted : an extra inch on the outer bolt-plate would have made all the difference. This action continued for about half an hour at a range of fifty yards when the *Hornet* fell away a little, and Commander Dickinson, seeing that gunnery could accomplish nothing, prepared to board. Before he could give more than the preliminary orders he fell, mortally wounded, but Lieutenant MacDonald carried out his intentions. The PENGUIN ran on board the *Hornet*, with her bowsprit between the *Hornet*'s after rigging, but then it broke, bringing down with it the PENGUIN's foremast with all its sails, blanketing the forward guns, while the after ones had been mostly dismounted. In this situation, and having no colours left flying, Lieutenant MacDonald hailed the *Hornet* that he was surrendering.

The PENGUIN had 10 killed and 30 wounded out of her 105 men and 17 boys. The *Hornet* out of her 163 men and 2 boys had 2 killed and 11 wounded, according to her report; but according to the British prisoners, losses were actually heavier, some killed having been put overboard before the British prisoners were brought aboard : certainly the proportion of killed to wounded is unusual for American reports. Immediately after the surrender the *Peacock* and the store-ship came up, and whatever news they had heard there was eagerness to pursue the Pacific voyage; so next morning the PENGUIN was fired and the American sloops proceeded on their way.

Not, however, for long. On 28th April, in the South Atlantic, halfway between Tristan da Cunha and the Falklands, they came in sight of what they took to be a fat East Indiaman, and immediately bore down in chase. What they hoped to devour was in fact the CORNWALLIS, 74, Captain John Bayley, with the flag of Rear-Admiral Sir George Burlton, KCB. The American sloops had never dreamt of meeting a line-of-battle ship in the roaring forties, and were quite close in before they discovered that they had made an error; they separated in flight, the *Peacock* going off to the SE, and the *Hornet* northwards, which ship the Rear-Admiral chose to chase. All day the pursuit continued, the battleship gaining, until she had to heave-to in order to drop a boat for a Marine who had fallen overboard. The remarks of the Rear-Admiral have not been recorded. Up again, on again, off again, the chase continued for two more days, the CORNWALLIS showing a remarkable turn of speed for her class; perhaps the Rear-Admiral had discarded some of the tons of guns on her upperworks, which were quite superfluous for her present work. The *Hornet* threw away her anchors, then her boats and spare spars, then her bell and forge, then her cables and her small arms, and finally all her guns and shot. In the long run she got away, and in fact made her home port, but no longer as a ship of war.

19

A Swarm of Wasps

The ostensible reasons why the United States of America declared war on Britain in 1812 had to do with stopping American ships to search for deserters, impressing American subjects, and the declaration of a general blockade of Europe; all matters which could very well have been settled by negotiation, and in fact were twice so settled, but first one side and then the other refused to ratify the agreement. The underlying reasons may have been territorial: America was always expansionist, like Russia; she had recently acquired the vast southern territories of Florida and Louisiania from Napoleon for dollars down, and may now have been looking northwards to Canada. Thirty years before, the Republic had won independence by a combination of several European powers against Britain; now that most of Europe was combined under Napoleon against Britain, might not Canada join the Union? Furthermore, since the French cruisers had been practically swept from the seas, great and rich British convoys were traversing the Atlantic with no other escort than a single frigate or sloop, to scare off casual pirates: handsome pickings.

To occupy Canada by land seemed a feasible enterprise, but to challenge Britain on the sea appeared the utmost temerity. The United States' whole Navy consisted of 8 frigates and 12 sloops, not a single line-of-battle ship; whereas Britain had at sea in full commission 102 line-of-battle ships, 124 frigates and about 400 sloops. In the outcome the land attack on Canada was totally unsuccessful, whereas at sea the American warships had an unbroken succession of victories for the whole of the first year.

The reasons were not far to seek. In the first place, the overwhelming Royal Navy was not there; almost the whole of its main strength was tied up in blockading Napoleon's fleets in the various European ports. It was the old story of the cat at the mousehole; the mouse can't get out, but the cat can't go away; so it is just as much a prisoner as the mouse. In this case it was a mighty dangerous mouse: outside Toulon lay Vice-Admiral Sir Edward Pellew, with sixteen ships of the line and three frigates, blocking Vice-Admiral Emeriau, with eighteen or twenty ships of the line and eight frigates. This situation was repeated all round the coast of Europe: it was impossible to slacken the blockade to provide even a few heavy ships to deal with a handful of frigates and sloops on the other side of the Atlantic. Let the frigates and sloops on the American stations get on with it.

This is where the second circumstance came into play: in almost every case the American vessels were larger, stronger and better built, better armed and far better manned than their British nominal counterparts. There were no rules governing the various types of ships, although the rigs were closely defined. Thus a sloop was a ship-rigged three-master, but might be almost any size consistent with the rig, so long as it was definitely smaller than the smallest frigate in its navy. A brig must always be two-masted and square-rigged, a schooner two-masted and rigged fore-and-aft; but there were no limits on size. Thus the British regarded a schooner as one of the very smallest warships, meant for winkling petty pirates out of their hidey-holes in the West Indies. Quite a large class of British schooner was 75 tons, with four 12-pounder carronades and 20 men and boys; while the Americans, with their incomparably greater experience of this rig, built schooners of well over 300 tons, with at least ten long 12-pounders and more than 100 men. During the war the new American sloops were of 540 tons British measure, about 100 tons larger than the largest British sloop.

As for building, the British sloops varied greatly, the best being those which had been captured from the French. Home-built ones were mostly run up by contract in yards used to building merchant ships, in contrast to the frigates and ships of the line, which were always built in the Royal Dockyards to the highest standards. For cheapness and speed the sloops were often, at this stage of the war, built of pine and other light timbers. The Americans, on the other hand, had a continent of splendid ship-timber to choose from, and only the best was chosen. During the whole period of building an experienced captain supervised the work, with full powers to reject anything not perfect. The timbers and planking throughout were much heavier, the masts and yards far stouter, than in the equivalent British ships.

The American Navy was by far the best-manned of the period, the nearest in quality being the Danish (at this time including Norway). While the British had to use the press-gang and the quota system, and the French were conscripting peasant boys, the Americans were accepting only the best of the volunteers. The New England states produced a race of mariners equal to the best in the world, and in addition they had a valuable stiffening of experienced men-of-war in the form of deserters from the Royal Navy (page 41). In general the American naval officers were all native born, but a large proportion of the petty officers and senior ratings were British. These could be relied upon to the last; they would never surrender of their own accord, for to be taken in arms against their native country was certain death.

It was this qualitative superiority of the individual American ships that was not understood, or at least not acknowledged, by Admiralty, and many a ship and many a man were lost before the lesson was learnt.

The name *Wasp* has long been honoured in the Navy of the United States, and is at present carried by one of the most powerful ships in the world. At the period of the 1812 war it was a small-ship cognomen, and to make things easier for the meticulous student it was borne by three quite different ships in one year.

The 18-gun British brig-sloop FROLIC, Commander Thomas Whinyates, had a long five-year tour of duty in the Caribbean during which she was sorely stricken with malaria, which seriously debilitated the survivors, amounting to 92 men and 18 boys. This extraordinary proportion of youngsters was owing to two reasons: the great difficulty in scraping a crew together, and the fact that the West Indies had been cleared of all French ships of war, and the only danger was an occasional small privateer or pirate, very unlikely to try conclusions with an 18-gun brig. It was with pleasure that the order was received to quit this pestilential climate and escort a convoy of fourteen merchantmen from Belize, British Honduras to England.

For sailing ships at that period the route from the Caribbean, after clearing the islands, was north on the wind and current, keeping west of the Sargasso weed, and picking up the southwester between 30° and 40° north latitude, according to the season. Commander Whinyates – but we should call him Captain, for he was gazetted post captain on 12th August 1812, although he did not know it for many months – sailed with his convoy from Belize on 12th September 1812, rather close to the hurricane season. Off Havana he spoke an outward bound Channel Island ship and was informed that the United States had declared war on 18th June, three months before, and had already captured the 38-gun British frigate GUERRIERE on 19th August 1812 (*The Frigates,* page 144–5). This was doubly bad news: although it was well known that the Americans had three big frigates, it was not believed that one of them could force a British 38-gun frigate to surrender; and if such was the fighting capacity of the Americans, Captain Whinyates could not but reflect that, with his weakened crew and tethered to his convoy, he would have little chance against a freshly outfitted American sloop of about his own gun-force; and yet he could not honourably avoid it.

The weather was rough, and before clearing the islands the FROLIC sprung her fore topmast. On the night of the 16th October, about 200 miles north of Bermuda, a hurricane scattered the convoy, sprung the main topmast of the FROLIC, carried away her main yard, and tore her sails badly. She hove-to all next day and night in a confused high sea to make what repairs were possible and to allow her convoy to rejoin her. Six of them did so before dark on the 17th, and at dawn on the 18th another sail was seen approaching and thought to be another of the convoy, until she failed to reply to the recognition signal. Ordering the convoy to make the rest of its way on its own, the storm-battered FROLIC turned to meet the approaching enemy, setting what sail she could. It was not much, with no main yard and with both topmasts sprung: a reefed topsail on the fore yard and her driver; enough to give her steerage way to steady her somewhat in that horrible sea, tossing from every direction.

The enemy was the 18-gun ship-sloop *Wasp*, Captain Jacob Jones, armed almost exactly as the FROLIC, with sixteen carronades, 32-pounders, and two long guns: 12-pounders in the *Wasp* and 6s in the FROLIC: There was nothing much to choose either in tonnage or weight of broadside; the difference was in fitness, of ships and of crews. The *Wasp* had a crew of 168 men, like their ship in perfect condition, five days out from Delaware Bay; the FROLIC had been five years in the West Indies, carried 92 men and 18 boys, almost all reduced in health, and the ship was so damaged that she had only two spars left on which to set sails.

Before the storm Captain Whinyates had sighted a Spanish brig-of-war escorting a Spanish convoy, and the possibility existed that they had also been seen from the *Wasp*; the FROLIC therefore hoisted Spanish colours in the hope of delaying, for the benefit of her convoy, the inevitable combat. The *Wasp* approached within sixty yards and then hailed; immediately the FROLIC hoisted British colours and opened fire with musketry as well as guns; the *Wasp* replied at once, closing the range. Although there was little wind, the sea was so tumultuous that on both sides the muzzles of the carronades were often under water.

The first ten minutes of battle were very much to the FROLIC: inside five minutes the *Wasp*'s main topmast came down, and a few minutes later the mizzen topgallant mast and the gaff of the driver. Had the FROLIC been fully rigged this would have given her a possibly decisive advantage; as it was, the most that offered was a chance to escape, and now this too was lost; a shot carried away the peak halyards, down came the gaff and with it the driver, leaving the FROLIC with no means of movement whatever, a mere hulk tossing on the seas.

The *Wasp* now took up an advantageous position across the FROLIC's bow, whence she was able to rake the brig from bow to stern with only one gun able to reply. This cannonade went on for half an hour, the FROLIC obstinately keeping her colours flying, until at last the *Wasp* came alongside and boarded without resistance, finding practically nobody alive on the deck except the man at the wheel and three wounded officers, including the captain. Lieutenant James Biddle of the *Wasp* now cut down the FROLIC's colours, which at the fall of the gaff had been lashed to the mainmast.

In all encounters between British and American ships the casualties were dreadfully heavy : both sides fought with the same tactics, the same principles of gunnery, and the same grimly tenacious courage. In this case the FROLIC was so shattered that both her masts went overside a few minutes after her surrender; she had 15 killed and 47 wounded, so that more than half her crew were casualties. The *Wasp* had the spar damage described, and her losses were eight killed and eight wounded.* Captain Jones has been criticised for prolonging the cannonade instead of boarding to finish the action with less loss

---

* It is to be observed that British casualty reports almost always show the wounded as more than twice the killed, whereas American reports show the numbers about equal. The reason is that the British sailor got 'smart money' for any wound he reported to the surgeon; in American ships this did not apply, so that the captain usually reported as wounded only those actually incapacitated.

of life, but it was no part of his duty to save the lives of the enemy so long as their flag flew; it was perfectly open to Captain Whinyates to stop the slaughter at any time by hauling down his colours, which he would have been perfectly justified in doing any time after the gaff fell and left the ship immovable.

There was little enough time given to either to exult or deplore. During the afternoon, while the two ships were lying together, the line-of-battle ship POICTIERS, Captain John Poer Beresford, came up and took them both without resistance, the spar damage to the *Wasp* making escape impossible. Captain Beresford very properly retained Captain Whinyates in command of the FROLIC. In due course he stood court-martial for the loss of his ship and was most honourably acquitted; indeed, it was his determined resistance and the damage inflicted on the *Wasp* which made possible the capture of that ship, which could otherwise have easily sailed away from the heavy 74.

Very different was the treatment of Captain Jones, although he came home without either his own ship or his prize. He and his crew received the thanks of Congress along with a present of 25,000 dollars, a gold medal for the captain and silver ones for all the officers: such is the enthusiasm of a young nation in the early stages of a popular war.

When it finally penetrated to Admiralty that the three American big frigates were superior in every respect to any British frigate afloat, steps were taken to 'abate the nuisance', among others the provision of really powerful fast ships. The smallest class of 74-gun line-of-battle ship was obsolescent, all were more than twenty years old; the Navy had started the wars with 54 of them, and there were still 20 left. Three of these, the MAJESTIC, SATURN and GOLIATH, were drastically cut down by removing poop, quarter-deck and forecastle; freed of all this superstructure and the 22 guns carried thereon, but retaining the full sail power of the 74, it was hoped that they would be as fast and as handy as the American big frigates. For armament they retained the lower battery of twenty-eight long 32-pounders, and on the upper deck mounted twenty-eight large carronades, 42-pounders, with two long 12-pounder chase guns. They were rated as 56-gun ships, but were much larger and more powerful than the earlier ships of the same rating, which were East India ships bought into the service. Thus fitted and armed, with excellent crews and experienced captains, they went forth seeking what they might devour.

On 2nd February 1814 the MAJESTIC, Captain John Hayes, was cruising in the Atlantic about a hundred miles east of the nearest of the Azores when a ship came in sight to windward bearing down towards her. This was the American privateer *Wasp*, from Philadelphia, of 20 guns, which at first mistook the MAJESTIC for a large Indiaman and scented a rich prize, but finding the mistake in good time made off to the NE under all sail. The MAJESTIC made after her, hoping she might be the big frigate *Constitution,* which was known to have sailed from Boston a month before. After chasing all night, at dawn she was within four miles of the *Wasp* and gaining when there appeared to the southward, about ten miles off, a squadron of two large frigates, another ship and a brig. This seemed a likelier proposition, and the MAJESTIC went off in chase of the two frigates, which turned out to be 40-gun French frigates, of which the MAJESTIC ran down and captured one; but the *Wasp* got clear away.

In 1813 three American sloops were launched, rated as 18-gun sloops, mounting twenty carronades, 32-pounders, and two long 18-pounders; these were larger than any previous sloop, being 540 tons (English measure) and carrying 175 men. Apparently to confuse future students, but possibly for some other reason known to themselves, these sloops were named *Frolic, Peacock* and *Wasp.** They were intended for long-distance cruising.

The REINDEER, 18-gun brig-sloop, Commander William Manners, was by no means the best of her class. She

* For elucidation, see Appendix 3.

had been run up of fir, quickly and cheaply under contract, during the invasion scare of 1803–5. She was intended to carry 32-pounder carronades, but after a few years these were exchanged for 24-pounders, sixteen of which, with two long 6s, was as heavy an armament as her timbers could carry. Of 385 tons, she carried a crew of 98 men and 20 boys. They had the advantage of long service together in the sloop, under the same commander, who had worked them up into a splendid crew who simply idolised their handsome, young and aristocratic commander. On account of this happy and united complement, the REINDEER, in her base town, was called the 'Pride of Plymouth'.

In June 1814 the REINDEER was cruising in the Western Approaches, about 500 miles west of Ushant. Trade was slack, for the war in Europe had ended; Napoleon was on Elba, and Allied armies had restored Louis *le gros* to his acquiescent subjects. The only war was with the United States, and the vast power of the Royal Navy was now available to crush that minor flotilla. The odd privateer might be picked up and there were rumours that some of the sloops had sailed with stores for a long cruise, but the big American frigates were all in their home waters.

At dawn on 28th June, with the wind light from the NE, a sail was sighted in the WSW, and the REINDEER went in chase to investigate; the ship was in fact the *Wasp* already described, commanded by Johnstone Blakeley, intent on bringing the war right to Britain's doorstep. A daring feat, this was made possible by the fact that the great fleets had been withdrawn from the Scheldt, the Channel and off Brest; some to be laid up, some to be paid off, and a few to go to American stations; so that there was some scope for bold raiders, although nothing like serious warfare could be undertaken.

As the REINDEER came up, the chase was recognised as one of the new large sloops, far more than a match for the brig; nevertheless the chase was continued, both ships trying for the weather gauge, at which the REINDEER was successful, and the action began about 3 p.m. A close and furious cannonade was kept up on both sides for more than half an hour, supplemented, on the American side, by a rapid and accurate musketry from the fighting-tops. Commander Manners was shot through the calves of both legs, but kept the deck. One of his men had a strange and fearful wound : an American Marine, in haste, left his ramrod in his musket, and this, fired at short range, transfixed the skull of a gunner; he went below to have the protruding shaft sawn off for convenience, and returned to his gun. After the action the rest of the ramrod was removed, and the heroic gunner made a complete recovery.

The REINDEER was now so battered as to be quite unmanageable, and she came against the *Wasp* with her bow against the enemy's larboard quarter, in such a position that she could be raked both by cannon and musketry, with very little capacity to reply. Most of the officers were down; the commander was again shot through both thighs, which knocked him down, but he sprang up again to lead his men in the only possible desperate attempt. 'Follow me, my boys, we must board her !' and, blood pouring from his wounds, leapt into the rigging to lead aboard, when two bullets from the *Wasp*'s maintop struck him through the head, and he fell back dead on his deck. The *Wasp*'s crew now boarded in their turn, and with their overwhelming numbers rushed the ship to the quarter-deck, where they received the surrender of the vessel from the commander's clerk, Mr Richard Collins, the senior man left on his feet.

What the *Wasp* had captured was a wreck and a shambles. Of her crew of 98 men and 20 boys, the REINDEER lost 25 killed and 42 wounded, most of them seriously; above the waterline, she had had been simply shot to pieces, although both masts were still standing, tottering. Seldom has a ship lost half her complement in half an hour, and such destruction shows the efficiency of the *Wasp*'s commander and crew. Out of 173 men and 2 boys she lost 11 killed and 15 wounded, showing the fight that the REINDEER's men had put up against odds which perhaps her commander should not have challenged;

but such amazing victories as that of the SPEEDY over the *Gamo* had given an unfounded idea of British superiority, and they had to find out the hard way that American ships and American crews were every bit as good as their British equivalents, and in many respects decidedly better.

The two ships lay together overnight, but in the morning the foremast of the wreck fell, and Commander Blakeley decided that she could never be made seaworthy; so taking out the wounded and prisoners he set her on fire, and made for Lorient, where he lay for almost two months repairing and refitting.

This very long repose in Lorient is a very odd thing, diplomatically. Britain and France were not only at peace but in alliance; the King of France had been for more than twenty years an honoured guest in Britain, and owed his restoration in great part to British tenacity; yet an enemy warship, after destroying a British ship, was allowed to enter a French port, land his wounded and prisoners, and enjoy every facility to refit in order to pursue the war. Stranger still, the British did not station a frigate off the port to intercept the *Wasp* when she came out. There may, indeed there must, have been some diplomatic accommodation, for when the *Wasp* emerged she had given up the idea of raiding in British waters and laid a course for home.

The 18-gun brig, such as the REINDEER, was something the Royal Navy was not short of: from two in 1793, the class had grown to 81 at the beginning 1814. The standard armament was sixteen 32-pounder carronades and two long 6s, although in the case of the REINDEER the armament had to be lightened. On the 1st September 1814 the AVON, of this class, Commander the Hon. James Arbuthnot, was cruising about between Madeira and Casablanca, at the time sailing SW with the wind fair from the SE. As darkness was falling she was overtaken by a strange ship on much the same course; this was in fact the *Wasp*, so little expected that more than two hours were spent on night signals and hailing until the AVON was satisfied that this was an enemy, and it was after 9.30 p.m. that she opened with her broadside, without much effect, the standard of gunnery being wretchedly bad. Not so with the *Wasp*: her first broadside cut the peak halyards of the AVON, letting the big driver sail fall over the after guns and blinding them; the next broadside brought down the mainmast, blinding most of the other guns with sails and wreckage, and leaving the AVON unmanageable and unable to make any effective reply to the rapid and accurate fire of the *Wasp*.

The AVON had nothing left standing from which to show her colours, so about 10.30 p.m. the *Wasp* ceased fire and came close, hailing to know if she had surrendered; the answer was 'Yes'. The *Wasp* now hove-to in order to take possession of her prize when she became aware of another sail coming up. This was the brig CASTILIAN, Commander David Braimer, a sister ship of the AVON. Recognising the situation, she opened fire on the *Wasp*, which did not reply but made off downwind under all sail, pursued by the CASTILIAN; but the AVON now made signals of distress and her sister ship turned back to her rescue. At midnight she got out her boats and took off the AVON's crew; no sooner was this completed, in about an hour, than the AVON heeled and sank, illustrating her determined resistance to the last and also the devastating fire of the *Wasp*. She had 10 killed and 32 wounded out of her complement of 104 men and 13 boys, including all her commissioned officers.

The *Wasp* did not appear to have much damage, and was out of sight when day broke. On the 15th September she was spoke off Madeira, but was never seen again: presumed foundered with all hands. The loss of the gallant ship was mourned not only in America but in Britain, where the daring audacity of her cruise had been widely admired by open-minded people, much as the cruise of SMS *Emden,* Captain Müller, in the Indian Ocean, exactly a hundred years later.

20

The Last Shots: Tragedy of Errors

In almost all wars, once the issue is no longer in doubt, there is noticeable a certain disinclination for heroic action on both sides, particularly among the victors. Nobody wants to get himself killed on the last day of a war, however valiant he may be and however fiercely he may have fought when his country was in jeopardy. Thus the last shots of a great war tend to be random and sporadic; yet those mopping-up operations are just as necessary and dangerous as the great decisive actions. Montaigne remarks, 'A man is not always on the top of a breach, or at the head of an army in the sight of his general, as upon a scaffold. A man is oft surpris'd between the hedge and the ditch, he must run the hazard of his life against a hen-roost, he must bolt four rascally musketeers out of a barn.'

On 12th March 1814, as the Allied armies were gathering around Paris, the 18-gun ship-sloop PRIMROSE, Commander Charles Phillott, was lying-to about a hundred miles west of Coruña, on the lookout for anything passing Cape Finisterre. At 2 in the afternoon, wind NE by E, a sail was reported to leeward, standing SW; she was observed to alter course more to the westward, avoiding the PRIMROSE, and sail was made in pursuit. What she was chasing was in fact the British packet brig DUKE OF MARLBOROUGH, from Falmouth to Lisbon with the mails and some military passengers. The trouble was that each mistook the other for an American privateer, or even a naval ship, because of the impression made by the incursions of the Americans into the Western Approaches. It was like the expectation of German parachutists in Britain in 1940; far from panic, or even alarm, but inducing an exaggerated state of suspicion and readiness.

About ten miles away the PRIMROSE fired a gun and hoisted a small blue ensign at the gaff, and when within seven miles hauled this down and put up a larger red ensign. It is unlikely that these could be distinguished at that distance, and if they had been they would have been ignored. The conventions of war at that time permitted the use of false colours up to the very moment of opening fire, and an American privateer in those waters was more likely to use British colours than any others. Then the business of hoisting first a blue ensign and then a red was exactly what one might expect of an American privateer, who could not be sure of the currently acceptable ensign. The DUKE OF MARLBOROUGH hoisted the private recognition signal, but her flags were much smaller than usual for King's Ships, and as she was dead ahead of the PRIMROSE and the wind almost astern, the flags streamed out ahead and could not be made out. Obviously this was another privateer ruse; after two hours the DUKE OF MARLBOROUGH, having had no answering signal, hauled it down, sure that she was being pursued by an enemy, and prepared for battle, fetching two long brass 9-pounders aft to her stern ports. As it came dark the commander of the packet, who had the well-known name of John Bull, ordered the private night recognition signal to be made, but nobody was quite sure what that was; and whatever signals were made, the PRIMROSE made no reply.

The wind now freshened, and the bigger ship began to over-take quite rapidly, at which the DUKE OF MARLBOROUGH opened fire with her stern chasers, doing some damage to the headsails and forward rigging of the PRIMROSE, which made no reply; but coming up on the starboard quarter, both the commander and the second lieutenant (who had Stentor's voice) hailed. Whether both ships hailed together and confused the sound, or whether the distance was too great, the only reply was by gunfire, which killed three men and wounded three. The PRIMROSE now began to fire as her guns could be brought to bear, but Commander Bull manoeuvred his ship with such skill that she suffered no damage. The PRIMROSE now ran upon her opponent's quarter, intending to board, but Bull had run out a spare spar as a boom, so that his big antagonist could not get aboard of him. At the same time the fire of the packet's stern guns still further damaged the sloop's rigging, and she had to fall away to re-fit. Coming up again on the beam, she was able to bring her broadside to bear, and the DUKE OF MARLBOROUGH ceased firing, on which Commander Phillott hailed again to know if she surrendered, and found out, to mutual consternation, that the fight was between allies.

Under other circumstances Commander Bull would have had great credit for the masterly manner in which he defended his ship against hopeless odds; he had two passengers killed, including the adjutant of the 60th Regiment, and about ten wounded. The ship was much damaged, had three and a half feet of water in the hold, and was practically sinking from heavy shot through the hull below the waterline. She was saved by the carpenter of the PRIMROSE and his mates coming on board to plug the shot-holes. The PRIMROSE had three killed and twelve wounded, and suffered moderate damage to her spars and rigging. Both commanders would have deserved praise had they been in fact engaged with an enemy; as it was, it may be imagined that they wrote up their logs and reports with something less than rapture. It was, however, neither the first nor the last time that so disastrous an error was made.

During the Hundred Days, while Napoleon's veteran soldiers flocked to rejoin his eagles, there was no such enthusiasm in the French Navy. Napoleon had not led *them* to victory after astounding victory; he had not made *their* leaders dukes and princes; and his severity towards unsuccessful naval officers was notorious. He refused to take wind and weather into account, just as he had done during his Moscow campaign. Moreover, the long years cooped up in harbours had as always sapped the morale. Still, there were captains who were proud to hoist the tricolour again, and one of these was Capitaine de fregate Nicholas Touffet, commanding the corvette *Légère,* twenty carronades 24-pounders, two long 12-pounders, and four 6s on the quarter-deck. She sailed from Toulon and about fifty miles west of the northern tip of Corsica fell in with the brig-sloop PILOT, Captain John Toup Nicolas, sixteen carronades 32-pounders and two long 6s, on the 17th June 1815, while a wet and weary British army was taking up positions in front of the village of Waterloo.

There was the usual manoeuvring to get the weather gauge, in which the PILOT was successful, coming up abeam about 2.30 p.m., when both ships hoisted their colours and the PILOT fired a single shot through the corvette's foresail. The *Légère* replied with a broadside, and the cannonade began; as usual, the French firing high at the rigging, the British firing low at the hull and the men. This went on for about an hour and a half, when the French fire became intermittent and random; shortly she was seen to back some sails in order to drop astern. The PILOT tried to do the same, but her rigging was so much cut up that she was unable to do so and could only keep on ahead. Wearing with the wind, she tried to cross the bows of the *Légère* and rake her, but immediately the corvette hauled as close to the wind as possible and made off to windward under all sail, leaving the PILOT virtually disabled for sailing. The crew set to work with a will, however, and within an hour had some sail set and went in chase, making more repairs en route. By this time the *Légère* was six miles off, with her rigging in good order, so the chances of catching her were slim; however, the PILOT chased all night, but in the morning there was no sign whatever of the *Légère.*

The casualties on board the PILOT amounted to 2 killed and 14 wounded; but those of the *Légère*, out of a much larger crew of probably 170 men, have been given as 22 killed and 78 wounded, which would indeed have given her good reason to flee from a much smaller ship. The PILOT was fought in a way to do every credit to her commander and crew, but it does not appear that much notice was taken of the action, since by the time the report reached Britain all attention was focused on Paris, where on 7th July Wellington marched in triumphantly at the head of a British Army, the first for 400 years. It is not enough to fight a fine action: it is necessary to do it at the right time.

I have already animadverted on the recklessness of the American government in despatching a squadron to the Pacific when they knew that peace negotiations were well advanced, the peace having in fact been signed a month before the squadron sailed. The only ship to get out of the Atlantic was the *Peacock,* 18-gun ship-sloop, Captain Warrington; without touching at the Cape she made her way across the Indian Ocean, making for the Sunda Straits, a fine locality for picking up richly-laden Indiamen. She hove-to off Anjier (now Anjer Lor) where the East India Company maintained a station, and where was lying one of the Company's armed ships, the NAUTILUS, ten carronades and four long 9s, Lieutenant Charles Boyce. He sent out a boat with his sailing master and an officer passenger to enquire if the American sloop had heard that peace had been declared on 24th December of last year, it being now 30th June 1815; and at the same time the Company's harbourmaster went out in his boat, with a copy of the declaration of peace signed by Mr Madison, which he had been given by an American merchant ship which had called. When the two officers from the NAUTILUS came on board they were instantly hustled below; when Mr MacGregor, the harbourmaster, came aboard he had time to show the declaration to the first lieutenant and the purser before he too, on the captain's order, was taken below.

These proceedings had been observed from the NAUTILUS, which now came alongside, and Lieutenant Boyce hailed Captain Warrington to ask him whether he knew that peace had been declared six months ago. The only answer he received was a brusque order – 'Haul down your colours instantly!' In view of the overwhelming superiority of the *Peacock* it would have been as well if Lieutenant Boyce had complied under the strongest protest, and it is difficult to see what Warrington could have done next. He could not long have pretended ignorance of the peace, and that any act of war was now piracy, a hanging matter; moreover the 22-gun VOLAGE, which had fought a frigate at the battle of Lissa, was approaching the straits with excellent means of persuading Warrington to keep the peace. However, Boyce refused, and the *Peacock* opened fire; the NAUTILUS replied, wounding five men, but shortly had such a fearful casualties for so small a ship that she hauled down the flag – of the Honourable East India Company, not a Royal Navy ensign.

The casualties the NAUTILUS suffered by this atrocity were dreadful: six killed, her commander frightfully wounded, her lieutenant mortally wounded and seven others wounded. Lieutenant Boyce had a large grape-shot through his hip, and his leg smashed by a 32-pound shot; he survived in great pain, but had to have his leg amputated at the hip and was of course crippled for life. His First Lieutenant Mayston lingered for five months after the action before he died. Wounds and death are inevitable in war, and every fighting man steels himself both to inflict or to receive; but so much the more does every fighting man abhor wanton slaughter. The NAUTILUS was a Company's ship, reporting to the Governor, and the news did not reach England for a long time, when the government was engrossed with post-war problems; but no doubt if the NAUTILUS had been a King's Ship, Admiralty would have pressed the government to insist on Captain Warrington being hanged, even if it meant renewing the war – which might have been not a bad thing to relieve the political situation at home.

These were the very last shots of the wars, which have never been renewed, although most early Victorian politicians and historians considered their renewal inevitable, and gave very convincing reasons for their predictions; but Time has his own way of dealing with prophecy. At the present time it is quite impossible to visualise Britain at war with either France or the United States under any circumstances whatever. That is a certainty. But I remember hearing in the House of Lords the late Duke of Bedford, an ardent pacifist, say to the House, 'You have had your way; you have totally destroyed your enemies : have you no enemies left?'

Glossary

ABACK: sails are aback when the wind is pressing them against the masts. To be taken aback; to find the ship unexpectedly in such a position, usually unmanageable.

ABAFT: towards the rear of the ship.

ABEAM: on one side of the ship, especially when the main-masts are in line.

ABOARD: any part of any deck of a ship, inside the hull. 'Come aboard' is the usual invitation into the ship. 'To run aboard' usually means an accidental collision.

ADRIFT: a ship without use of her sails, anchors or boats, drifting about with the winds and currents.

ALOFT: anywhere in the ship higher than the main-masthead.

ANCHORS: the best bower is stowed at the cat-head nearest the bow on the starboard; the second bower in the same position on the larboard; the sheet anchors are stowed immediately aft of these; all four anchors are of the same size and weight, usually 4 to 5 tons in ships of the line, and about $1\frac{1}{2}$ tons in a sloop. The kedge anchor is usually lighter and has more than two flukes, being intended to drag off a ship that has run aground or is otherwise helpless.

BACK: a wind backs if its apparent source changes in a counter-clockwise direction.

BEATING: proceeding to windward in zig-zag fashion, each of the beats as close to the wind as the vessel will sail.

BAR: a shoal to be expected across the mouth of a river.

BRACES: ropes fastened to the yardarms for the purpose of swinging and fastening them.

BOW: the most forward part of a ship's hull. An object is reported to be 'on the bow' if it lies within 45° of the line to which the bow is pointing.

BINNACLE: the strong box built immediately forward of the wheel to contain the compass, lights, etc.

CABLE: the heaviest rope on the ship, being the thick strong rope by which the anchor is attached, usually made up in lengths of 120 fathoms.

CAT-HEADS: the short strong beams projecting from the forecastle, to which the anchors are made fast.

CLEW: the lower corner of a square sail or aft corner of a fore-and-aft sail.

CLEW-EARRING: the loop by which the clew of the sail is made fast to the yard.

CLOSE-HAULED: sailing as close to the wind as possible.

CRANK: unstable in the hull, requiring great care to prevent capsizing.

DRIVER, or spanker: the largest fore-and-aft sail on a full-rigged ship, spread by boom and gaff on the mizzen mast.

FISH: to repair a spar by lashing smaller timbers strongly around it.

FLEET: more than ten warships under a single command. See 'squadron'.

HEAVE-TO: to check the movement of a ship by setting one or more of its sails aback (q.v.).

KNOT: a denomination of speed, signifying one nautical mile per hour; measured at this period by heaving over the stern a log attached to a knotted cord, the number of knots being counted while a sand-glass was running, the knots being 50·57 feet apart for a 30-second sand-glass.

LARBOARD: the left side of a ship when looking forward; now called 'port'.

LATEEN: a large triangular sail set on a long sloping yard; a favourite Mediterranean rig, especially for smaller ships.

LIE-TO: having hove-to (q.v.), to continue to lie with as little motion as possible by adjusting the sails.

LOOM: an indistinct appearance, at night or in fog.

MUSKET-SHOT: an inexactly estimated distance, usually taken as 200–300 yards.

MIZZEN: the aftermost mast of a ship having more than two.

OFFING: in the vicinity. In the case of land, at a safe distance offshore. In the case of a vessel, within topmast sight but well out of shot.

PINTLE: the bolt by which the rudder is attached to the stern.

PISTOL-SHOT: an estimated distance, usually taken as about 50 yards.

QUARTERDECK: that part of the ship's deck, usually raised, extending from the mainmast to the stern. Reserved for officers, except for ratings on duty.

RAKE: to cannonade the whole length of a ship, either from astern or forward.

SLIP THE CABLE: to allow the whole of the cable to slip through the hawsehole, having attached a buoy by a rope longer than the depth of water, so as to pick it up later. To be distinguished from CUT the cable, when the cable is cut through with axes and the anchor abandoned.

SPLICE: to unite two ends of rope by twisting the strands together.

SPRING: when anchoring with a spring, a rope is passed out of a stern-port and passed forward, where it is made fast to the anchor ring. After the anchor has taken hold, the ship may be swung in any direction by means of the spring rope.

SPRING: a spar is sprung when it has partially split longitudinally.

SQUADRON: a number of warships less than ten, under one command. See 'fleet'.

STARBOARD: the right-hand side of the ship, looking forward.

STAYS: a ship is said to be in stays when the sails are temporarily aback when changing course.

TACK: tacking is used in the same sense as beating (q.v.), but is also applied to each straight course between changing direction: e.g. a ship beating to windward might make long tacks so as to keep as great an area as possible under observation, or she might make short tacks so as to arrive sooner at her destination.

WEATHER: the weather side of a ship is that from which the wind is blowing.

WEATHER-GAUGE: to be on the weather side of an enemy, almost always a tactical advantage.

WAY: a ship is under way when it is moving through the water under full control. Steerage way is just enough movement to allow the rudder to do its work.

WEIGH: to pull up the anchor. If more than one anchor is down the ship is 'moored' and has to be brought to a single anchor before she can weigh.

Notes on the Plates

Jacket illustration Probably a convoy collecting in the Downs; more probably for the West Indies than the East. The Deal galley punt in the left foreground was the principal ship-to-shore boat, and was remarkably weatherly. All detail is remarkably accurate in this oil by Brooking.

Plate 1 The French chasse-marée was the pest of the English Channel. With her enormous sail-power and her large crew of skilled Breton mariners, she could run away from anything more powerful and capture any merchantman. On this occasion she has come rather close inshore to pillage and fire a merchantman, and the brig is going to get her in this weather.

Plate 2 The SCOURGE and the *Sans-Culotte*. This was the first action of the war. The British brig, half-gunned and with 20 less than her complement, engaged the French privateer *Sans-Culotte*, and after a battle of three hours captured her and brought her into port. See Chapter 3.

Plate 3 The ANTELOPE and the *Atalante*. The ANTELOPE, carrying mails in the West Indies, was intercepted by the much larger *Atalanta* and actually brought her as a prize to Jamaica. The drawing, unfortunately, is by no means a model of correctitude. See Chapter 3.

Plate 4 The VIPER. A remarkable class of ship intended especially for the carrying of despatches in all weathers. Note the four rows of reefing points. She could also carry another large jib and a large square-sail on her topmast. See Chapter 8.

Plate 5 The WOLVERINE. An experimental type of vessel, she gave an excellent account of herself off the French coast, and was eventually sunk in a magnificent but hopeless action in the Atlantic, which allowed her convoy to escape. See Chapter 11.

Plate 6 Aristocratic Captain. Thomas, Lord Cochrane, in the full uniform of a captain at the age of 27. The worthiest successor of Nelson, he fell foul of Authority. See Chapter 4.

Plate 7 Plebian Captain. James Cook, greatest of all navigators, in the uniform of a lieutenant, to which he had just been promoted, at the age of forty, in order to command a ship of war, and map the world.

Plate 8 The *Wasp* and the REINDEER. There were a number of *Wasps* in the American Navy, which are elucidated in Appendix 3. The last *Wasp* made a daring sally into the English Channel and sank two British brigs under the noses of the Channel Fleet. This *Wasp* was lost with all hands on the passage back to America. See Chapter 19.

Plate 9 The *Hornet* sinking the PEACOCK. Immediately after the PEACOCK surrendered, both ships anchored in 33 feet of water, and the PEACOCK hoisted a flag of distress, correctly shown as the ensign upside down. She sank in minutes, but the prompt action of the *Hornet*'s boats saved all but five of the survivors. The action took place much further from the shore than depicted. Four British sailors made off in a boat (eventually reaching Demerara) and these are seen in the middle distance. The brig on the extreme right is the ESPIEGLE, among the sands off the mouth of the Demerara River; as shown, the position agrees with most American accounts, but in the shallow water the foretop of the PEACOCK stood up for years, and subsequent survey showed her to be at least 20 miles from the nearest possible position of the ESPIEGLE.

APPENDIX 1

Effect of Cannon Fire on Wind

Ever since the introduction of cannon as the main weapon of naval warfare it had been noticed that light breezes died away to a calm when a cannonade was opened. This happened so often that it was accepted by all naval authorities as axiomatic. Later generations, which did not use the wind for propulsion and were accustomed to a few high-velocity guns per ship, have been inclined to criticise this as merely empirical and capable of other explanation. For a light wind to die away to a calm is nothing unusual, with or without a cannonade, and cordite in rifled guns produced no perceptible effect on the wind. It is, however, to be explained theoretically as well. Smooth-bore guns used enormous quantities of propellant— 15 pounds for a 32-pound shot, 4 pounds for a 4-pounder; a big ship like the VICTORY would blaze off a quarter of a ton of powder in a single broadside, while two sloops alongside firing at each other would be discharging a hundredweight of powder a minute into the confined space between the ships. This produced enormous quantities of hot gases, causing an area of comparatively high atmospheric pressure around the ships, quite enough to nullify any slight wind pressure.

Effect of the War on American Trade

All expressed in terms of current pounds sterling

Year	Total exports	Total imports
1807	£22,571,488	£28,869,765
1812	8,026,506	16,047,916
1814	1,443,216	2,701,041

British Trade in the Same Years

1807	£31,015,526	£26,734,425
1812	38,041,573	26,163,431
1814	53,573,234	33,755,264

M

Elucidation of the Sloop Names
Frolic, Peacock and Wasp

FROLIC. Brig-sloop, 18 guns actual, Commander Thomas Whinyates. 384 tons. Captured 18th October 1812 by *Wasp* (1) and recaptured the same day by POICTERS, 74.

Frolic. American sloop, ship-rigged, 18 guns nominal, 22 actual, Commander Joseph Bainbridge (*not* Commodore Bainbridge of the *Constitution*). 509 tons English measure. Launched early in 1813, first of the three. No particular history. Captured 20th April 1814 between Cuba and Florida by the frigate ORPHEUS, 36 guns nominal, Captain Hugh Pigot, and the 12-gun schooner SHELBURNE, Lieutenant David Hope.

PEACOCK. Brig-sloop, 18 guns actual, Commander William Peake. 386 tons. Captured and sunk 24th February 1813 by the American ship-sloop *Hornet*, Captain James Lawrence (Chapter 19) off Demerara.

PEACOCK. Ship-sloop, 18 guns nominal, probably 24 actual, Commander Richard Coote. Foundered at sea with all hands, Northern Caribbean, August 1814.

Peacock. American ship-sloop, 18 guns nominal, 22 actual, Commander Lewis Warrington. 509 tons American, 540 tons English measure. Launched early 1813. Several successes (Chapter 19). Penetrated the East Indies, and on 30th June 1815 engaged and captured the Honourable East India Company's 10-gun schooner NAUTILUS, Lieutenant Boyce, unfortunately some months after peace had been declared. Survived the war.

Wasp. American ship-sloop, 18 guns actual, Commander Jacob Jones. 434 tons. Captured FROLIC (see above and Chapter 18) and was the same day captured by the POICTERS, 74, 18th October 1812. Taken into the Royal Navy as LOUP-CERVIER; served on the American coast. Foundered with all hands 1815.

Wasp. American privateer, 20 guns actual, of Philadelphia. Chased off Azores by the MAJESTIC, Captain John Hayes, 2nd and 3rd February 1814, but escaped.

Wasp. American ship-sloop, 18 guns nominal, 22 actual, Captain Johnston Blakeley. 509 tons American, 540 tons English measure. Launched early in 1813. Conspicuously successful in several courageous actions. Last sighted 15th September 1814 off Madeira, returning to US after a most creditable cruise in British waters. Foundered at sea with all hands, latter half of September 1814 (Chapter 18).

TABLE I

Strength of the Royal Navy in sloops, brigs, etc. in 1793 and in 1814

The following classes commanded by a Commander

	1793	*1814*
Ship-rigged sloop, quarter-decked, 18 guns		33
flush-decked, 18 guns		7
quarter-decked, 16 guns	13	10
flush-decked, 16 guns		3
quarter-decked, 14 guns	7	
Brig-sloop, 18 guns	2	81
16 guns	5	32
14 guns	7	14
10 guns		28
Bomb-ketch, 8 guns and 2 mortars		8

The following classes commanded by a Lieutenant

	1793	*1814*
Gun-brig, 14 guns		3
12 guns		67
10 guns		1
Cutters and Schooners (all fore-and-aft rig)		
14 guns	11	8
12 guns	6	8
10 guns		24
8 guns		2
6 guns		1
4 guns	1	10
Totals	**52**	**340**

This table refers only to ships in full commission.

Omitted are all ships in reserve or under repair, armed transports and storeships, and all ships, armed or not, which had not the primary purpose of seeking battle with the enemy.

The gun-force given is the nominal rating; in the case of the larger sloops the actual force was greater; see Chapter 1.

TABLE II

Losses of the Royal Navy, for the years 1793 to 1815 inclusive, in the classes of vessels named in Table I

Year	By enemy action	By perils of the sea
1793	2	3
1794	6	3
1795	2	2
1796	1	10
1797	2*	8
1798	3	6
1799	2	7
1800	1**	10
1801	5	6
1802†	none	2
1803§	2	5
1804	5	9
1805	5	14
1806	7	10
1807	9	19
1808	11	15
1809	4	21
1810	1	8
1811	7	9
1812‡	4	14
1813	7	12
1814	7	13
1815	2	5
Totals	95	211

Grand total 306

*One ship lost by crew mutinying and taking ship into enemy port.
**Lost by crew mutinying and taking ship into enemy port.
†Peace of Amiens ratified 10th October 1801.
§War resumed 18th May 1803.
‡After this date, most losses by enemy action were to American ships.

TABLE III

Sloops and brigs, etc. of the Royal Navy, lost by foundering or capsizing at sea between 1793 and 1815 inclusive

Year	Name	British-built or captured	Guns	Area where lost	Fate of crew
1794	Actif	captured	10	West Indies	all saved
	Spitfire	captured	6	West Indies	all lost
1796	CURLEW	British	18	North Sea	all lost
	SCOURGE	British	16	North Sea	all saved
	Bermuda	captured	14	West Indies	all lost
	HELENA	British	14	North Sea	all lost
1797	SWIFT	British	18	China Seas	all lost
	Vipere	captured	16	West of Ireland	all lost
	Hermes	captured	16	uncertain	all lost
	Pandora	captured	14	North Sea	all lost
	RESOLUTION	British	14	uncertain	all lost
1798	Braak	captured	16	Delaware Estuary	35 lost
1799	Orestes	captured	18	Indian Ocean	all lost
1800	Chance	captured	18	uncertain	25 saved
	Trompeuse	captured	18	English Channel	all lost
	Railleur	captured	14	English Channel	all lost
1801	Babet	captured	20	West Indies	all lost
	Utile	captured	16	Mediterranean	all lost
1802	Scout	captured	18	North Atlantic	all lost
	FLY	British	14	North Atlantic	all lost
1803	CALYPSO	British	16	West Indies	all lost
	AVENGER	British	14	North Sea	all saved
1805	Hawke	captured	18	English Channel	all lost
	Imogene	captured	18	West Indies	all saved
	Orquixo	captured	18	West Indies	95 lost
	SEAGULL	British	18	uncertain	all lost
	Redbridge	captured	10	West Indies	all saved

Year	Name	British-built or captured	Guns	Area where lost	Fate of crew
1806	MARTIN	British	18	West Indies	all lost
	SERPENT	British	18	West Indies	all lost
	SEAFORTH	British	14	West Indies	only 2 saved
	CLINKER	British	12	off Havre	all lost
	Papillon	captured	10	West Indies	all lost
1806	Berbice	captured	4	West Indies	all saved
1807	BUSY	British	18	North Atlantic	all lost
	PROSPERO	British	Bomb-ketch	North Sea	uncertain
	SPEEDWELL	British	14	English Channel	uncertain
	Elizabeth	captured	12	West Indies	all lost
	Fire-fly	captured	12	West Indies	only 4 saved
	CASSANDRA	British	10	North Sea	all saved
	Maria	captured	10	West Indies	all lost
1808	TANG	British	8	West Indies	all lost
1809	LARK	British	18	West Indies	only 3 saved
	FOXHOUND	British	18	North Atlantic	all lost
	HARRIER	British	18	East Indies	all lost
	CONTEST	British	12	North Atlantic	all lost
	PELTER	British	12	West Indies	all lost
	Dominion	captured	14	West Indies	only 3 saved
1810	SATELLITE	British	16	English Channel	uncertain
	CONFLICT	British	12	Bay of Biscay	uncertain
1811	FANCY	British	12	Baltic	all lost
	Fleur-de-la-Mere	captured	10	North Atlantic	all saved
1812	Magnet	captured	16	North Atlantic	all saved
	NIMBLE	British	10	Kattegat	all saved
	CHUBB	British	4	North Atlantic	all lost
	PORGY	British	4	West Indies	all lost
1813	SARPEDON	British	10	West Indies	all lost
	RHODIAN	British	10	West Indies	all saved
	SUBTLE	British	10	West Indies	all lost
1814	ANACREON	British	18	English Channel	uncertain
	Peacock	captured	18	West Indies	all lost
	CRANE	British	18	West Indies	all lost
	Vautour	captured	16	uncertain	all lost
	Dart	captured	10	uncertain	all lost
	CUTTLE	British	4	North Atlantic	all lost
	HERRING	British	4	North Atlantic	all lost
	Elisabeth	captured	10	North Atlantic	uncertain

Total of sloops, brigs, etc., lost by foundering at sea 66

Of these, total British-built 36

Of these, total captured previously from enemy 30

Areas in which lost	Number of ships
West Indies	26
North Atlantic	13
North Sea	7
English Channel	7
Eastern waters	3
Baltic and Kattegat	2
Delaware Estuary	1
Mediterranean	1
Uncertain	6
	66

Losses of crews	Number of ships
All lost or 4 or less saved	48
All saved	9
Heavy loss	3
Uncertain	6
	66

INDEX

Names of British vessels are in SMALL CAPITALS, names of other ships are in *italics*.
Abbreviations: Adm–Admiral; Cmdre–Commodore; Cdr–Commander.

371